W9-BMJ-362

# THE
# JESUS
# OF THE
# PARABLES

# THE JESUS OF THE PARABLES

## CHARLES W. F. SMITH

### REVISED EDITION

A PILGRIM PRESS BOOK
FROM
UNITED CHURCH PRESS
PHILADELPHIA

**Library of Congress Cataloging in Publication Data**

Smith, Charles William Frederick, 1905-
  The Jesus of the parables.

  "A Pilgrim Press book."
  "In this edition the revised version texts [of the
Bible] have been replaced by those of the revised
standard version."
  1. Jesus Christ—Parables. I. Bible, N. T.
Gospels. English. Selections. Revised standard. 1975.
II. Title.
BT375.S735   1975      226'.8'06      74-26816
ISBN  0-8298-0267-3

United Church Press, 1505 Race Street
Philadelphia, Pennsylvania 19102

To the memory of
**Beverley D. Tucker**
**R. Cary Montague**
**Noble C. Powell**
and to
**William H. Laird**
ministers of Christ and his gospel
to whose interest and assistance I have been
indebted for my share in this ministry

# ABOUT THE AUTHOR

Charles W. F. Smith, a native of London, England, is a graduate of the University of Virginia and the Episcopal Theological Seminary in Virginia (M. Div., D.D.). He has been Rector of Christ Church, Exeter, New Hampshire; Canon of the Washington Cathedral (1941-45); Rector of St. Andrew's Episcopal Church, Wellesley, Massachusetts; and for twenty-one years was Edmund Swett Rousmaniere Professor of the Literature and Interpretation of the New Testament at the Episcopal Theological School, Cambridge, Massachusetts. Dr. Smith is now retired and living in New Hampshire. He is the author of several books, including *Biblical Authority for Modern Preaching* and *The Paradox of Jesus in the Gospels,* and numerous journal articles.

# CONTENTS

# PREFACE TO THE REVISED EDITION

In the twenty-five years since this work was first published, a greatly intensified interest has arisen in the parables of Jesus and in the Jesus who used them. The studies of Jeremias, Fuchs, Linnemann, Perrin, G. V. Jones, Amos Wilder, Funk, and Via have all appeared in the interim, along with the work of Derrett on the law of the time. In addition the discoveries of the scrolls at Qumran and the gnostic library of Nag Hammadi have had to be taken into some account. The work done has established both a line of criticism and appreciation and its questioning and modification in the interest of new approaches to the "historical Jesus" and to hermeneutics and existential understanding, some of which were anticipated.

Since 1948 many new translations of the Bible have appeared, and in this edition the *Revised Version* texts have been replaced by those of the *Revised Standard Version*. Italics have been added to some of the biblical quotations to lift up certain words.

The original aim—to help the minister in study, preaching, and pastoral concern and the lay person in appreciation of the parables—has been retained. The notes have been completely revised to bring the discussion more up to date and with the intention of helping the serious student know where to turn for guidance to exegesis and further bibliographical resources.

The chapters have remained essentially the same except for the last, which has been replaced by a largely new study. In the others, apart from revisions to take account of new interests, there has been extensive rewriting of a few of the interpretations, notably those of the Tenants of the Vineyard, the Dishonest Steward, and the Friend at Midnight. It is hoped that this revision will serve the preacher and student of a new generation as the original, I am thankful to say, did the last.

I would thank the ministers, seminary students, undergraduates, and lay people who in many seminars, conferences, and discussion groups across the country have provided lively criticism and renewal for the theme and confirmed the vitality of the subject in rapidly changing times.

It is always impossible adequately to thank my wife for her loving and patient endurance and for constant practical help and spiritual encouragement in the preparation of the original book and of this revision.

The final stages of the revision were accomplished under the rigors of a storm of unprecedented proportions which deprived us of the use of our home, during which we took refuge in the Plymouth Inn of Plymouth, New Hampshire, and were provided with the necessary seclusion and facilities to complete the copy. To its proprietor, Mr. Calvin Carpenter, we shall always be grateful for his Christian understanding.

Charles W. F. Smith<br>
Bridgewater Hill<br>
New Hampshire

# ONE THE PARABLES AND THE CRUCIFIXION

Jesus used parables, and Jesus was put to death. The two facts are related, and it is necessary to understand the connection. How important the death of Jesus is to the Evangelists is shown by the proportion of space each Gospel gives to the last few days in Jerusalem. Modern Christian teaching, with its reflection in popular notions, gives no answer to the question which the Gospels so largely set out to answer: Why was this man crucified? Yet any view of Jesus' work or teaching that does not account for his death would appear to be totally unrealistic and inadequate. There can be little doubt that the preacher is often to blame for failing to make this clear. Even the teaching of Jesus suffers when it is presented in isolation from the crucifixion and the resurrection, since these events are essential to the Gospel. The Evangelists are all concerned to bring this out. The parables must be understood as part of the drama. No one would crucify a teacher who simply told pleasant stories to enforce prudential morality. He would be a very unlikely victim if it could not be known what his stories meant—if, in fact, they were deliberately designed to conceal his meaning. If our reading of the parables does not help to account for the crucifixion, we have scarcely come to grips with them.

The implacable enmity of Jesus' opponents, let it be said with all justice and even sympathy, was not malicious. The truth seems to be that they "rejected" him *because they understood* him—better, in some respects, than his own followers. Far from seeking to allay their opposition, Jesus appears to have stimulated it. He did this largely by parables. His enemies and even the public found him and his claims, his teaching and its demands, incredible in the radical meaning of the word. It was not their failure to comprehend but their refusal to accept what he made inescapable that led to his death. In the pursuit of his work and the presentation of his challenge so that it could not be ignored, the parables played no small part. It is our contention that, as a means of elucidation, they were vitally important to the process. In short, the prime reason for Jesus' crucifixion was Jesus himself. The struggle in which he engaged was clarified and brought to a head by his parabolic teaching. (See Preliminary Note, page 223.)

The method of teaching by parables was not new. It had been extensively developed by the rabbis; scholars of the last eighty years have rendered a great service by drawing attention to the rabbinic parallels. Jesus, however, used parables not simply as a means of illustration but as weapons. They were, for him, instruments to be used in warfare, the chief weapon he resorted to when challenged and when, to meet that challenge, he invaded the preserves of his enemies and fought them upon their own ground. Our understanding of Jesus has deteriorated from many causes, most of them rooted in the nature of the New Testament and its use by the Christian church. He has become largely a passive figure or one removed entirely to the heavenly realm. Yet the Gospels are inexplicable on either basis. A study of the parables reveals a Jesus who was constantly under attack, an attack aroused by his own activities and the teaching by which he justified them. His usual response to attack was to assume the offensive. His public career occupied a period of manifold tensions and urgent decision from which Jesus cannot be abstracted. When the parables are studied with this in mind, we are less inclined to demand that Jesus reason with the cold logic of an armchair philosopher or weave fancies with the literary skill of a penman. We cannot agree with Leslie Weatherhead that Jesus perfected his parabolic stories by constant telling and retelling.[1] Their origin was more dynamic, their occasion more spontaneous, their purpose more militant. They were, for the most part, struck off in the heat of debate. They were pointed to pierce an immediate situation. They were designed to confront men with an issue to be decided. They are related to action rather than to rationalization, to life rather than to literature. Yet, although they are spontaneous and occasional, they retain a meaning that escapes from the moment, and they yield truths that show no signs of being outmoded. While Jesus was not a philosopher or a theologian (in the accepted sense), his parables alone provide material that neither the philosopher nor the theologian can exhaust. This is the mark of Jesus' supreme genius. We have a curious tendency, even in dealing with Jesus' humanity, to overlook his sheer intellectual stature.

The enduring value of the parables lies in Jesus' skill with the method. His teaching is inseparable from his person. He transformed everything he touched and revealed its possibilities. The parable involved a technique supremely fitted to his needs. It is so flexible an instrument, capable of being tempered to the occasion, that it is not surprising that simple and adequate definitions of a parable are hard to come by. It is not possible, probably, to produce a neat sentence that covers all the variations found even in the Gospels.[2] What a parable is can best be understood from a detailed study of the parables themselves.

The parable or similitude was a means by which a comparison was made. An observed fact or an imagined situation in common life, on the one hand, was laid beside a spiritual relationship or a religious truth on the other. In the process, the judgment formed concerning the first was shown to have its relevance concerning the second. Conviction, vindication, or elucidation was sought through stimulation of the hearer's own intellect and emotions. The parable had neither the carefully constructed detail of an allegory nor the precision of a syllogism. Precise meaning became more evident from the context of its utterance or the situation in which it played a part. Where it was necessary to underline the meaning by adding a moral, the parable was less effective as parable.

When the principles of this form of teaching are grasped, it will be seen that the parables were valuable instruments in disputation. Because the parable depended for its success upon the familiarity or reasonableness of its material, drawn from common life, it could appeal for an opinion. Many of the parables open with the typical rabbinic question: "With what can we compare the kingdom of God?" (Mark 4:30; cf. Luke 13:20). Or the question may take a more specific form: "But to what shall I compare this generation? (Matt. 11:16)." It may answer a question or lead to a question—Luke 10:29ff. is both. The parable may itself take the form of a question or series of questions (Luke 5:34; 17:7-9). When parables begin with the question "Which of you . . . ?" (Luke 11:5-8; 15:4-6; 15:8-9; etc.), we can see that this more or less rhetorical device expects but one response. The judgment of the audience on the situation is asked, as in Matthew 21:28-31 (the parable of the Two Sons), and obviously expected in such parables as the Pearl Merchant, the Treasure in the Field, the Prodigal Son, the Barren Fig Tree, the Unmerciful Servant, and others. The hearer is expected to say or think "Of course," or "Certainly," or "He was right," or the like. The judgment will be obvious and inescapable in proportion as the parable is vivid, familiar, and true to life.

By demanding an opinion on its own human level, the parable provided an opening which left the hearer defenseless.[3] A truth which might be rejected or not even listened to in the form of a straightforward assertion could thus be pressed home before the hearer was aware that he had lowered his guard. To admit the validity of the principle on one level was to be open to the suggestion that it applied equally or with even more force on another. Even where an opponent "held his peace," the point was clear to other bystanders, and silence must be seen as an admission of discomfiture.

Jesus often made use of this device, and the parables appear as the tactical weapons in his strategy. The impact they made is to be measured by the ultimate violence of the response. This impact depended upon the familiarity and verisimilitude of the theme and the inescapable answer it elicited. We more clearly grasp its force when we consider the final step by which the argument was pressed home, since it affords a clue to the interpretation of many of Jesus' stories. The clear statement of the method is found in Matthew 7:9-11, where two little similitudes in the form of questions asking for and expecting a judgment are followed by what is called the argument from the lesser to the greater, or the a fortiori argument, based on the question, How much more?

> Or what man of you, if his son asks him for a loaf, will give him a stone? Or if he asks for a fish, will give him a serpent? If you then, who are evil, know how to give good gifts to your children, *how much more* will your Father who is in heaven give good things to those who ask him?

The obvious answer to the two questions is "None." The application then turns on lifting the comparison to the divine level with the argument that what is true among men will be infinitely more true for God in heaven.

This helps to avoid what seems to many a real difficulty, but it lands the unwary in another difficulty of a theological nature. It helps to explain the means by which those parables may be interpreted which tell of unscrupulous or worldly characters—as in the Dishonest Steward, the Widow and the Judge, the Treasure in the Field, and others where the problem is as real though less obvious. The solution is not that the text is corrupt or that they are falsely attributed to Jesus but that the stories move on a frankly human and even immoral level. The a fortiori principle must be applied. The characters are not to be admired; they obviously cannot be allegorized; we are expected to reason that if such a man in his human concerns shows (let us say) so much energy, how much more should the child of God, or does God . . . ?

The danger of the principle arises when we make further deductions from it. It is clear that Jesus found it possible to use scenes and events of the world and common life as he knew them and to draw from them comparisons in the realm of the kingdom of God. This is not to say that there was no difference in his mind, but that the principles that apply at one level are not utterly foreign to those that operate on the other level. The two realms, while sundered "as far as the east is from the west," have points at which they are akin. The experiences we have of love, fellowship, and concern are but faint shadows of those that arise from the heart of God, but they are shadows. God has not left himself without witness; the image of God is a reality, though distorted by sin. It does not mean that man and his affairs raised to an enormous degree equal God. Jesus notes the difference when he says, "If you then, *who are evil,* . . . how much more will your Father *who is in heaven*?" There is real discontinuity between the realm of evil and the realm of heaven, but the eye of faith may still trace the parallels and, in doing so, become even more sensitive to the distortions.

We must remember that Jesus addressed Jews who had no empty conception of God but had inherited the Old Testament knowledge that God is One, the Holy One of Israel, who is "of purer eyes than to behold evil," the Judge of all the earth, full of loving-kindness and truth. His use of the "how much more" principle is aimed at those who, by their traditions and practice, had seemed to forget this God. By it he reminds them that God could not be less merciful, less just, less worshipful than man. It is an instrument used in debate, and this is its limitation. The point involved is pressed home by forcing the hearers to come to a conclusion in the realm of everyday experience.

That Jesus chose his subjects with this in mind is suggested by the probability that the parables were designed for the times and places and the audiences with which Jesus was presented. The Dragnet may well have been delivered by the lake, the agricultural parables in the countryside, the commercial parables to town or marketplace audiences, the vineyard stories in Jerusalem or its environs where vines were common, and those that deal with womanly activities (the Lost Coin, the Leaven in the Meal, etc.) when numbers of women were present. If this be so, it argues against their artificial and premeditated character. They were also adapted to the circumstances of his struggle. The parables were struck off in the course of action, in the presence of critics and foes, under the pressure of making a point clear as Jesus responded to his audience, not in seclusion. It is conceivable that parables like the Prodigal Son, the Good Samaritan, the Tenants of the Vineyard, and many others might have taken quite a different form had the occasion been other than it was.

To read the parables in this way will make it apparent that they are not merely moral tales, pious illustrations, or "example stories," not fables or allegories or myths, not conscious works of art. There is much that is immoral and far from pious in the parables—the rascally steward, the shrewd merchant, the callous judge, the churlish householder, the father who entrusts a third of his wealth to a prodigal, the inconsiderate guests, the unscrupulous tenants. They deal with the real world of actual men. The situation depicted may be an everyday observation concerning the sowing and reaping of crops, the culture of a vineyard, the duties of servants, the tending of sheep, or the baking of bread. The greater part of Jesus' material is drawn from household and business affairs. The stories move in more imaginative realms, but the imagined plots and scenes are credible and within reason—a son goes away and returns, a traveler is assaulted and rescued, guests decline an invitation and the host seeks substitutes, bridesmaids skimp their preparation, and tenants refuse to pay their rent.

This verisimilitude is essential to the parable and serves to distinguish it from the fable and the allegory. Faithfulness to nature is not expected in a fable, where plants and animals speak and act as human beings (cf. the fable of the trees and the bramble in Judg. 9:8-15); the Gospels are free of fables. In an allegory, naturalness is not essential. In a parable, a familiar or credible situation on the plane of ordinary life is laid alongside a situation or truth on the plane of spiritual things. The relationships involved are in some respects parallel, but there is no confusion or substitution of the one for the other. A parable differs from an allegory as a simile differs from a metaphor. In a metaphor, the language of one realm has been transferred to another. In a simile, a comparison is expressed without transfer. In a parable, the thing depicted does not become the thing intended, as it must in an allegory. The known remains what it is and by doing so throws light on the unknown. Each member of the comparison must remain true to itself. The shepherd is a shepherd and does not become a missionary; the father of the prodigal remains an indulgent father—he does not become God; the leaven remains yeast and does not become the kingdom of God. This is not so in an allegory, where there is no demand for verisimilitude, because the substitution of terms is determined from the start. Parables are properly termed "similitudes" (though the term is usually reserved for brief examples) and the Hebrew and Greek words used, *mashal* and *parabolē*, mean to lay alongside or to compare.[4]

Parables were a characteristically Jewish form of teaching, unlike the fable, which we associate with Aesop, or the myth, classically developed by Plato. These serve their purpose, but we can see that they were not adapted to the needs of Jesus in his warfare. John

Bunyan, whom we associate with allegory, wrote his *Pilgrim's Progress* in prison. The construction of allegory demands leisure. The real events about which he wrote there and in *The Holy War* are events in the spiritual life and the warfare of the soul. The details are chosen because they can be transferred to the realm of the real events, where their meaning is clear. They need not be realistic in the story and may make doubtful sense until the transfer is made. The clue, in Bunyan, is often found in the names: Christian, Sloth, Giant Despair, Mr. Great-heart, Doubting Castle, Mansoul.[5] There are allegories in the Old Testament. We find, for example (in Dan. 8:3-12), a ram which pushes in all directions of the compass and a goat which grows four horns in place of one and a fifth out of one of the four. This is not characteristic of the animals and is not intended to be, because they deliberately represent something other than themselves and must act like that which they represent. When the key is given us (vs. 20-21), we find that the two-horned ram is the Medo-Persian Empire and the much-horned goat is Greece.

Allegory is not *characteristic* of Jesus, and to burden him with allegorical constructions is to take him out of his warfare. His parables have, with unfortunate results, been for centuries interpreted allegorically; the new day of parable interpretation dates only from Jülicher.[6] The great difference in the two methods is that in an allegory the details are important because each has individual meaning and is to be interpreted; in a parable the details are important for other reasons. First, they add reality; they have the general effect of scenery, making the characters and events lifelike. A woman takes a broom and a lamp to find a lost coin. The broom and the lamp are needed in the search, to give light and to clear the floor. We do not have to identify them and find out what they mean. Or, secondly, the details may guide us to the central point and make the emphasis clear. The traveler from Jerusalem to Jericho is designedly vague, but the priest, Levite, and Samaritan are clear. In the parable of the Banquet the more original (Lucan) version details the excuses in order to show their artificiality, and the host sends his servant twice to search for guests in order to underline his determination to fill all the seats. A great deal of distortion can be imported into the parables and will lead us on false scents when we try to smell out allegorical meanings. There is one central point, one intended comparison to be looked for, and the rest of the detail contributes to it or is pure realism.[7]

Two points are likely to confuse us. One is the mode of expression characteristic of the rabbinic schools. Thus Jesus seems to say, "The kingdom of God is like . . . a man . . . leaven . . . a grain of mustard seed." Actually we must not stop here. We must follow the whole parable if we are to discover the point of comparison. We are to find out what the man does; what happens to the leaven and the meal; what it is about mustard seed that makes it useful as a similitude. The second point is that when a good subject of comparison has been chosen and the right point of departure has been found, it will often prove that the details fall into place as exceedingly appropriate, reinforcing the main point and tempting us to use the details in allegorical fashion. It is a temptation we should in most cases resist, for while useful homiletical results may follow, the pressure of centuries of allegorical interpretation may ensnare us again in a distorted use of similar material elsewhere. Jesus was a master at the choice of an appropriate comparison, or it would not have been possible to turn his parables into allegories.

Jesus, at least in the parables, was not a systematic theologian. The effort to make him one means that we pour his teaching into our own mold and modernize him: westernize or hellenize or even Christianize him. But Jesus was a Jew, and as a Jew he was understood by the Jews who heard him. Inevitably they connected what he said with the concerns uppermost in their own minds and interpreted his activities in relation to the issues that confronted their generation. This is important when we remember that the parables were used in disputation and served to focus the issue under debate. We cannot understand the parables without reference to the circumstances of the times, and we should not try to understand the rest of Jesus' teaching without weighing the most probable meaning of the parables. When we set out to study them we are faced with the problem of where to begin. Prior theological demands or homiletical schemes will impose upon them an order of treatment which very likely has little or no reference to the original situation.[8] The order in which they are treated should arise rather from a study of each parable in isolation and an attempt to discover its own meaning, even apart from its context in the Gospels.[9]

When we attempt to do this, we are impressed that Mark's first major example is deliberately introduced at a certain point and serves to open up the subject of parabolic teaching. When we study the Sower, however, apart from its Marcan interpretation, we shall discover that it has a place in his scheme which does not appear on the surface. Studied in its broader setting, the parable proves a good starting point, though with a sense other than that imposed upon it by Mark. Each parable in turn raises other questions, and, when we have examined the parables independently for their own meaning, we find one or more which in turn seem to answer the problems raised. This is a better guide and one more likely to be original than the dictates of theological or homiletical schematology.[10]

In the face of modern analysis of the Gospel material, it is no longer possible to attempt a biography of Jesus in the ordinary sense of the word. The sections are fitted, in the Synoptics, into a chronological outline which depends upon Mark and must be judged in a great many instances to be artificial. At the same time there are certain broad marks of progression from crisis to crisis, and it is difficult to believe that even a generation after Jesus' death there was not some recollection of the general phases of his career.[11] This seems to be endorsed by certain internal marks in the parables themselves. Their nature and Jesus' characteristic use of them makes it all the more necessary to ask what their relation is to his general strategy. To do so makes it frequently necessary to remove them from the setting given by the Evangelist.

Very early in the Gospel of Mark stands a collection of incidents having to do with opposition to Jesus (Mark 2:1 to 3:6). It is obviously a collection and not chronological. It is nonetheless clear, however, that Jesus' initial mission of preaching, healing, and exorcism aroused opposition which undermined his initial popularity. His response was a change of method: an itinerant, outdoor mission in place of synagogue preaching. The change was accompanied by parables which express his reasons for continuing his efforts and which serve to analyze and illuminate the situation. They constitute an attack upon the assumptions that give rise to the opposition and a criticism of the attitudes his contemporaries take to the kingdom of God, which is the prime dictate of his own work. These parables have been preserved, no doubt, for other reasons, but they are illuminated and made more illuminating when we see them as the opening of Jesus' counterattack upon the situation that confronted him. His teaching here constitutes a dynamic response which could not be ignored and in turn precipitated a series of critical developments which inevitably led to the cross.

The indictment against him necessarily crystallized into specific counts, and the vindication thus called for is found most clearly in parabolic form. His change of method brought him into immediate and widespread contact with the populace, and his vindication is not directed merely at the official opposition but constitutes an appeal to the people to judge between himself and his enemies.

If the opposition made specific charges, Jesus was not unwilling to make his countercharges also specific. Hence we find in the teaching of the parables an indictment and an appeal which become more and more insistent as parable follows parable and the scene changes from Galilee to the environs of Jerusalem. His physical retreat beyond the border served only to prepare his descent upon Jerusalem itself. The growing intensity of the situation is reflected in the parables, which, better than any other mode of teaching, were fitted to press home his demands. He thus created for the authorities a dilemma that could not be resolved except by drastic action in one direction or the other. The issue is confused in the Gospels as we have them because the ultimate results dictated a change of viewpoint, which we will explore. But this should not blind us to the realities of the situation or to the necessity of discovering what it was about Jesus that made him so offensive to Jerusalem that he must be removed in haste and once and for all. Something more than the treachery of an obscure disciple is needed to explain the situation. Because the crucial parables could be adapted to later needs, we should not ignore the probability that the situation that emerged after the resurrection was the direct result of Jesus' own impact—and his intention. The parables have too many marks of supreme genius to make credible the theory that they are largely the construction of later hands. When we read them as instruments in a desperate campaign, we find that both parables and situation become more clear. Once again, the men who rushed Jesus to the grave were not simply perverse.

It is assumed in this approach to the parables that they could be understood by those who first heard them. On the theory that they held an esoteric meaning which needed to be elucidated, it is difficult to see why they aroused the response they did and to understand why Jesus used this form of teaching. When we examine the inner meaning claimed for the parables, we find that they must be turned into allegories to yield it. This is true of the prime example on which the theory is based, the parable of the Sower. If the judgment expected on the situation depicted in a parable is necessary to the interpretation, the method is reduced to an absurdity if the story does not mean what it seems to mean. A reply addressed to critics which can properly be understood only by friends and not by the critics is not likely to stir the latter to violent action but rather to leave them indifferent. The persistence of allegorical interpretation, and the prevalence of theological contortions in dealing with the parables, is largely owing to the uncritical acceptance of the theory of a meaning reserved for the initiated. The correlative position, that Jesus was hiding his real meaning and his real nature, is influenced by theological speculation about his own person and is subject to the same criticisms.

The problem probably would not arise except for the fact that it is embedded in the earliest Gospel at Mark 4:10-12. Jesus has here delivered the parable of the Sower, and the disciples are made to ask about it privately. Jesus' answer is, "To you has been given the secret of the kingdom of God, but for those outside everything is in parables; so that they may indeed see but not perceive, and may indeed hear but not understand; lest they should turn again, and be forgiven (vs. 11-12)." This is followed by the "interpretation" of the parable. At once we are struck by the phrase "for those outside," which seems to cut across Jesus' normally inclusive attitude. We are reminded also that for Mark there is a "messianic secret" to be withheld from the populace, which those who stumble upon it are not to publish. The esoteric treatment of the parables fits into this scheme.

By comparing the parallel passages we find that Luke 8:9-10 follows Mark and, if anything, makes the theory more explicit. In Matthew 13:10-17 there is a more extended treatment. The first statement is, "To you it has been given to know the secrets of the kingdom of heaven, but to them it has not been given"—a statement of fact. Those close to Jesus ("the disciples," v. 10) understand the subject of the teaching. They have a gift which in itself perhaps explains why they are disciples. Others have not the same facility. The subject of the kingdom of God is difficult and mysterious to them. In Mark the disciples ask about the parables; in Matthew they ask why Jesus *uses* parables in his public teaching. Matthew then gives the reason (v. 13): "This is why I speak to them in parables, because seeing they do not see, and hearing they do not hear, nor do they understand." Here again is a statement of fact—the people seem to see but do not see; they seem to hear but do not hear—and not a statement of purpose. The contrast is further brought out in verse 16: "But blessed are your eyes, for they see; and your ears, for they hear." Unlike the disciples, the people need to have the teaching explained to them by analogy with something they can understand.

It appears that Matthew is deliberately modifying Mark's statement. A Jew would certainly detect in Mark 4:12 and Matthew 13:13 an allusion to Isaiah 6:9-10, which Matthew proceeds to quote. We note that Matthew has not copied Mark 4:12 ("lest they . . .") but has substituted the passage from Isaiah. This is a statement both of a fact and of the purpose by which the fact is explained. The word translated "that" in Mark 4:12 (*hina* with the subjunctive), a statement of deliberate purpose, becomes in Matthew 13:13 the word translated "because" (*hoti* with the indicative), or a simple statement. The Old Testament quotation is from the Septuagint version, which itself modifies the more harsh Hebrew (in which the prophet is to make the ears of the people heavy *lest* they hear, etc.). The Hebrews made no clear distinction between an observed fact and the divine providence of which the observed fact might be the result. Thirdly, it is usual for Matthew to introduce Old Testament quotations in the interest of showing Jesus to be the fulfillment. The passage is sufficiently alluded to for Jesus' purpose in verse 13. Verses 14 and 15 may be taken as an addition by the Evangelist. The sense is improved by reading verse 16 after verse 13 and by omitting verse 12 as an accretion.

When we weigh all the considerations, there is nothing conclusive in the Marcan theory beyond the statement that the disciples could better understand the difficult subject about which Jesus was teaching than could the multitude. It was therefore necessary for Jesus to teach the people as a whole by means of parables. Indeed this (more original?) viewpoint is expressed in the same chapter of Mark. At verse 33 (if not at vs. 21 or 26) the public situation that obtains at the beginning of the chapter is resumed, suggesting that the withdrawal to instruct the disciples privately is an insertion into a previously continuous narrative. Here we read, "With many such parables he spoke the word to them, as they were able to hear it; he did not speak to them without a parable (Mark 4:33-34a)." Here again Matthew has dropped Mark's further statement, "But privately to his own disciples he explained everything" (v. 34; cf. Matt. 13:34). This again reads as an interpolation intended to harmonize with the insertion above. The impression is further confirmed by the little similitude of Mark 4:21—"Is a lamp brought in to be put under a bushel, or under a bed, and not on a stand?"—clearly in this setting a parable about the use of parables. There is no designed obscurity: "For there is nothing hid, except to be made manifest; nor is anything secret, except to come to light (Mark 4:22)."

There remains, however, the fact that a parable needs to be interpreted. Those against whom it was deliberately directed would be more likely to grasp its relevance than casual listeners (cf. Mark 12:12). It would also be possible to hear the parables merely as illustrations or stories without grasping the comparison, even as common illustrations are retained apart from the points they were intended to make clear in a sermon. The multitude might in this sense hear the story but not see the meaning of it and fail to be moved by it to the essential activity of repentance. In view of this there are the added warnings, "If any man has ears to hear, let him hear (Mark 4:23)" and "Take heed what you hear (v. 24)," more correctly given in Luke: "Take heed then how you hear (Luke 8:18)." To understand the words of Matthew 13:13, "nor do they understand," to refer to the parables is to make nonsense of them. Referred to the nonparabolic teaching and as an explanation of why Jesus turned to parables, the words make sense, and all that we know of parables and their use endorses them.[12]

On the assumption that the parables are what they seem—a means of elucidating, not of obscuring, the teaching—it is essential to seek their original meaning. This cannot be done without some sense of the occasion on which they were used, and in order to approach that we must discriminate between the purpose of the Evangelists and the original intention of Jesus. Here it is that the crucifixion must be kept in view and, as we shall see in the next chapter, the resurrection. If the parables were understood by others than the disciples, then they cannot be ignored in the comprehension of Jesus' warfare and fate. We must also not be led astray by the urgency to find something helpful of a theological or homiletical nature. Current application must await the decision as to original meaning. The immediate usefulness, we shall find, will be by no means absent, but it must not be allowed to determine our interpretation. The first concern is to find the central point and its bearing. We may then be justified in making expansions of the application which arise out of a sense of the aptness of the details and not simply when we are charmed by the detail and find it homiletically stimulating. The discovery that the details of a parable support or determine the central point makes us confident that we have found the point—and we should be in no hurry to lose it by uncontrolled indulgence of our delight with the scenery or the psychology.

There is much popular preaching that just here loses all claim to be an exposition of the parable as parable. Consequently, it seems necessary to suggest the abandonment of many homiletical approaches that have become traditional and are often made enticing. Nothing, except possibly entertainment value, is lost by substituting for themes that allow for homiletical skill the power that comes from closeness to our Lord's own message and the desperate and hopeful issues of the kingdom of God. The parables in their central points come close to people and close to the issues of history. When God is mediated to people at the point of their deepest need or highest joy, their response will be more significant than if they have been simply entertained. Our situation, even in the churches, is not essentially different from that of those who first heard the parables of Jesus. The dilemma of human life is not other than that with which Paul dealt. Both are illuminated by the parables. The seriousness of our need to return to the sources is made clear by the fact that the parables are the parables of the Crucified. There is but one Gospel, and it is the Gospel of what God did through Christ. That, too, is the theme of the parables.

# TWO THE PARABLES AND THE RESURRECTION

Without the resurrection, the parables would not have been preserved. The resurrection of Jesus is central to any understanding of Christianity. To say so is a truism, yet unless it is kept constantly in mind the key to the nature and meaning of the Gospels is lost. Obviously no book of the New Testament was written before the resurrection had worked its change in the followers of Jesus. They became, thereby, new men, and their interest in the work and teaching of Jesus became a new thing. The events of Jesus' career were seen from the standpoint of the early church; *they were seen always in the dazzling light which broke upon his disciples at the first Easter.* The sayings of Jesus were then no words of a mere man, no matter how gifted, or of a human teacher, no matter how skillful. They had come to be the words of the Messiah of God's true Israel, the Lord of the Christian church.

The account of the events that led up to the crucifixion and the teachings that had a share in producing that result were not recorded by a diarist or taken down verbatim. They were received by the Evangelists, who embodied them in the Gospels after a period during which they were passed on by word of mouth. But the account of events and the uttered words were preserved, not by those who mourned a defeated and deceased leader but by those who had come to worship a living Savior and victorious Lord—though he was outwardly the same person, as were they. It is part of the record that the primitive church believed the Jesus who had been known and mourned, and who was now worshiped, to be "the same yesterday and today and for ever (Heb. 13:8)." The earliest preaching concerned the Jesus of intimate historic experience: "God has made him both Lord and Christ, this Jesus whom you crucified (Acts 2:36)." Indeed, the first Christians looked for the return of "this Jesus, who was taken up from you into heaven (Acts 1:11)."

If we do not lay sufficient stress on the postresurrection viewpoint at the outset, we may find it difficult to understand why a study of the parables of Jesus—or of the Jesus who taught by parables—must involve us in questions of criticism applied to the Gospel records in which the parables are now preserved. Only by giving full weight to the radical transformation caused by the resurrection can we understand why the clue to the original meaning of the parables appears so soon to have been lost—or, if not lost, at least overwritten. It is as if we were dealing with a palimpsest.

The oral tradition embodied in the Gospels by the Evangelists arose from two main interests and assumed a double form: first, the form of Christian preaching and constant repreaching, with the primary purpose of winning converts to the new faith and of justifying that faith by apologetic; second, the form of instruction given to members of the earliest Christian communities as they tried to develop a new way of life in a pagan, unsympathetic, and sometimes hostile environment.[1] These interests superseded the detailed discussion of Jesus' warfare. That issue was, in a sense, closed—for the Jews by Jesus' death; for the disciples by his resurrection. Parables, which had been the prime instruments in his campaign, tended after the resurrection to become vehicles of apologetic and of Christian nurture. It is the resurrection that accounts for the Marcan theory of the parables as veiled teachings. The glory of Christ had been revealed by his rising from the dead, and Mark attributes to Jesus the meaning that the church found in his parables after that experience.

The New Testament shows on its own pages the marks of the mental and spiritual struggle out of which the resurrection faith was born, and the Gospels as we have them are the deposit of that struggle. The events cf Holy Week and Easter revealed to Jesus' followers how seriously they had failed to understand him. Adjustment to that discovery was not easy. New factors had to be assimilated, and new solutions were demanded. The significant thing is that the solution was resolved by a new understanding of *the ancient tradition.* The marks of this are clear in the record, along with discernible signs of historic "controls."[2] The risen Christ expostulates with two disciples on the road to Emmaus: "O foolish men, and slow of heart to believe all that the prophets have spoken! Was it not necessary that the Christ should suffer these things, and enter into his glory?" (Luke 24:25f.; cf. vs. 44-46). The appeal to scripture is foremost in the Pentecostal speech of Peter (Acts 2:14-36) and in his other utterances (e.g., Acts 1:20; 3:20-25), in the apologia of Stephen (Acts 7:1-53), in the discussion between Philip and the Ethiopian (Acts 8:30-35), and in the references by Paul to the Gospel which had been transmitted to him wherein he saw the death and resurrection of Christ to be "in accordance with the scriptures (1 Cor. 15:3f.)."

The transitional period of the Judeo-Christian church (as it may be called) came to an end when the church emerged as an autonomous and distinctly Christian institution. This reorientation of viewpoint meant that the Gospel material was adapted to the new interests and functions of a body which experienced expansion and persecution and which had to justify the one and protect itself amid the other. The material was the same but, if we may so phrase it, the "terms of reference" were changed. We must try to discern where the parables have been provided with a setting dictated by the interests of the church and see their relevance to the situation of Jesus and his people. It is necessary to change the terms of reference again, back to Jesus' own time. The parables must be understood as the efforts of one who sought to make an issue inescapable rather than as the utterances of a triumphant victor. Matters of intense concern to the early Christians overlaid the actual development of Jesus' strategy and the immediate impact of his teaching upon the contemporary leaders as he pursued his determined way to the final climax in Jerusalem.

The first concern that occupied the developing church was the person of Jesus. The crucifixion and apostolic testimony to the resurrection were the core of the church's message and the center of its life. But it was "folly" to the gentiles and a barrier to the allegiance of the Jews (1 Cor. 1:23). "Form criticism" makes clear that this need for an apologetic explains the early development of the Passion narrative which, in each Gospel, occupies so prominent a place. It was necessary to justify to the Jews the preaching of a crucified Messiah, and to the Greeks the following of a condemned and executed criminal.

Apart from the impact of the resurrection and the revolution produced by that experience, Jesus, judged by any normal human standard was a failure—or, at the most, a martyr. How great a failure tends to be obscured because, again, the record was set down a generation after the resurrection. It was hard for the early Christian preacher or even the Evangelist who collected the preaching to focus his mind on this point. There were no "objective historians," and "straight biography" was impossible. They desired to present the Faith and its grounding in the work and person of the Lord. It may be thought remarkable, then, that the record is as extensive or as reliable as it is. The validity of the record is a tribute to Jesus and to the force of the impact he made—and this is particularly true of the parables. Because of their concrete, vivid, literary form, parables are likely in any case to be the best-remembered parts of Jesus' teaching and among the most frequently used in preaching. Where they can be stripped of elements of modification inevitable to their use during the oral period, they reveal additional testimony to the dynamic quality of Jesus' ministry.[3]

As interest in Jesus moved from his human history to his eternal meaning and nature—his significance for faith—it is natural that increasing weight was given to the "moments" that set forth his supernatural character and authority and less attention given to his warfare and to the process by which his execution became inevitable. This meant a lessened interest in the "offense" which his presence and work presented to his political and religious opponents. The offense was felt also by the common people and, to an extent not fully revealed, by his own friends. The Gospels still show that Jesus' contemporaries were offended at his claim to forgive sins (Mark 2:7) and by his association with the "sinners," that they attributed his power to perform exorcisms to a league with evil spirits (Mark 3:22), and that they were scandalized at the authority pretended to by a carpenter whose family connections they knew (Mark 6:3). One community at least felt him an undesirable person to have in the neighborhood (Mark 5:17). John the Baptist was doubtful of Jesus' calling (Matt. 11:2f.). The crowd complained when he accepted the hospitality of the publican Zacchaeus (Luke 19:7). The demand was constantly made that he validate his claim, and we shall see that the parables take up the demand and answer it. His own companions took it upon themselves to rebuke him (Mark 8:32) and found his words something of which to be ashamed (cf. v. 38). They became afraid of the course he pursued, and probably of him (Mark 10:32), and tried to restrain him as one not in his right mind (Mark 3:21).[4]

Again it is remarkable that so many traces of this doubt and uneasiness, even unpopularity, are left in the record set down by a worshiping community. Although the apostles were leaders to whom increasing honor was paid, clear admissions remain that even this inner circle of disciples had failed to understand him. It is recorded that they could not comprehend his plans or his reasons for them. "They did not understand the saying, and they were afraid to ask him" (Mark 9:32; cf. v. 10, and Luke 18:34; 24:21a, etc., and the note in John 6:66). The connection of these explanations with references to the resurrection indicates the revolution in the thinking of the disciples which that event brought about. Incidents like the dispute over who should hold high office (Mark 9:33ff.; 10:35ff.) and the final words of Mark's original Gospel (16:8) are similar traces of a confusion that the subsequent triumph did not completely obscure. This is again a testimony to the fact that Jesus is no creation of the church or of legend, not a "cult figure" but a solid fact of history.[5]

A second factor of absorbing concern to the church was material that justified the autonomy of the new community and vindicated its newly realized task of a mission to the gentiles. The marks of the controversy with the Judaizers are clear in The Acts and in the Epistles of Paul—even though the exact chronology of the stages in the controversy is by no means obvious. Modern scholarship has made a great deal of this factor. Luke in particular reveals an interest in justifying the mission beyond Israel which leads him to modify and adapt the record.

Interest in the universal mission developed in the early church and can be traced only indirectly to Jesus himself. The largely unresolved debate about Jesus' precise view of the future is a factor here. Once more the crucifixion-resurrection transition must be allowed full play. The task of Jesus was accomplished, but it was accomplished only by his death and resurrection. Since his aims could not be established before his death—and, indeed, without his death his attempt had failed—the disciples could hardly be expected to understand the full implications of his work. The tradition emphasizes the point that even after the resurrection there was no immediately clear comprehension. It was only after Pentecost and when the church had achieved autonomy that the real implications of the situation began to dawn. Even so, it was the acute process of controversy that clarified the issue.

This transition is also marked in the record. Until we grasp the cause of the confusion attendant upon it, we remain in doubt as to whether Jesus had any interest beyond Israel or whether signs of this interest are all to be attributed to the Evangelists. The wonder is, not that the Gospels show traces of the vindication of the universal mission, but that they show so few. They contain material that might have been so used. There are also indications that Jesus' immediate mission was confined to his own people. We must consider whether this necessarily excludes a wider purpose. As we shall see in the detailed study, Jesus faced a situation in which a vindication similar in principle though not in detail was necessary. The response he made was perfectly susceptible of elaboration. His problem was the extension of God's mercy beyond the *accepted* Israelite. The passages that deal with his mission to the outcasts probably owe their preservation to the interest of the church in reaching all men. In certain places we need only to substitute the word "gentiles" for "publicans and sinners" to discover that the task of the church could find a real basis in Jesus' own practice.[6]

The universalizing tendency of the church also wrought another change in the use of the Gospel sayings. When they were made applicable to all men, they became interesting in their application to the individual. *But Jesus spoke originally to a particular nation in a definite historical situation.* There seems every likelihood that sayings that had their first application to the Jewish people, with their sense of corporate responsibility, were, when the nation was no longer the important factor, applied universally to the individual or in particular to the Christian disciple. To take but two examples: "You are the salt of the earth" came to be understood to have general reference to followers of Christ, yet there can be little doubt that originally it concerned the particular people to whom Jesus was speaking and referred to their national vocation. "Whoever would save his life will lose it" has come to be understood of every human soul, yet there can be little doubt that it was addressed to a definite and critical issue that confronted Jesus during his ministry.

The needs of the early church, itself the product of the resurrection, often obscure the realization that Jesus stood face to face with an actual situation to which he responded or which he precipitated, and this is frequently forgotten or given insufficient attention. An interesting example is the Gospel of Matthew, where we shall see that the Evangelist's concern with the presence of unworthy members in the church probably accounts for his "parable" of the Tares Among the Wheat and the allegorical interpretation of it, for his interpretation of the Dragnet, for his addition of the wedding-garment scene to the parable of the Banquet, and his inclusion of the parable of the Ten Virgins in its present form.[7] Behind such adaptations may often be found the real situation that called forth the original parable, a situation that was tense and demanded complete attention to the exclusion of general moralizing. As Dodd suggests, Jesus is sometimes treated as though he had the leisure and detachment of a Greek philosopher, able systematically to organize and present his "philosophy of life."[8] Or he is presented as one who moved publicly about a secret task, hiding his real purpose and disguising his real meaning in a form of teaching to which only the initiated would have the key or which only those who came after could understand. To adopt either viewpoint appears to me to be false—and nowhere so decidedly misleading as in treating the parables.

Those who observed Jesus' activities were by no means passive, nor were they silent before his teachings. They raised objections, made demands, took action. But neither was Jesus passive. He answered their objections; he too pressed a claim and rejected the demands made of him. He took counteraction; even his surrender to the cross was counteraction. The parables are a phase of this exchange. They offer no apologies or excuses for his work; they justify it. They do not conceal his meaning or purpose; they affirm it. Where friends or enemies offer superficial agreement, the parables pursue them. They force the unwary to commit themselves to an opinion on one ground and do not allow them to escape a decision on another. As a weapon the parables could be provocative. To catch anew the drama and its enduring significance, we must put Jesus' teaching again into the historic situation and see those among whom he moved as Jews whose past history and present situation were engrossing preoccupations making for violent reactions.

The main factor in Jesus' own position is that he was a Jew among Jews. As the Hebrew scholar J. Klausner says, "Jesus was a Jew and a Jew he remained till his last breath."[9] His education was that of a village child, and he probably spoke and read no languages other than Aramaic and possibly classical Hebrew. His experience was narrow, confined to the scenes referred to in the Gospels and reflected in the simplicity of the parable settings. He was a religious Jew—that is, a good Jew. His interest was centered where the religious Jew's interest was always focused: on the Torah, the Holy City, and the destiny of God's chosen people. The kingdom of God absorbed attention, along with the Law which was to be its formative factor and its constitution. Upon Israel lay a special vocation. It was chosen to be a holy nation; it had been preserved among the peoples of the earth; it was central to God's purpose. Thus ran the covenant. The constant confusion of this sense of destiny with imperial ambition is one of the chief clues to the real meaning of the Old Testament. It is a major clue to the elucidation of Jesus' teaching and of his strategy.

This fact is of prime importance. In spite of subsequent tendencies of Christian theology and the appeal to the Gospels in its support, Jesus was not and could not be a Hellenic philosopher. His training had been from infancy in the canonical Jewish scriptures, presumably under the rabbis and therefore in their normal treatment of those traditions. The story of his childhood visit to the temple (Luke 2:41ff.) suggests, however, that he approached the canonical scriptures and traditional commentary in a searching and questioning frame of mind and was accustomed to apply to it his own critical discrimination. This becomes clear by a study of his use of the Old Testament and is further illustrated by the parables.[10]

His audiences, likewise trained in the scriptures from youth, were apt to discern at once a reference to them and to supply the background for themselves. The allusions do not always come readily to our minds, and it must be a first principle of interpretation that we remember this contact and seek to supply it. For example, the amount of meal in the parable of the Leaven would doubtless remind the audience of certain Old Testament scenes. In the parable of the Tenants of the Vineyard (Mark 12:1-12), the opening description is suspected by some scholars as an assimilation to Isaiah 5:2. It is omitted in the Lucan version. This may well be an addition used in preaching and written in by the Evangelists, but it is by no means irrelevant since the passage from Isaiah would, in any case, be at once suggested to Jesus' audience. Parallels to his teaching in extra-canonical literature and rabbinic parables would also perhaps be suggested, but a primary reference to the canonical literature must always be considered.[11]

There existed at the time a large body of apocryphal writings, and modern scholars make frequent appeal to them for light on the background of Jesus' times. Certainly from these sources we may sense the atmosphere of the thinking world. The apocalyptic expectations which already appear in the canonical Old Testament later developed a wealth of literary forms and represent the reactions of the Maccabean and Roman periods. They do not represent, as some have supposed, a complete despair or an abandonment of the ancient faith in a righteous God.

There is a dualism present, but not an eternal metaphysical dualism, equal and unresolvable. This is testified to by the Qumran scrolls (e.g., the "Manual of Discipline"), where the dualism is ethical rather than cosmological and limited to a term. The confidence in the triumph of Yahweh and his people is unimpaired, though its realization moves from the temporal realm to the eternal, from the mundane to the supramundane. It is an affirmation of the invincible power of God's justice in the face of every disillusionment of earth. No hope can be seen for the worldly order; the kingdom of God will nevertheless be established. There opens the vision of an invasion from without, the possibility of the imposition of a heavenly order upon the disorders of earth.

We can see in this one of the major elements of Jesus' situation. It is a reflection of the agony of his times. There is a "bookish" tendency in the reading of the Gospels that might well lead us astray. To be too exclusively concerned with the Gospels as texts is to stand apart from the history of which they are but reflections. To be absorbed in them as literature is to forget the agonized ferment of the times, to which they are only an immediate foreground. Even to be engrossed with Jesus, commendable as that must always be, is to make the mistake of ignoring the people to whom he belonged. His teachings were designed for the actual people he addressed. They were heard and understood by folk who stood in a certain historical position. As V. G. Simkhovitch has written, "The more limited is our knowledge of the one, the more important is the light that may be shed by the many."[12]

Simkhovitch's essay was important for this emphasis, which has not received the attention it merited. All of Jesus' life was lived in a period of violent political tension, the clue to which is the attitude toward Rome. This determined the national policy of the Jews. Simkhovitch pointed out that the Jews themselves sought annexation by Rome and that the purpose of this move was clear. "In reality they were trying to save their culture and their religion."[13] The familiar parties of Jesus' time had their own attitudes toward this question. For the Sadducees, peace with Rome and noninterference from outside promised security in their official position as the ruling caste. Anything that was likely to draw unfavorable attention was to be discouraged. For this reason they rejected any expansion of the tradition and adopted the protective coloration of a Hellenistic way of life. For the Pharisees, it was all-important that advantage be taken of the well-known liberality of Rome toward the religion of its provincials. Until the heaven-sent Messiah should appear, revolt was fruitless. It was essential to "keep the Law." In the end, to do this the Roman yoke must be broken. The Pharisees were the noblest product of Judaism (much as our view of them is distorted by denunciations in the Gospels) and as such were admired by the people. Their very enthusiasm and strictness, however, had led to the creation of a large body of outcasts, among whom were the "publicans and sinners" who received a large share of Jesus' attention. The Qumran community seems to have originated in an extreme wing of the pietistic movement which had completely withdrawn itself to prepare for the eschaton. The Zealots represented an emerging group out of favor with the dominant parties—for obvious reasons. Their resistance to the taxation and impositions of Rome and their advocacy of an armed struggle for independence could not but be an embarrassment. Yet in the end they were destined to force the nation into a disastrous war. During Jesus' youth and manhood their policy had already issued in bloody revolts, the traces of which appear in the Gospels.[14]

This violent unrest and state of nervous tension must have had an immediate bearing on Jesus' work. It is certain that wherever his sayings had relevance to the vital issues under debate his hearers must have detected it. Far from being unaware of such relevance, the probability is that they would read into his teaching attitudes subject to violently controversial reaction. Dr. John Knox, in a reference to this point of view, says of Jesus, "That he was aware of and sensitive to the political situation goes without saying; that he was on the whole silent about any particular technique for solving it seems likely."[15] This is a useful caution against looking to Jesus for a political (or economic) program. The important point is that Jesus offered a radically different analysis of the situation, and his words suggested most emphatically his rejection or trenchant criticism of the solutions then being pursued or being considered. Sayings like "No one can serve two masters" must have been heard by those of that day as a comment on policies to which many hearers were committed. The parables, especially the "later" ones, deal with factors that had been ignored, as it seemed to Jesus, and he in effect warns that God's solution might be radically different from those currently popular. The Gospels bear witness that this was the case at the trial of Jesus.[16] False or true, the issues were such that the procurator must take note of the charges made. We must therefore bear constantly in mind this charged atmosphere in which Jesus' work was done. It is an element that cannot be neglected in trying to understand the original impact of his teaching. The issues were not literary; they were matters of life and death.

The parables arise out of real situations and are frequently instruments of controversy, forged for the moment and produced to meet, to develop, or to create an issue. It becomes apparent that, once the situation has changed, the occasion has passed, and the issue is no longer felt as paramount, the clue to a parable so produced would be mislaid. It was only natural, therefore, that the church should be in doubt about the original meaning of the comparison or indifferent to it. It is a tribute to the genius of Jesus that Christians found a way to apply the parables, and sometimes more than one way; that his spontaneous creations produced in the heat of debate should have valid meanings long after the moment had passed. While this of course must be discussed in detail in actual instances, let us observe here that one danger was likely to arise.

Many of the parables thrust sharply against sins or failings of religious classes and groups, most conspicuously the Pharisees. Here we would class not only the parable of the Pharisee and the Tax Collector but the Two Sons, the Banquet, the Barren Fig Tree, and many others. Now it is characteristic of the failings Jesus attacked that those susceptible to them are unable to see themselves as they are. Not only are they incapable, they are unwilling to recognize the diagnosis of their own disorder as a diagnosis at all. It is either resented as an unjust and unwarranted attack or, more usually, it is applied by them to someone else. Yet this is one of the clues to the diagnosis, and Jesus so assesses it in his saying, "Why do you see the speck that is in your brother's eye, but do not notice the log that is in your own eye?"

This tendency to reject self-criticism helps us to understand why the church failed to apply as it should the primary teachings of Jesus' parables. It was willing to see their application to others while it missed the application to itself. The tendency would be to preserve clearly the teaching that applied to current opponents but to be less clear about the relevance of teaching that was a warning to the church. This could be only a potential danger in the first generation. The book of The Revelation of John refers to situations in existence at the time it was written of which this would be true (especially Rev. 3:1, 7). After the "triumph of Christianity" over the Roman Empire, in successive eras of papal supremacy, and in the era of "national churches," the tendency must become aggravated. It exists too widely in our own time for our own comfort, and to rediscover the primary meaning of the parables is to be painfully aware of the need of modern Christianity for the teaching they conveyed when first spoken. It was because the initial hearers could not escape the meaning for Israel that they hurried Jesus to the cross.

In the last analysis, an estimate of Jesus' teaching in relation to his situation must necessarily deal with Jesus' own presence in that situation. Neither political nor theological necessity determined the nature of the Gospel but, as Paul rightly understood, the presence of Christ. The course pursued by the Jewish nation remained essentially unaffected by his work except as the emergence of the Christian church may be considered part of Jewish history. To understand his teaching would be difficult without some sense of the historical atmosphere of the times; it would be impossible without observing that he himself considered his own presence critical. There is an atmosphere of crisis about his words and work which is not explained simply by the disturbances abroad. He was manifestly a figure of destiny, and the destiny of men was in some sense determined by their reaction to him. This was his own view of the situation, and his consciousness of high mission is a prime factor in the story.

A prime factor—yet when we come to investigate we find it possible to arrive at no definitive conclusions as to what that consciousness was. Here, more than at any other single point (because it is the central point), the hand of the Christian community can be detected at work. It became clear to the Christian mind that Jesus was no ordinary man. It therefore seemed impossible that Jesus should not clearly have referred during his ministry to his own peculiar place in the purposes of God. In recent works we find controversy raging about the question of messiahship, about the terms Son of Man and Suffering Servant, and concerning Jesus' filial consciousness.[17] When the evidence has been sifted free of later interpretations, we are left with no certainty. Perhaps no conclusive answer is possible except the testimony of the Christian soul who knows Jesus as living Lord and Son of God. Certainly, in the last analysis, no other assurance can be convincing, nor, I think, would Jesus himself consider it of value. Until we are committed to him he must in some sense be always an enigma.

The parables as such seem to contain nothing by which the issue raised may be finally determined. If this mode of teaching was intended by Jesus to be the means of making his message clear, it is striking that no parable should have survived that put the nature of his own person beyond all doubt. The conviction arises that no such parable was told, for that very parable certainly would have been cherished and it would not have been necessary to adapt those which originally had clearly another purpose. The parables, however, present the kind of challenge that in itself constitutes a claim. This becomes more apparent where we can take them out of the "life situation" of the early church and apply them again more directly to the position in which Jesus stood. Parable after parable confronts those who are addressed with a message and a person that demand a radical response. In this Jesus appears as a prophet, and this was the testimony of his contemporaries (cf. Mark 8:28; Matt. 21:11). But there was something more than prophecy. The testimony to that "something more" is the violence of the reaction in Jerusalem and the extremity of the charges laid against Jesus, of which he was apparently judged guilty and for which, therefore, he was crucified. The Jews were confronted with something they called "blasphemy" and the Romans with something they labeled "treason." The chances are that the two designations refer to a common element of offense—as it seemed to them—in that which confronted them. Increasingly it became impossible to separate message from messenger, the demand from him who made it. This is seen nowhere more clearly than in the parables. It appears that no final conclusions can be arrived at concerning "the messianic secret" or the precise eschatological expectations of Jesus until the parables have been studied for their bearing on those themes. To do this they must be divorced as far as possible from the adaptations of the early church.

Even on the assumption of a "messianic secret" in Mark, we are forced to ask whether Jesus was not quite reluctant to claim messianic honor.[18] If we do not accept the theory of a secret, the reluctance remains. No claim, in any case, could have been more subject to misunderstanding or more subject to exactly the sort of interpretation Jesus must reject. The title Son of Man, as can be seen by the reading of any of the works on the subject, was well-nigh enigmatic. The reading back into the Gospels of the theory of the Suffering Servant may well be a fruitful clue and may indeed correctly interpret Jesus' inner consciousness, but it remains a reading back. All these solutions may represent elements in Jesus' own thought. Certainly they were elements in the thought of the times. Some or all of them serve to illuminate the situation and may to some extent be true guides. But Jesus himself is strangely silent. *Of God and God's kingdom the parables are full. Of the Messiah they have nothing directly to say.*

Once again the gulf represented by the resurrection experience faces us. The parables lend themselves in many cases to interpretation by the church, which finds in Christ its Lord and Judge. We have no quarrel with this, but our purpose is to find their original meaning in the hope that Christian interpretation and use will be extensions of that meaning.

This suggests the method we shall follow. While we cannot in every case follow all its strands, we can endeavor to apply it in general. It is first necessary to see what the parable is as parable. The essential content can be arrived at by comparison of parallel versions. We can eliminate introductions, appendages, and interwoven elements which appear to have been added in transmission or arise from the particular interests of the compiler. This will enable us to study the incident, the observed fact, the drama, or the narrative that the resultant parable sets forth. Here we must ask whether its terms may not have suggested a connotation to the Evangelist, or to those through whom it passed before reaching him, that was not necessarily the connotation suggested to the original audience. We must also ask what observation or judgment it elicits or was designed to draw from those who stood in the position of the original hearers.

This raises the question of the controlling setting—a double question. From the secondary material it may be possible to tell what was the situation that prompted the inclusion of the parable in the Gospel or the choice of the context in which it now stands or the application that has been associated with it. Against this we must weigh the contexts and interpretations in other Gospels, where they differ, and whatever we can recover of the possible position of Jesus and his contemporaries. We must ask what—in view of the concerns and policies of the moment, in view of the interaction between Jesus and his opponents, and in view of the traditional background—those to whom it was directed may have been expected to understand. It may then be possible to suggest what the original interpretation may have been, taking account of Jesus' teaching elsewhere. We must also weigh what bearing the teaching arrived at may have had on Jesus' eventual fate.

Our attempt in most cases ought not to stop at that point. The interpretations given in the early church, reflected in the Gospel record, are of interest even where they differ from what we deduce to have been the original meaning. We may consider whether they are more or less arbitrary adaptations or whether they are legitimate extensions to a changed situation. This will determine our own use of the parable. We can ask ourselves in all seriousness whether the attitude or situation to which the parable and its teaching were first addressed still exists or represents a real possibility. In that case we must take its meaning to heart, and the preaching of it will be in relation to the current form of attitude, situation, danger, or hope that first gave it force. We can ask whether the teaching, though addressed to a situation that no longer obtains, is not susceptible of application in more general terms to universal weaknesses or potentialities of human individuals or groups. Here is the danger point in preaching—that we shall so generalize the truth taught that it becomes simply a moral counsel, involving at no point the eternal issues of crucifixion and resurrection, of judgment and redemption. The cure does not lie in allegorical identifications but in examining our own hearts and probing our corporate life to see whether, after all, the parallel does not exist where we had missed it. We are all too prone to overlook the failings of the churches, of organized Christianity. When we recover the directness of the application of the parables to the historic Israel, we recover also the duty to apply them to "the people of God" before we apply them to "those outside."

We therefore seek to understand the Jesus of the parables in order to discover his significance for us and for his church in our day. We may not expect by study alone, whether study of the parables or of the whole New Testament, ever to solve the problems that arise when we are confronted by Jesus. The reactions of his contemporaries as these problems were met and answered by the action of God produced the New Testament church. Membership in that church represented a radically different reaction to Jesus. It was a response to God manifested in Christ. In any study of the Gospels, we do well to recall the words that stand at the end of a monumental investigation of Jesus and his interpreters:

> He comes to us as one unknown, without a name, as of old, by the lake-side, He came to those men who knew Him not. He speaks to us the same word: "Follow thou me!" and sets us to the tasks which He has to fulfil for our time. He commands. And to those who obey Him, whether they be wise or simple, He will reveal Himself in the toils, the conflicts, the sufferings which they shall pass through in His fellowship, and, as an ineffable mystery, they shall learn in their own experience Who He is.[19]

# THREE THE CALL OF GOD'S KINGDOM

According to the earliest Gospel (Mark), Jesus first appeared in public at the baptism of John. This was the point at which the Gospel preached by the primitive church began (Acts 10:37). Jesus' baptism marked his consecration to the messianic task—"anointed . . . with the Holy Spirit and with power (Acts 10:38)"—in terms of what was first represented probably as a Davidic type of Sonship. He was then "led by the Spirit" into the wilderness. For accounts of "the temptation" we are dependent on Q in Matthew 4:1-11 and Luke 4:1-13. These stories clearly mean that at the outset Jesus is interpreted as having weighed carefully the traditional forms of the messianic expectation—material prosperity, wonder-working, and imperial dominion—and once and for all rejected them as clues to his own vocation. Whatever positive decision he may then have made could be revealed only as events unfolded and were met at every point by his own decisive response. Though it is not expressly set forth, a strategy is involved in which the parables are tactical weapons.[1]

Jesus' message concerned the kingdom of God and was delivered at first through the natural medium, the synagogues of Galilee. His sabbath appearances there afforded opportunity to engage in works of healing and exorcism as well as to preach (Mark 1). It was not long, however, before opposition developed within synagogue circles (Mark 2:1–3:6), and it appears either that Jesus was no longer considered an acceptable teacher or that he himself found the medium no longer served his purpose. There followed a period of ministry out of doors in Galilee, marked at first by wide popularity but later by a decided falling away. It may be a simplification to represent this as a simple progression. In all probability it was a repeated experience in each new area to which Jesus carried his message, failure following initial popularity as the stay was prolonged and the people found Jesus unwilling to adapt himself to their views. The indication in John 6:15 (cf. vs. 66f.) that the loss of followers was due to disappointed political hopes has much to commend it.

Mark assigns the first use of parables to the beginning of the outdoor ministry. The major example is the parable of the Sower, and around it Mark arranges the theory of parabolic teaching criticized in the preceding chapter. To it he has assimilated other parables. The interpretation offered below, which treats as secondary his theory and explanation, suggests that this parable offers the best starting point. If the interpretation is correct, it provides an important aid to our understanding of Jesus.

## THE SOWER

### Matthew 13
*¹That same day Jesus went out of the house and sat beside the sea. ²And great crowds gathered about him, so that he got into a boat and sat there; and the whole crowd stood on the beach. ³And he told them many things in parables, saying:* "A sower went out to sow. ⁴And as he sowed, some seeds fell along the path, and the birds came and devoured them. ⁵Other seeds fell on rocky ground, where they had not much soil, and immediately they sprang up, since they had no depth of soil, ⁶but when the sun rose they were scorched; and since they had no root they withered away. ⁷Other seeds fell upon thorns, and the thorns grew up and choked them. ⁸Other seeds fell on good soil and brought forth grain, some a hundredfold, some sixty, some thirty. *⁹He who has ears, let him hear."*

### Mark 4
*¹Again he began to teach beside the sea. And a very large crowd gathered about him, so that he got into a boat and sat in it on the sea; and the whole crowd was beside the sea on the land. ²And he taught them many things in parables, and in his teaching he said to them:* ³"Listen! A sower went out to sow. ⁴And as he sowed, some seed fell along the path, and the birds came and devoured it. ⁵Other seed fell on rocky ground, where it had not much soil, and immediately it sprang up, since it had no depth of soil; ⁶and when the sun rose it was scorched, and since it had no root it withered away. ⁷Other seed fell among thorns and the thorns grew up and choked it, and it yielded no grain. ⁸And other seeds fell into good soil and brought forth grain, growing up and increasing and yielding thirtyfold and sixtyfold and a hundredfold." *⁹And he said, "He who has ears to hear, let him hear."*

### Luke 8
*⁴And when a great crowd came together and people from town after town came to him, he said in a parable:* ⁵"A sower went out to sow

his seed; and as he sowed, some fell along the path, and was trodden under foot, and the birds of the air devoured it. ⁶And some fell on the rock; and as it grew up, it withered away, because it had no moisture. ⁷And some fell among thorns; and the thorns grew with it and choked it. ⁸And some fell into good soil and grew, and yielded a hundredfold." *As he said this, he called out, "He who has ears to hear, let him hear."*

This is one of the three best known parables and perhaps the least understood. It seems easily comprehended, because in each of the Synoptics there is an interpretation ascribed to Jesus. The Sower is one of the most popular parables because the "interpretation" so readily lends itself to sermonizing. This very use of the parable "in the pulpit" accounts for Mark's explanation of its meaning. The Gospel exposition has led some recent writers to prefer the designation "the parable of the Soils." Yet the traditional title, the Sower, persists and is correct. The misunderstanding of the parable is explained by the fact that the interpretation offered in the Gospels is popular and more apparently useful than the parable itself. Critical scholars have held that the parable leaves so much uncertainty about its original meaning that we must be satisfied with conjecture. It is hard to escape from the traditional treatment, but must we abandon the attempt to elucidate it?

The basic version is Mark's. The opening word, "Listen! (Mark 4:3)" and the conclusion, "He who has ears to hear, let him hear (v. 9)," may be set aside as depending on each other. The latter is a floating saying reiterated in Revelation (chs. 2:7, 11, 17, 29; 3:6, 13, 22; 13:9) and used rather extensively by the Evangelists (Mark 4:23; cf. 8:18; Matt. 11:15; 13:43; Luke 14:35). It prepares for the application supposed to have been given in private and may be dropped. The parable then stands without the traditional Jewish introduction and lacks a specific context apart from Mark's use of it to introduce the whole subject of parabolic teaching.

The bare parable (Mark 4:3-8) is the account of what quite normally happened when a sower of that time sowed his seed. It is important to note that it is an account of a normal process which happens constantly. It is not about a particular sower (as against those who have supposed—perhaps from "Behold" [RV]—that Jesus pointed to an actual sower within view). The use of the generic article, *ho speirōn* ("the sower"), indicates that it deals with the sower as a class. Like the parable of the leaven, it is put in concrete narrative form for the sake of vividness.[2]

The sower, Jesus observes, sows his seed, and for specific reasons (three, as in folk tales) some of it bears no fruit. But, by contrast, the rest falls where it can produce a harvest. There is perhaps an element of Oriental hyperbole in the "thirtyfold and sixtyfold and a hundredfold" of Mark (inverted by Matthew and confined to "a hundredfold" by Luke). Mark emphasizes, in verse 8, the abundance of the results as the other Evangelists do not, and yet multiplication of the seed by the harvest is not beyond the reasonable expectation of the farmer.[3]

The difficulty arises when we ask what we should have made of this parable if we had received it without interpretation. Should we find our attention focused on the varieties of soil, on the failure of the seed in three instances to grow to fruition, or on the assurance of an abundant harvest? The question seems difficult only because we find it hard to dispossess our minds of the interpretation in the text and of the many sermons the ordinary churchgoer has heard devoted to the unfruitful soils. It is a question that cannot be answered without first considering what it might have meant to the Jews who heard it and treated it as a parable rather than as an allegory of homiletic value.

There is in the Old Testament a certain tradition of God as the Sower. The priestly account of creation (Gen. 1:11-12) asserts the fruitfulness of the earth and the reproductive power of the vegetable world as originally ordered. In Jeremiah and elsewhere God speaks as the Sower. "I will sow the house of Israel and the house of Judah with the seed of man and the seed of beast (Jer. 31:27)." "I will sow him for myself in the land (Hos. 2:23)." There is also the passage in Isaiah 5:2 where God expects a vintage from his planting: "He looked for it to yield grapes." In Isaiah 55, the fruitfulness of God's word is likened to the operation of the rain and the snow that the earth may "bring forth and sprout" and that it may give "seed to the sower and bread to the eater" (vs. 10-11), and the emphasis is upon the certainty of its accomplishing that for which God designed it. "It shall not return unto me empty, but it shall accomplish that which I purpose."

We may remind ourselves, moreover, of the nature of parables—they were designed to prompt a judgment and were often interpreted by the principle "how much more." In this parable a common experience is depicted. Everyone knew the characteristic hazards of sowing by hand on rocky soil where weeds were prolific, near the haunts of men who trod paths along the edges of the fields. But everyone was equally aware of the truth in the climactic end of the parable, the abundant harvest which is achieved in spite of all the natural hazards. It might well be the hearer's observation that the mischances that befell a portion of the seed were incommensurate with the certain results. He would indeed be a strange sower who sowed so carelessly that the bulk, the half, or even, in fact, any considerable portion of the seed fell on unprofitable soil. He would be either a curiously careless sower or a most indifferent plowman.[4] The listener might well observe that in spite of the inevitable loss of some of the seed the rewards are so great that the sower finds it worthwhile, abundantly worthwhile, to sow his seed year after year, persistently, knowing that the harvest far outweighs the loss. This is the clue to the parable.[5]

Did Jesus intend to convey the idea that what was sown was the word of God? I think we must hesitate here, since this is too easily to be deduced from the interpretation. Further, in the Marcan version the use of the word "seed" is altogether absent, though whether this is deliberate avoidance or a fortuitous textual circumstance it is impossible to say. Jesus spoke of both his words and his acts as signs of the invasion of the kingdom of God, and in any case his "word" was the "word of the kingdom"; it was the burden of his message.

Those who doubt that the parable could be understood without an explanation seem to ignore the fact that the hearers were familiar with the parable method and may be presumed to have been aware of the circumstances under which it was spoken. They might well understand it as Jesus' response to that situation and his reason for it. There is nothing in the parable to indicate at what point in Jesus' ministry the parable was delivered, though it seems safe to assume that it was in the Galilean period during his outdoor teaching. The surmise that it was late in the ministry depends entirely on the assumption that the parable was related to the effects of Jesus' preaching—or, rather, to the astonishing lack of effect.

As several scholars have pointed out, it is the interpretation, and not the parable itself, that stresses the loss rather than the gain. The parable ends on a positive note, a note of superabundance. We shall find the original meaning here. To put ourselves in the place of the hearers is to reason that, just as the sower expects to lose a proportion of his seed and is not thereby discouraged or deterred from sowing but expects a plentiful crop, so in the spiritual realm God also is persistent. The spiritual unfruitfulness of some areas is manifest, yet his work has an abundant result. He never gives up but by constant perseverance secures a harvest. It seems clearly a parable of *persistence.* The principle "how much more" has also its use. If the sower of ordinary seed, we may argue, does not become discouraged by losses but, with the harvest in view, persists always, how much more will God persevere in setting forward his kingdom in the certainty (since his kingdom must rule over all) that it will come to fruition?

If we seek for a setting in Jesus' ministry, we may find it in his determination to persist in his work in spite of opposition, in spite of the closing of the synagogues to his message. We might well conceive of the parable as the counterpart of his message to John the Baptist (Matt. 11:4-6; Luke 7:22-23). In that, he pointed specifically to the work being done. In the parable, he lays down the principle that his persistence is justified by the certainty of results. What is presented to John as an appeal to the facts becomes, in the parable, a challenge from both the facts and the will of God—the facts being more abundantly clear to Jesus from his assurance of God's intention than they could ever be to the eye of the onlooker.

Later, when the remnant of Jesus' followers who had survived pondered on the failure both of Jesus and the church to win the majority, the emphasis shifted, as in the interpretation, from the persistence of the sower (which arises from the certainty of harvest) to the unfruitful aspects of the soil. Both Dodd and Cadoux connect the parable with Jesus' saying in Matthew 9:37-38 and Luke 10:2, "The harvest is plentiful, but the laborers are few." This may well be granted but, in the light of the parable, the saying would seem to be less an observation of fact than an act of faith. The attention of the parable, in any case, falls upon the sowing (which is persistently undertaken because of the harvest) as well as upon the harvest. As an observation upon history it would read that, in the story of Israel, in spite of many barren periods and unfruitful areas of national life, God had never ceased to raise up his prophets and leaders to continue the sowing unto harvest. In the parable Jesus expresses in the face of incipient rejection his determination to continue. It is a necessity required by the will and purpose of God.

If we may see here, then, Jesus' proclamation of his purpose to pursue his task in the face of all opposition and failure, we may understand anew the position of the parable in Mark. It follows the series of "opposition incidents," the withdrawal from the synagogues to the sea, the appointment of the Twelve, the charges of the scribes "from Jerusalem," and the separation from his mother and brethren. If opposition and distrust made it, to say the least, expedient for Jesus to work outside the normal channels, the appointment of the Twelve was a proclamation of his intention to continue his work— whatever else it may have been. And the parable may well be another form of the proclamation and the parabolic expression of the basis for his determination.

Interpreted in this sense, it finds points of contact with Jesus' progress to the ultimate climax in Jerusalem. Thus there is the urgency to embark on the task without distraction which he presented to would-be disciples in Matthew 8:19-22 and Luke 9:57-62; the charge to the seventy missionaries in Luke 10:1-16, which contains the harvest saying just quoted; the joyous cry with which Jesus greeted the return of the Seventy: "I saw Satan fall like lightning from heaven (Luke 10:18)"; his response to the warning about Herod: "Go and tell that fox, 'Behold, I cast out demons and perform cures today and tomorrow, and the third day I finish my course. Nevertheless I must go on my way (Luke 13:31-33)' "; and the saying in the passage already cited (9:62), cast also in an agricultural metaphor, "No one who puts his hand to the plow and looks back is fit for the kingdom of God."

The place Mark has given to the parable, following his "opposition" sections, is obscured in the Gospel because of his double interest in the parable as a basis for his theory of the use of parables and as an ecclesiastical analysis of problems current in his day. When these are stripped off, the other and perhaps earlier connection begins to appear, and it becomes of more interest when we allow the parable to speak for itself, as we have tried to do.

We are then left with the problem of the interpretation given in the Synoptics (Matt. 13:18-23; Mark 4:13-20; Luke 8:11-15). Attempts have been made to accept it at face value or to treat it as a second parable based on the first. More convincingly, the commentators have laid down the grounds for treating it as a secondary development of oral tradition.[6] The grounds may be summarized as follows.

Anyone reading (even in English) the interpretation and then the parable, along with other parables, finds an entirely new atmosphere. The parable is simple, direct, and naturalistic; the interpretation is developed (awkwardly at the outset) as a studied allegory. In the parable everything belongs to the scene, while in the interpretation outside interests come in at every point. The language makes this clear. In the introductory verse Cadoux sees the Christian preacher at work. As he points out, the words, "Do you not understand this parable? How then will you understand all the parables? (Mark 4:13)" sound strange on the lips of Jesus, particularly at that point in the Marcan story, for they assume the existence of a body of parabolic teaching and would be reasonable in a sermon on the parables but not on the lips of Jesus after the first of his parables. Words and phrases appear which are characteristic of a church that is a numerical minority, engaged in expansion by preaching, sorrowing over lapsed converts, and undergoing persecution for the faith. Think, for example, of "the word," "receive it with joy," "no root in themselves," "endure for a while," "tribulation," "persecution," "fall away," "the cares of the world," "the delight in riches," and "the desire for other things." In Luke the Greek words used are even more clearly characteristic of the early church.[7] The atmosphere of the interpretation is that of the Roman (Mark) or the gentile church (Luke), and a situation more developed than that by the lakeside is in the background. Moreover, the need to interpret the parable defeats the purpose of a parable, which itself is designed to be an elucidation.

The need for interpretation does arise when the situation to which the parable is addressed no longer obtains.[8] After the resurrection, the persistent determination of Jesus to pursue his course had become clear and his incarnate work was accomplished. The task resting upon the church was that of preaching him and his gospel. It soon became apparent that the results were by no means automatic, nor were they always enduring. To allegorize the incidental details about the unfruitful pockets of soil not only illuminated the causes of failure but afforded vivid and valuable homiletic material to use in warning the hearers of the dangers involved for them. How fruitful this line of thought has proved, how truly evangelical and salutary, is illustrated by all preaching since. The constant association of parable and interpretation in the oral tradition explains quite naturally the incorporation of the latter in the Gospels.

It is not our purpose to advocate the abandonment of this homiletic treatment. It has its enduring value, and it has the most ancient sanction. What we plead for, however, is a recognition that it is a homiletic development, legitimate though secondary. It should be safeguarded always by holding it in relation to the original purpose of the parable suggested above and allowed to throw light upon our Lord. The tendency of preachers is to devote too much attention to the negative aspects of the church's adventure in the world. To go behind the interpretation to the parable itself, behind Mark's theory to the situation of Jesus, reminds us of the sovereignty of God, of his unfailing purpose to "give you the kingdom," and creates in us an unflagging zeal and an invincible hope.

This is important, and succeeding parables reinforce it. It is important because to escape from the traditional homiletic uses puts the preacher where he ought to be—in the place of the hearer. By following the Gospel interpretation concerning the word, the preacher preaches about hearing and receiving the word of God; he preaches *about* the word of God instead of preaching the word of God. It is hard to escape the danger of identifying oneself with the sower and the people with the soils, a dangerous position of superiority for the preacher. The net result is likely to be negative. To turn back to the more direct meaning is at once to be preaching about God and his Christ, the persistent, eternal God whose sovereign purpose is expressed in Christ. His kingdom does not fail, but neither is it a juggernaut. It meets opposition, it experiences failure, but it triumphs over both and amid both. The opposition and the failure belong to history, as unproductive pockets of soil belong to sowing. But the kingdom belongs to the eternal realm, and the harvest is to be kept in view, not the failures. It is the Christian's duty to cultivate the field—and to keep his mind on the harvest. The first interest of the parables is the sovereignty of God. The Sower is primary in more senses than one. What it teaches must be kept in view in dealing with the others.

This, however, raises the question as to why the progress of God's kingdom in history is so confusing. Answers are found in the parables of the Leaven in the Meal, the Mustard Seed, and the Farmer and the Growing Seed. These too have been considered parables of growth, but each deals with an aspect of the kingdom and the primary thread that unites them is not that of growth.

## THE LEAVEN IN THE MEAL

**Matthew 13**
*33He told them another parable.* "The kingdom of heaven is like leaven which a woman took and hid in three measures of meal, till it was all leavened."

**Luke 13**
*20And again he said,* "To what shall I compare the kingdom of God? 21It is like leaven which a woman took and hid in three measures of meal, till it was all leavened."

No doubt this parable has been preserved because it could be interpreted as a forecast of the growth of the church in scope and influence. But this reason for preservation suggests a reinterpretation, and our question is how it differs from the original meaning.

The Leaven is missing in Mark, while in Q (as preserved in Matthew and Luke) it forms (with the Mustard Seed) the second member of a pair. Nothing beyond this editorial circumstance requires us to interpret each exactly alike. The attempt to find a parallel meaning causes us to seek a common feature as the clue and draws unnecessary attention to something purely incidental—namely, that in each case there is a species of expansion—while ignoring the more fundamental differences.

A second caution is necessary: to remind ourselves that the comparison is not between leaven and the kingdom of God but "like leaven which. . . ." It is important to repeat this because an initial difficulty faces those who would, in the traditional way, make the kingdom of God (or Christianity) equal leaven. The difficulty is that leaven elsewhere in scripture represents not something good but something evil. In Judaism leaven came to have unfortunate connotations, probably because the process of fermentation which yeast induces was thought of as corruption. It is only fair to say that to the ancients the process was mysterious. They lacked a scientific explanation.

Leaven was prohibited during the Passover celebrations, the "feast of unleavened bread (Exod. 12:17)." Jesus is reported to have said, "Beware of the leaven of the Pharisees and the leaven of Herod (Mark 8:15)." In Galatians 5:9 we find, "A little yeast leavens the whole lump." Again Paul writes (1 Cor. 5:6-8), "Do you not know that a little leaven ferments the whole lump of dough? Cleanse out the old leaven that you may be fresh dough, as you really are unleavened. For Christ, our paschal lamb, has been sacrificed. Let us, therefore, celebrate the festival, not with the old leaven, the leaven of malice and evil, but with the unleavened bread of sincerity and truth." Evidently Paul did not think of leaven as a symbol of the kingdom.

It would have been difficult also for Jesus' hearers to understand the leaven as a straightforward simile for the kingdom of God. Attempts to avoid the difficulty without suggesting whence the difficulty arises are not too convincing. It has been suggested that Jesus is here making a new and unexpected use of a familiar illustration. This does not seem characteristic of Jesus, since it expects too much of the audience. The rest of the New Testament shows no awareness of such use. The transition from leaven as inimical to good is documented in Ignatius, *Epistle to the Magnesians,* X.2., "Put aside the evil leaven, which has grown old and sour, and turn to the new leaven, which is Jesus Christ."[9] There is no real solution when the leaven is taken in an allegorical sense. The difficulty disappears, however, and the confusion is removed when it is not so taken. Like Jesus' audience, we must treat it as parable. Then the comparison is not between the leaven and the kingdom but between *what happens* when leaven is put into a batch of meal and *what happens* when the kingdom of God enters history.

The parable is that when a woman puts an unspecified amount of yeast into a specified amount of meal, all the meal is affected. Three seahs is the specified amount, and three seahs made one ephah. This was a large baking; as we might say, a party baking. In the Old Testament the same amount of meal was used when Abram and Sara entertained the Lord at Mamre (Gen. 18:6) and Gideon the angel under the oak at Ophrah (Judg. 6:19). Hannah offered an ephah when she presented Samuel at Shiloh (1 Sam. 1:24). It is therefore a very large but not an impossible amount that Jesus specifies, and this gives us a clue to the interpretation.

Everyone knows what happens when leaven is used. All the meal becomes leavened (indeed, it may be used as leaven to leaven other meal). The leaven loses its identity, becomes part of the dough and cannot be extracted. Jesus puts the emphasis on what happens to the meal and not on what happens to the leaven.[10]

The parable, then, lifted to its spiritual plane, must mean: *When the kingdom of God enters the world, nothing is unaffected by it*—no part of human life, no part of history. This is not to speak of a universal spread in the sense of a universal *acceptance*, but of universal disturbance by a new element. The effect is felt throughout; nothing is secure from it. It is highly probable that the hearers would think of the action involved as a fermentation, a ferment involving the whole. This is a case where, once the clue is found, the aptness of the figure used is apparent. A new age has opened and everything is determined by that fact. It is recorded that Jesus said, "Do not think that I have come to bring peace on earth; I have not come to bring peace, but a sword (Matt. 10:34)," and, "I came to cast fire upon the earth; and would that it were already kindled! (Luke 12:49)." The emphasis is not a missionary one, nor is it eschatological in the sense of something belonging to a distant future. It speaks rather of a present and continuing reality. Jesus' own presence on the scene was the new factor introduced into history, from which history would never be able to escape. "But if it is by the finger of God that I cast out demons, then the kingdom of God has come upon you (Luke 11:20)."

We must not make the mistake, when we carry forward the meaning of this parable into subsequent history, of supposing that the parable is prophecy. Jesus is not here foretelling the experience of successive ages. Forecasting the future is a limited view of prophecy in any case. The principle here enunciated as a present truth is so true and so universal that illustrations of it and testimony to its insight can be found over and over again. Moreover, to grasp the principle is to find that assurance in the midst of change which enabled Jesus to abandon his ministry and die on the cross in the faith that the impending defeat was also part of his work under the will of God.

There have been times in history, for example, when an almost ideal situation seems (in retrospect) to have obtained. One thinks of the fruition of the Middle Ages or the apparent calm and outward respectability of the Victorian era. But in each case a ferment was at work which disrupted the age and led to new and more complex possibilities of growth. Under the church-dominated feudalism of the Middle Ages, the masses of people lived in serfdom. The revival of learning and the expansion of exploration destroyed a synthesis that we can characterize only as premature. Under the Victorian prosperity was a seething proletariat produced by the industrial revolution, and within society new scientific and historical studies created a ferment. Men always wish for a period of calm, for deliverance from wars and depressions and strikes and revolutions. But, in the language of the parable, *there is a ferment at work which no time and no society can escape.* As in the assertion Dr. Van Etten once quoted in a sermon, "Nothing is ever settled until it is settled right."[11] The kingdom of God does not *possess* the whole—perhaps it never will in history—but it always and everywhere *disturbs* the whole. The kingdom of God, the absolute rule of the All Holy, is not necessarily a blessing. It is a blessing to those who seek God's will. To those who reject his rule, his kingdom means condemnation and loss. But it is inescapable, as no part of the meal can escape the influence of the leaven that has been inserted in it. Jesus issued his challenge, and, though men tried to remove him, history ever since has had to come to terms with him. It is along these lines, I am sure, that the parable is to be interpreted. Here preachers and students are offered a more fruitful, more trustworthy, and more hopeful theme than the inevitable growth of the church or of the kingdom.

After a period when a false oversimplification of science deluded many into thinking that the kingdom of God was to be a steady approach to utopia, pessimism has taken hold of the human spirit. In the face of constant upheavals people have turned away from the church, supposing its gospel to be ineffective or literally untrue. They will be won again (and should be won again only) by a realistic message. What is needed is the realism Jesus expresses in these parables, a realism that is honest but triumphant, that discerns in the very facts of opposition and disturbance the present activity of God, immanent in the process but not contained within or frustrated by the process. To interpret the Leaven as a parable of inevitable, undisturbed permeation with good is to be blind to the facts. It is difficult to find, behind the Gospels, a Jesus who taught that doctrine. To do so he would have needed an entirely supramundane and quite romantic view of the future. Actual history would prove him mistaken. This is not the Jesus of the cross, and neither is this Jesus' view of history. The disturbance he himself created is still, fortunately, the source of our disturbances. Once we grasp this, we have a message to deliver to which people who live in the midst of upheaval will give ear. It may, by the grace of God, save them from cynicism and despair. "The whole creation has been groaning in travail together until now (Rom. 8:22)." "Not that I have already obtained this or am already perfect; but I press on . . . that I may know him and the power of his resurrection, and may share his sufferings (Phil. 3:12, 10)."

We found that the parable of the Sower was used in relation to the rise of opposition and expressed Jesus' determination to proceed. He well knew that to continue his work meant further attention from present opponents and new enemies. The next parable is perhaps another development of that thought and suggests why the impact of the kingdom is not steady triumph but disturbance.

## THE MUSTARD SEED

### Matthew 13
*³¹Another parable he put before them, saying,* **"The kingdom of heaven is like a grain of mustard seed which a man took and sowed in his field; ³²it is the smallest of all seeds, but when it has grown it is the greatest of shrubs and becomes a tree, so that the birds of the air come and make nests in its branches."**

### Mark 4
*³⁰And he said,* **"With what can we compare the kingdom of God, or what parable shall we use for it? ³¹It is like a grain of mustard seed, which, when sown upon the ground, is the smallest of all the seeds on earth; ³²yet when it is sown it grows up and becomes the greatest of all shrubs, and puts forth large branches, so that the birds of the air can make nests in its shade."**

### Luke 13
*¹⁸He said therefore,* **"What is the kingdom of God like? And to what shall I compare it? ¹⁹It is like a grain of mustard seed which a man took and sowed in his garden; and it grew and became a tree, and the birds of the air made nests in its branches."**

Once again, it is to be noted that this parable places no emphasis on the *process* of growth, though it is normally included under the "parables of growth" in an attempt to find a meaning parallel to the Leaven, its "twin" in Q.

The occurrence of the parable in each of the Synoptics presents problems of literary criticism. In Mark it is placed in the collection of "seed" parables. This tells us nothing except that the Evangelist so grouped it. In Luke it occurs in a non-Marcan setting and in isolation ("therefore" in Luke 13:18 is but an artificial link with the passage it follows). In the Lucan form the parable appears to be derived from Q. Matthew, like Luke, pairs it with the parable of the Leaven but seems to have combined Mark and Q.

We note the following: The introductory phrase, characteristic of rabbinic parallels, appears in both Mark and Q (Luke). In the three cases a man is pictured as sowing the seed, but this is the device of verisimilitude. The comparison is based on the nature of the mustard herb, not on the man or his sowing. Matthew is correct in saying that herbs of this kind were generally sown in a field.[12] Mark avoids the question by using the more general term gē ("earth" or "ground"). The Marcan form then proceeds to state the case for the smallness of the seed with some precision—"the smallest of all the seeds [viz., sown] on earth." Mustard was the smallest seed in general use. Luke ignores the point or assumes it or is unaware of its significance. Matthew's *ho mikroteron men estin pantōn tōn spermatōn* ("it is the smallest of all seeds") draws attention to the symbolic sense in which it is used. As a matter of fact, though it may not be literally the most minute, the mustard seed was proverbial for its smallness; Oesterley gives typical examples.[13] "If you have faith as a grain of mustard seed (Matt. 17:20)" is a Gospel parallel. In rabbinic lore it indicated something almost, as we should say, microscopic.

With regard to the result (there is no indication of time, long or short, much less emphasis upon it), it is again the Marcan form that is the more precise ("and becomes the greatest of all shrubs"). Matthew follows Mark. It is an observation of relative size. Mustard bushes or "trees" are known to grow to comparatively large size, standing up conspicuously above surrounding herbs of other varieties. Mark not only avoids the word "tree" but speaks of the birds lodging in its shade and not specifically in its branches. All use concluding words reminiscent of the Old Testament ("The beasts of the field found shade under it, and the birds of the air dwelt in its branches (Dan. 4:12)." "Under it will dwell all kinds of beasts; in the shade of its branches birds of every sort will nest (Ezek. 17:23)."[14]

In general, scholars prefer the Lucan form of the Q saying as likely —for its brevity and unity—to be more original than Matthew, who conflates Mark and Q. Mark, by breaking into the sentence in Mark 4:31 with an explanation which leaves his syntax incomplete (breaking off at *tōn epi tēs gēs*), appears to be introducing an explanation for the benefit of gentile readers. The care with which he states the whole parable confirms the impression.

It appears that the literary problems, carefully weighed, lead us back to the core of the parable and away from superficial similarities with the Leaven. The Evangelists are agreed that the parable concerned mustard seed and the fact that, full grown, the bush attracts birds. The other detail is gathered in the course of transmission. The variants read like the normal comments, qualifications, and explanations likely to be made in preaching. Nothing is to be decided about the meaning from the context—particularly since Luke feels free to use it virtually without context.

The mustard seed would suggest to any Jewish hearer something small and inconspicuous. But, when it has reached maturity, it is significantly no longer small in relation to its natural surroundings but actually *conspicuous*. It is so conspicuous that it attracts the attention of birds, which find it something they can use for their own purposes. Here is the original element in Jesus' treatment. He points out this proverbial feature of the mustard seed and then sharpens its meaning by drawing attention to the mature bush which gives shelter to life outside itself.

The actual comparison depends, then, not on the *growth* from small to large, but on the relative smallness of the seed, so small as to be easily overlooked, and the relative size of the herb when grown, so large as to attract attention—a midget of a seed among seeds, but a veritable tree among herbs. That the conspicuousness of the grown plant is the point is well attested by the fact that, with all their variants and with a double source, the Evangelists agree that this was the conclusion of the parable.[15]

What then, we ask, could this mean to Jesus' audience at that time and under the conditions that prevailed? That the kingdom of God is further understood when it is seen that, though at first inconspicuous, it is finally so conspicuous that it attracts attention from those who can put it to their own use.

There can be no doubt that every Jewish hearer would relate this point to Israel's own experience. It was part of the racial tradition that Israel had had small beginnings—more than inconspicuous, indeed—had been destitute and enslaved. Yet God did not overlook this people but had chosen and called it. "It was not because you were more in number than any other people that the Lord set his love upon you and chose you, for you were the fewest of all peoples; but it is because the Lord loves you (Deut. 7:7-8)." Under God's care Israel had prospered until it could not escape the attention of the nations. But it was disastrous attention. The nations sought to use Israel for their own purposes, and when Israel refused, so much the worse for Israel. The Northern Kingdom for a while, and then Judah, had looked out across a highway along which contending empires marched. Jerusalem became not only a strategic and therefore dangerous fortress but the focus of the conflicts of the ancient world. "For, lo, the kings assembled, they came on together (Ps. 48:4)." After the return from exile Israel had no desire but to be allowed to live its own life. This could not be. Greece, Syria, and finally Rome had taken notice of it; Rome, so to say, with a vengeance. The parties for the moment dominant in Jesus' time asked only to be let alone to develop their own religious culture. In effect, they wanted to reverse the situation suggested by the parable and use Rome as a protecting tree under which they might dwell undisturbed. Jesus implies that this is impossible for those who possess the secret of the kingdom of God. So unique a culture as Israel's, so high a calling, so necessary a possession as the kingdom, rises above all others as a tree overtops the bushes!

This must have been the line of thought suggested to the hearers, who were Jews, deeply disturbed about just such questions. But the Evangelists preserve the parable as useful to the church. All the sources make it a parable of the kingdom.

The application, then, is that the kingdom of God, having come into the world, *must attract attention.* This is again Jesus' observation: "A city set on a hill cannot be hid (Matt. 5:14b)." In a more tragic and gloomy setting he is represented as quoting the proverbial (?) saying, "Wherever the body is, there the eagles will be gathered together (Matt. 24:28)." His own movement and his own position with relation to it, though inconspicuous, must soon attract attention. We know well that it did, and the issue was the cross. The implications of his whole teaching are that since the kingdom cannot escape attention, the fact must be welcomed as providentially ordained and used as an asset for the furtherance of God's purposes.

The Old Testament figures of birds sheltering under the tree are interpreted as allegories of small states seeking shelter in the hegemony of an empire. To carry the parable in the same direction, only in more general terms, is not to strain it. It is, however, to extend it beyond the primary reference. Cadoux's suggestion that the lodging of the birds implies that Israel (then the kingdom and church) should extend its shelter to all people is an extended application rather than the primary one. It is certain that the primitive church found the parable applicable and in all probability interpreted it as a prophecy of the growth of the new religion.

Looking back with the perspective of Christian history, even without these tempting extensions of the application, we find how acute is Jesus' observation. The church, like Israel, was bound to attract the attention of the empire—and did. From that time to this the problem has persisted; the "Holy Roman Empire" is the classic exercise in it. The Christian culture raises its head above all others, and there is inevitable interaction. Secular forces take notice and try to take advantage. Religion adapts itself to the civilization in which it finds itself in hope of improving the environment but is never entirely one with it. When it becomes too closely adapted, it begins to lose its character as the "earnest" of the kingdom—losing the very characteristic of which Jesus here speaks. It must not overadapt itself, for all other cultures are but birds (if we may so pursue the figure) sheltering under the branches of the kingdom.[16]

The working out of the problem—that the kingdom of God attracts attention, undesirable as well as desirable, and that those who are attracted use it for their own purposes—is the task of the Christian preacher. For here, once again, the usual homiletic point vanishes to yield in turn a richer and more dynamic theme.

## THE FARMER AND THE GROWING SEED
### Mark 4

[26]*And he said,* "The kingdom of God is as if a man should scatter seed upon the ground, [27]and should sleep and rise night and day, and the seed should sprout and grow, he knows not how. [28]The earth produces of itself, first the blade, then the ear, then the full grain in the ear. [29]But when the grain is ripe, at once he puts in the sickle, because the harvest has come."

This parable has received a number of titles. We might be reluctant to add to their number, except that some of the titles determine the interpretation in advance, just as the title "the parable of the Soils" suggests a particular interpretation of the Sower. This brief parable, found only among Mark's ten examples, has many phases, each of which might be selected as a title. The one used has the simple virtue of generality.

Like the Mustard Seed and the Leaven, this is designated as a parable of the kingdom of God. There are seven others so designated by Matthew,[17] but we are not to suppose that the theme is limited to those clearly marked. The introductions are probably the work of the Evangelists or the deposit of tradition. The kingdom was Jesus' constant theme, and in some sense all his parables are related to it—if not to its nature, then to entrance into it, or to the way of life expected of "the sons of the kingdom." Had we the setting of all the parables we should probably observe this to be true. Failing this, we should be in error to assume that only those so designated refer to the kingdom of God. The question must often await the interpretation of the parable as parable, even in the cases where tradition makes specific use of the introduction. There is sufficient ground for believing that Jesus frequently used parables to answer the question, "With what can we compare the kingdom of God?"

In Mark 4:26-29 the kingdom is likened to the business of sowing, growing, and reaping in the experience of the farmer. The danger of allegory arises at every point. We must not equate the kingdom of God and the man, or fasten on either the seed, the growth, the soil, or the harvest as the clue. Rather, we must look at the parable as a whole.

The text needs little comment except to note the actual language. In verse 28 the word translated "of herself" or "of itself" is *automatē*. Automatically, spontaneously, the process goes on, apart from outside agency or interference. This is reemphasized in verse 29, *hotan de paradoi ho karpos*—"but when the grain is ripe"; the independence of the process determines when the next step shall be taken. And the timing is absolutely determined: *euthus apostellei to drepanon*—"*at once* he puts in the sickle"—and delay is as unfortunate as premature action would be. This emphasis is underlined by the concluding phrase, "because the harvest has come."

The activity envisaged, then, is the sowing of the seed, followed by inactivity (in relation to the seed) while the agency is transferred from sower to soil, and the resumption of action, at a moment determined by the maturity of the process, in the act of reaping.

Interpreted quite generally, this would seem clearly to indicate that the kingdom of God is neither crisis nor development but both crisis and development. It is like growing a crop in that there are times of activity and times of inactivity or, to be more exact, times of noninterference. After the seed is sown, direct activity is likely to be dangerous rather than helpful. The seed develops from stage to stage of its own volition. Meanwhile, life pursues its normal course: not that nothing is happening but, in the simplified terms of the parable, the locus of activity has shifted from the farmer to the earth. Interference, attempts to hurry the process or to change it, and the temptation to harvest too soon or to wait too long are all fatal. The independent activity of the seed in the soil, proceeding by its own laws, determines the resumption of activity on the part of the farmer. If he is a good farmer, he will be guided by the stages of the process inherent in its nature.[18]

This very general observation, like all interpretations of the parables that issue in general truths, seems inadequate. The inadequacy stems from the lack of a setting that would make the parable timely. We are forced to ask, therefore, to what in Jesus' ministry or to what concern of his strategy this applied. If the parables are elucidations, it will not do to make them either so obscure as to be more difficult than the teaching or so general that they are innocuous and irrelevant.

We have seen that there were in the days of Jesus, as in any age, those who were fretful for results and advocated the use of violent methods. In the charged atmosphere of the times, the Zealots were on the increase and the people of Galilee were all too easily persuaded to follow a political messiah who would lead them against their oppressors. The rulers were apprehensive and on their guard, ready to snuff out the first flicker of rebellion. But for Jesus, the kingdom was the kingdom of *God* and the times and seasons were in the Father's hands. The question and answer represented in Acts 1:6-7 ("Will you at this time restore the kingdom to Israel?") are here dealt with in another way. The parable is Jesus' answer to those "men of violence" described in Matthew 11:12 (Luke 16:16?) who would take the kingdom "by force." To his followers, Jesus counseled perseverance in the faith that it is "your Father's good pleasure to give you the kingdom (Luke 12:32)." We may compare a statement attributed to Guthlac of Crowland in the eighth century: "Know how to wait, and the Kingdom of God shall come to thee; not by violence nor by rapine, but by the hand of God."[19]

A saying that occurs in the apocalyptic section of the Gospels is illuminated by this parable: "Of that day or that hour no one knows, not even the angels in heaven, nor the Son, but only the Father (Mark 13:32)." The timing of eschatology, about which so many of Jesus' contemporaries, like modern scholars, are so concerned, must become for us what it apparently was for the Jesus of the parables— an issue beyond our scope. The times and seasons of the kingdom of God are part of the inherent nature of the kingdom itself and, ultimately, of the sovereign will of God, just as the time of harvest is determined by the inherent nature of the seed and its growth in the soil. To put in the sickle too soon is to destroy the very purpose of the whole process. The only attitude possible is that of watchfulness, and "Watch!" is a constant exhortation on Jesus' lips.[20]

We must be careful to avoid seeking to match each element in the comparison. The sowing of the seed and the seed itself are not to be narrowly identified. Neither sower nor reaper is necessarily God, nor Jesus, nor the church. The whole process is the concern of the parable, and for reality's sake the seed must be sown. The oft-debated question, how to reconcile the gradual growth of the kingdom with its near approach or its apocalyptic inbreaking, does not here arise, since the stages in the growth of the seed—blade, ear, corn—are not the point of the parable.[21] It is not the *length* of the process that is emphasized but the *givenness* of it, and the three stages serve to underline it by marking the necessarily inevitable order of progression. Here the point is the importance of avoiding debates about times and places. The parable suggests a given quality about the kingdom of God that stands apart from our fretful concern. Without it the kingdom would not be God's but ours; the parable lends little support to the nonbiblical phrase, "building the kingdom of God." We might object that the parable tells us nothing (except that he sleeps and wakes) of man's proper activity in relation to the kingdom. We are not at liberty to add details concerning weeding and cultivation. The emphasis is on the spontaneity and uncompelled nature of the growth. Jesus' whole message is not contained in any one parable, and we must look elsewhere for the answer to our questions—which themselves so often show signs of the fretfulness against which this parable is directed.

It is clear that this parable must present a difficulty, both to those who affirm definitely that Jesus taught or adopted a catastrophic eschatology and to those who commit themselves to the theory of a steady progressive development. The implication is that both are mistaken when they take an absolute position, but that both are partially true. It is perhaps a paradox; there is no reason why the attempt to deal with issues which lie ultimately in God's hand should not, humanly speaking, issue in a paradox. Is it not the task of the Christian preacher to lead his people to commit ultimate matters to God and, in doing so, to be prepared both to expect a catastrophic inbreaking and a development by crisis and growth? The acceptance of God's sovereignty is the vital point. Men are to watch and to work and, in each case, to pray.

The temptation to add details in the light of the experience of the church is revealed in the parable of the Tares Among the Wheat.

## THE TARES AMONG THE WHEAT
### Matthew 13

[24]*Another parable he put before them, saying,* "The kingdom of heaven may be compared to a man who sowed good seed in his field; [25]but while men were sleeping, his enemy came and sowed weeds among the wheat, and went away. [26]So when the plants came up and bore grain, then the weeds appeared also. [27]And the servants of the householder came and said to him, 'Sir, did you not sow good seed in your field? How then has it weeds?' [28]He said to them, 'An enemy has done this.' The servants said to him, 'Then do you want us to go and gather them?' [29]But he said, 'No; lest in gathering the weeds you root up the wheat along with them. [30]Let both grow to-

gether until the harvest; and at harvest time I will tell the reapers, Gather the weeds first and bind them in bundles to be burned, but gather the wheat into my barn.' "

In following Mark, Matthew has omitted the parable of the Farmer and the Growing Seed as a sequel to the Sower and has substituted at that place the parable of the Tares. After having dealt with Mark's version we are led to ask (with many commentators) whether the Tares is not another version of the Marcan similitude. Several points come to our attention. The sowing of the seed here becomes the sowing of *good* seed—a fact assumed in Mark but here specified for the purpose of the story. The sleeping and waking of the patient farmer here becomes a sleep which provides an opportunity for his enemy. Those whom the Marcan parable by implication rebukes here become vocal, though the interference is now applied only to the admixture of weed. The result, however, as the farmer points out, would be the same—the destruction of the harvest. The question asked has a suggestion of artificiality about it. Experienced laborers would know what answer the farmer would give. For the purposes of the story, nonetheless, it must be asked. The question and answer guide us to the interpretation. The growth is allowed to go on, but here the emphasis is on the combined growth of seed and weed. The farmer in both parables decides when the reaping shall be done, though here he speaks in the first person. The new feature is the separation of tares from the wheat.[22]

A striking feature of the parable is that it attributes the presence of tares to the activity of an outside person, an enemy. This suggests a theological consideration (the origin of evil) uncommon on Jesus' lips, except in the Fourth Gospel. It seems almost a direct contradiction of other parables (e.g., the Dragnet) which have to do with the *inclusive* nature of the kingdom. The parable, in the form it has come to us in Matthew, represents the problem posed by the inclusiveness of the kingdom after some experience of expansion, namely, in the gentile church. This is a problem that occupies Matthew's attention in several places.[23]

The parable, however, does not represent so late a stage in the tradition as the interpretation which follows in Matthew 13:36-43. This takes up the items of the parable in an allegorical manner and substitutes for them apocalyptic terms. We see clearly here the hand of the Evangelist. The emphasis falls on the separation at the judgment. An important feature of the parable is omitted, indeed, a feature that (as we noted) seems unnecessary unless it be included in order to determine the meaning: the question of the laborers regarding the pulling up of the tares and the farmer's reply. In other words, the allegorical treatment changes the meaning of the parable *by failing to allegorize the determining element.*

When the allegory is forgotten and the question and answer admitted, the point of the parable then becomes the same as the parable given by Mark, except that here the point is made with reference to a definite phase of the problem, a phase that becomes of more importance in the developing church. In the parable of the Farmer and the Growing Seed the lesson is taught in general terms as a response to a historical situation. When the situation changed the parable proved adaptable, but the adaptation forms practically a new parable.

It seems quite plausible to say that three stages in the development of the tradition are evident: (1) the parable in Mark; (2) the amplification of detail and the application *of the same truth to a particular problem* in the Matthaean parable; (3) the allegorical interpretation which centers attention on the judgment and neglects the original point. If this be so, Matthew has produced the later version (as more relevant to conditions in his time) and has added the interpretation after the analogy of the interpretation supplied in Mark to the parable of the Sower.[24]

In view of these considerations, we may omit further discussion. The exploration has served to emphasize the point which the parable of the Farmer and the Growing Seed set forth, namely, that the "times and the seasons" of the kingdom of God are determined by its own inherent nature. Hence, to try to take the matter into our own hands is, eventually, to be found rebels against God, since it is God's will that, in turn, provides the kingdom with its nature and laws.

If the Farmer and the Growing Seed was aimed at those who would offer violent interference with what is essentially God's affair, the next parable to be treated offers criticism of another type or group of persons who exhibit the opposite tendency.

## THE CHILDREN IN THE MARKET PLACE
### Matthew 11
[16]"But to what shall I compare this generation? It is like children sitting in the market places and calling to their playmates, [17]'We piped to you, and you did not dance; we wailed, and you did not mourn.' [18]*For John came neither eating nor drinking, and they say, 'He has a demon'; [19]the Son of man came eating and drinking, and they say, 'Behold, a glutton and a drunkard, a friend of tax collectors and sinners!' Yet wisdom is justified by her deeds."*

³¹"To what then shall I compare the men of this generation, and what are they like? ³²They are like children sitting in the market place and calling to one another, 'We piped to you, and you did not dance; we wailed, and you did not weep.' ³³*For John the Baptist has come eating no bread and drinking no wine; and you say, 'He has a demon.' ³⁴The Son of man has come eating and drinking; and you say, 'Behold, a glutton and a drunkard, a friend of tax collectors and sinners!' ³⁵Yet wisdom is justified by all her children.*"

A direct question introduces this parable from Q in rabbinic manner: "But to what shall I compare this generation?" The immediate cause of the question is the discussion of John the Baptist, in the context of which in Q the parable occurs. It seems to me that the verses (Matt. 11:18-19) that follow the parable are not so much an interpretation of the parable as an explanation of the occasion for the parable, an expression of the difficulty from which, by the similitude, Jesus seeks to draw a lesson. Verses 18-19, then, may be taken as setting, but as setting they help to determine the meaning of the parable. I see no reason to question them. I think we must say that verse 18 reflects a later period when John the Baptist and his movement appeared as a dangerous opponent of the church (an attitude reflected elsewhere in the four Gospels) or that it is a characteristic of only one section of the community. The people at large admired John, but those leaders who opposed Jesus also opposed John. Perhaps their opposition was based on no single unmixed motive. They may very properly have feared an uprising or quite naturally the loss of their own influence and position. In any case there were those who opposed both Jesus and John but for different reasons (as far as they gave expression to their reasons).

Elsewhere Jesus refers to the men of this "generation" (cf. Mark 8:12; Matt. 17:17, etc.), and in each case he is characterizing not the people as a whole but his opponents and critics—those, for example, who demand "a sign." No doubt he knew that in the end their attitude would determine the actions of all, rather than the spontaneous but untested and temporary popularity he himself achieved among the common people.

The parable itself is not difficult, but the interpretation it seems to require poses one problem. The parable appears to be a criticism of the children who sit in the market and call the tunes without response from their fellows. Cadoux concludes this to be the meaning and finds that Jesus' opponents are satisfied by neither John nor Jesus because they (the opponents) want always to call the steps to be danced or the game to be played. This is very tempting, except that while the parable *appears to* require this treatment, rabbinic parallels indicate that the transposition of terms is only apparent. What we have said earlier leads us, in any case, away from straightforward identification. The meaning of the parable is to be learned from the whole relationship. The rabbis apparently did not feel it necessary to set out their comparisons as though it were otherwise. B. T. D. Smith gives the following excellent illustration, in which the point of comparison seems to be the ink but is actually the state of the paper that is written on: "He who learns as a lad, to what is he like? To ink written on fresh paper. And he who learns when he is old, to what is he like? To ink written on used paper."[25]

In the parable the meaning is, to paraphrase, "as children playing in the market place will sometimes be peevish and play at neither weddings nor funerals, so are the men of this generation who will respond neither to an ascetic like John the Baptist nor to a companionable person like myself." The attitude depicted is self-satisfied pride and aloofness. Jesus characterizes it more than once (for instance, in the parable of the Pharisee and the Tax Collector), and there can be no doubt that it arises from his own experience. In the story of the man with the withered hand (Mark 3:1-6), Jesus is met with the same noncommittal aloofness in response to his question, "Is it lawful on the sabbath to do good or to do harm, to save life or to kill?"—although the situation that prompted the question was presumably provided by those who were questioned. "But they were silent." In another instance also connected with John the Baptist (Mark 11:27-33), Jesus poses a question which is met by the noncommittal response, "We do not know."

The parable is, then, a characterization and condemnation of an attitude among Jesus' contemporaries. In effect it made those whom it characterized the enemies of the kingdom of God and therefore actually opponents of Jesus' mission. In more explicit terms Jesus denounced the attitude as it was related to specific issues. "They bind heavy burdens, hard to bear, and lay them on men's shoulders; but they themselves will not move them with their finger" (Matt. 23:4; cf. Luke 11:46b). "You shut the kingdom of heaven against men; for you neither enter yourselves, nor allow those who would enter to go in (Matt. 23:13)." Of like emphasis is Jesus' "woe" on Chorazin and Bethsaida (Matt. 11:21-23a; Luke 10:13) and his discourse on the "sign of Jonah" in which the men of "this generation" are judged by "the queen of the South" and by the men of Nineveh because of the former's failure to respond to a greater occasion than that to which the two latter responded in their day (Luke 11:29-32; Matt. 12:39, 41-42).[26]

The saying with which the parable concludes, "Yet wisdom is justified by her deeds," is in all probability a floating saying or proverb not inappropriately added by the Evangelist.

The late President Franklin Roosevelt, speaking of attitudes toward the formation of the United Nations, declared that perfectionism was a danger to world peace. He was dealing with the same variety of peevish aloofness. It besets the church on every hand. There are those who belabor the church for its interest in political and economic issues, and there are those who condemn the church for the ineffective role it plays in those fields. They are sometimes the same people. Here the parable becomes relevant since it deals with just that case. It is a further indication that Jesus was in no sense indifferent to the tensions and passionate issues of his day. We may assume him to teach that his followers also cannot stand aside. But he also indicates the nature of the response they are likely to meet. They will not be able to please everyone, nor even to please the same person on different occasions. It was this that made the great prophets, notably Isaiah and Jeremiah, seem inconsistent to their contemporaries. The follower of Jesus must often be willing to appear inconsistent to the man of the world or to the partisan because the Christian's consistency should lie at a deeper level than that on which his inconsistency is judged. It must find its base at the supernatural level of the will of God.

Jesus, however, did not preach a negative doctrine. His condemnation of a calculated aloofness which is essentially noncommittal raises the question of the proper attitude to be expected of those who see the kingdom of God as a reality. This attitude is depicted in the following parables.

## THE TREASURE IN THE FIELD

**Matthew 13**
**44"The kingdom of heaven is like treasure hidden in a field, which a man found and covered up; then in his joy he goes and sells all that he has and buys that field."**

With the parable of the Pearl Merchant which follows it, this little saying occurs in Matthew exclusively. It gives rise to no particular difficulties except to question the morality of the purchaser of the field in not disclosing to the owner of the land the fact that a treasure was hidden within it. The parables were not tales of specific individuals, yet they were true to life, and the man in the parable behaves as men of that kind behave. We do not draw a moral from the man's behavior. "The kingdom of heaven is like treasure hidden," it opens, but the parable deals with the action of the man in relation to the field and the treasure, and we may be led into strange bypaths if we ask in what sense the kingdom is hidden.

The story is simple. A man finds a buried treasure, hides it again, and shrewdly purchases the field, though doing so involves the sale of all that he owns. From the fact that he finds the treasure in the field and from the fact that it takes all that he owns to buy *the field,* we assume that he is a laborer without capital and that he does not disclose the presence of the hoard during the negotiations. We learn from Derrett's study of the law involved that if the treasure were an ancient one, its presence unknown to the owner of the field, found by accident and not as part of the finder's prescribed task, the one who found it would have the *legal* right to act as he did in the parable.[27]

The meaning of the parable is: If a man will in this situation dispossess himself of everything in order to secure a treasure of worldly goods, how much more must the man who sees the kingdom of God be prepared to give up all else in order to possess it. It is a parable that clearly reveals Jesus' demand for an attitude of complete commitment as opposed to the aloof, noncommittal attitude condemned in the parable of the Children in the Market Place. The kingdom must be valued beyond all else. Commitment to it must be complete and irrevocable.

Matthew indicates (v. 36: "He left the crowds and went into the house. And his disciples came to him") that this, with the parable that follows, was addressed privately to the disciples. Many commentators have so interpreted it. Certainly the missionaries of the church found it to be true that they must "leave all" to serve the Gospel. This would no doubt in part explain the preservation of the simile and its setting. We should ask, however, whether it has any specific place in the ministry and strategy of Jesus. I think we can see its relevance if we assume it to belong to that aspect of Jesus' work which consisted primarily of an appeal to Israel. His sense of Israel's mission was high and determinative. In his day the nation was still torn by doubts, the doubts which had marked its whole history as God's chosen people. There were those who wished only to maintain the status quo, who feared that commitment would lose for Israel what it precariously held by the grace of Rome. Jesus' call was not to a political program but rather to a scorn of politics. He called the church, which was his own people, to a complete commitment to God's purpose and a wholehearted surrender to its unique mission. The Israelites must be willing to give up all that they had ever hoped for or gained by struggle if it stood in the way of total absorption in the task committed to them by God.

It was difficult for the Jews to think in purely personal terms. The kingdom of God was a corporate concept. The parable, if it applies to the kingdom, must have had for them this primary meaning. When Israel had rejected Christ and his claim, the same teaching must apply likewise to that church which inherited the task of Israel. And it must apply to every member of it. Neither can the meaning be confined to the primitive church or to missionaries. Surrender must precede service; he cannot be said to have prepared himself to enter the kingdom who does not evaluate it as worth more than all else he knows. (For homiletic purposes it may of course be observed that the securing of the treasure opens up new possibilities which more than compensate for what has been sold, but this is an expansion based on the aptness of the figure and not part of the primary interpretation.) Without a readiness to give up all else, there can be no possession of what God offers. This means for the church in every age that considerations of an ecclesiastical or political or even dogmatic character that prevents its full response to God's call must be given up or it forfeits the name of church of Christ.

Jesus was to return to this theme more than once in direct appeal to the Israel of his time, and other parables will bring it to our attention. The personal appeal is summed up in his words, "Let him deny himself"—for that, in the end, is the key to all-inclusive surrender, to deny self-centeredness and self-regard.

To the noncommittal a second and similar parable is added.

## THE PEARL MERCHANT
### Matthew 13
[45]"Again, the kingdom of heaven is like a merchant in search of fine pearls, [46]who, on finding one pearl of great value, went and sold all that he had and bought it."

Once again we note that the comparison is not intended between the kingdom of heaven and the man but between the relationship of men to the kingdom and the relationship of the pearl seeker to the pearl of great value. Neither, of course, do we equate kingdom of God and pearl, for the same reason.

The man is designated a merchant. He is not to be thought of as a collector or connoisseur of pearls but as, we should say, a dealer. The characteristic exhibited is not extravagance or enthusiasm, but shrewdness; not that Jesus commends shrewdness here any more than he does in the previous parable. This is a parable, not a moral tale. The assumption is that the dealer is not himself a collector but knows a collector who will pay so much for this pearl that the investment of all the dealer's wealth (including, we suppose, his present stock of pearls) will be more than repaid by a handsome profit. The point of the story is the merchant's decision to take the risk of loss in his determination to secure the pearl in question.[28]

The meaning of the comparison, then, is: If a shrewd merchant can value one pearl so highly that he is willing to commit everything he has to its purchase, how much more highly should men value the kingdom of God and commit all to securing a place in it.

What has been said of the setting in the Gospel and the setting in life of the parable of the Treasure in the Field applies here also. The corporate and personal meaning are the same here as there. The existence of two similar parables may, as suggested in Chapter One, be attributed to Jesus' dealing with the same problem before different groups of people—perhaps in country and town—and varying his simile as a good teacher would. This is not necessarily so, however, since there is no reason to think he may not have used two similitudes at a time for emphasis.[29]

It has sometimes been observed that in the previous parable the treasure is found by accident, while in this parable the pearl is found as the result of deliberate search. There are obvious homiletic opportunities here which, while not based on the primary purpose or intention of the parables, might be considered legitimate extensions based on the aptness of the details.

The prime importance of the pair of parables lies in their relevance to a particular situation, and they are examples of Jesus' use of the form as an implement in his strategy. They stand as correctives to those who might suppose from the parable of the Farmer and the Growing Seed that no activity is possible, and they represent the positive attitude which is to be opposed to the negative attitude condemned in the parable of the Children in the Market Place.

We cannot fail to note in conclusion that Jesus' parables lead us back again and again to a fundamental element in the kingdom of God, the will of God himself. The important element in the phrase "the kingdom of God" is "God." No response could be made to the call of God's kingdom that did not begin and end in complete surrender to God. This appears first as a fact in Jesus' own religious experience and then as an element in his strategy. Out of this his teaching emerges. He himself is impelled by the will of God. When this brings him into difficulty, this is his defense and it is the basis of his future plans. It must also be the attitude of those who would follow him. It does not originate in a dispassionate metaphysical cogitation but in a life experience. This, in any case, is the origin of all true theology; when it is forgotten, theology becomes scholastic and barren.

# FOUR THE WIDENESS OF GOD'S MERCY

Jesus' message was addressed to all Israel, not to one class or group. "Outcasts"—those who were considered by the "elite" as worthless—received his attention as readily as the Pharisees. When his ministry was exercised outside the synagogues, "publicans and sinners" became more accessible to him and he to them. It is well known that "scribes and Pharisees" attacked him for forming these associations, and it is wrongly assumed that they represented only a minority opposed to a majority who applauded Jesus. The fact is that Jesus during his ministry was an offense to his own people. In the glory of the resurrection this fact was largely overwritten in the record. Yet clear traces of the earlier situation remain. Jesus was not crucified without reason.

We can too readily assume that Jesus' polemic against the Pharisees had popular support. But the law-abiding and orthodox among the populace looked up to the Pharisees and probably admired in their leaders what they themselves did not pretend to achieve. The support of the people which Jesus had in the early days in Galilee and again in Jerusalem did not come primarily by winning away the followers of the Pharisees but from other causes. In Jerusalem we must make allowance for the presence of many pilgrims, both from Galilee and from "the Dispersion." These sat more lightly to the demands of the Law and found it possible to respond—up to a point— to Jesus' teaching. The Galilean following is largely to be explained on the ground that they took him to be a potential revolutionary leader. The falling away would then be explained by disappointed hopes.[1] In Jerusalem the popularity which made the leaders act with caution may be explained by Jesus' attack on the hierarchy (temple cleansing, etc.). And the consistent part of his following probably came from those on the fringe, including many who were, actually or in effect, "outcast." Even his disciples followed him from mixed motives, as the near approach of the cross was to make clear. These observations are made in order to safeguard us against supposing that it was simply to the scribes and Pharisees that Jesus had to vindicate his activity and teaching. The necessity of so doing was also a necessity required by the large following the Pharisees commanded. A defense addressed to them was necessarily a defense addressed to a large part of the populace. That the people shared in the Pharisees' distrust of Jesus' dealings with those "outside the Law" is shown by a comment in the story of Zacchaeus (Luke 19:1-10). "And when they [the crowd] saw it they all murmured, 'He has gone in to be the guest of a man who is a sinner (v. 7).'"

This is the most frequent criticism made of Jesus, and it was one which it was vitally important to meet. It was important from his opponents' point of view, for it involved the deep issues of religion and national life. The meal was, to the Jew, a sacred occasion, which united those who partook of the one table and, for the devout, presented an obligation to engage in elevated discourse.[2] To break bread with those outside was therefore questionable from several points of view. As Dr. Montefiore has written:

> This we may regard as a new, important and historic feature in his teaching. And it is just here that opposition comes in and begins. To call sinners to repentance, to denounce vice generally, is one thing. To have intercourse with sinners and seek their conversion by countenancing them and comforting them—that is quite another thing.[3]

Jesus' activity in this direction, as much as his "violation" of the sabbath and his claims to forgive sins and cast out demons, called in question the basic assumptions of the practice of the Torah, its expansion in "the tradition," and the hopes based on the satisfaction of its demands. Jesus' persistence in his strategy was deliberate, and his defense was equally important. His justification rested not on expediency or considerations of strategy but upon an urgent sense of the will of God which implied definite beliefs as to God's very nature.

We have already seen how some of the parables express this determination and call for a faith in God's invincible purpose inherent in the kingdom itself, a faith that demands a complete commitment. We now turn to some parables that explain Jesus' practice. There seems no good reason to question the statement of the Gospels that they were presented in answer to the charge of association with "publicans and sinners." The first to be considered has no setting but provides a good starting point.

# THE DRAGNET
## Matthew 13

[47] "Again, the kingdom of heaven is like a net which was thrown into the sea and gathered fish of every kind; [48]when it was full, men drew it ashore and sat down and sorted the good into vessels but threw away the bad. [49]*So it will be at the close of the age. The angels will come out and separate the evil from the righteous, [50]and throw them into the furnace of fire; there men will weep and gnash their teeth.*"

It is marked as a parable of "the kingdom of heaven" and in its present form has affinity with the interpretation of the parable of the Tares Among the Wheat. We detect at once that verses 49-50 are interpretation, and the language is in the same apocalyptic vein as verses 40b-42 ("So will it be at the close of the age"). It is to be regarded as secondary, not for this reason alone but because it does not really interpret the parable. In verse 48 the sorting of the fish is done by those who caught the fish. The substitution of the angels which "come out" (v. 49) is an importation from apocalyptic literature, just as the reaper angels in the interpretation of the other parable (vs. 39, 41) take the place of the laborers in the parable proper. Further, the reference to the fire is clearly out of keeping with the situation. The fish that were not edible or fit for the market were more likely thrown back into the sea or at the most put aside to be used, perhaps, for fertilizer. Cadoux humorously remarks that it is the good fish that reach the fire and not the bad.[4]

Indeed, it may be questioned whether the separating of "the evil from the righteous" is the central point of the parable. The sorting at "the close of the age" deals with a problem of the developed church rather than the situation faced by Jesus in his ministry.

Otto[5] and other scholars reject all but verse 47 ("The kingdom of heaven is like a net, which was thrown into the sea, and gathered fish of every kind"). The justification for this is not too certain, although the similitude then has unity and force. On the other hand, the process of sorting depicted has reality in its favor and could be observed on every hand along the shores of Gennesaret. The point remains that the parable is not justly treated if the method of fishing is ignored in favor of the sorting. The sorting is made possible and made necessary only by the gathering in "of every kind."

As distinct from the throwing net operated by one man from the shore[6] (cf. Mark 1:16—in the Greek), the dragnet involved the use of boats and crews. It enclosed a large area of water and gathered up all the fish moving in the area (cf. the scene in Luke 5:4-7). Designed principally for use where a school of desirable fish was located, it embraced other fish that happened to be there and made the subsequent sorting necessary. The essential preliminary was the widespreading, all-inclusive enclosure. The point clearly is the indiscriminate first step (as against a more selective type of fishing practiced, let us say, by the modern fisherman with a line and specialized lure). To attempt to discriminate before netting the fish meant to fail to make a catch at all.

The parable asks an opinion. In effect it says, Do not the fishermen spread their nets to enclose every kind of fish before they can be sorted? There can be only one answer. Just so, the kingdom of God embraces every human kind, and discrimination is a later and not the first stage. We may say that here Jesus is justifying his own appeal to men as a whole, whoever they may be, wherever they may be found, as against his opponents, whose policy condemned certain ones in advance and made no further effort to include them within God's purposes. This "universal" appeal was what it meant to be "fishers of men."

If we wish to extend the meaning in the light of subsequent knowledge of men's response to Jesus, we can see that after the first attraction a deeper understanding of God's demands or of the rigors of the disciples' way would, of itself, cause many to fall away. But we must not allegorize it and press the identity of those who fish with those who sort. In the growing experience of the church the parable would be preserved as a justification of the gentile mission and then adapted to use in solving the problem of the presence of the unworthy as in the parable of the Tares Among the Wheat. Its immediate and central significance, however, is as a statement of Jesus' policy—a policy that the church, to be true to its Master in any age, must consistently follow.

But Jesus was not content to state it as his policy. In answer to specific charges, he grounded his strategy in the conviction that it was necessitated by the very nature of God. This is set forth in the three famous parables grouped by Luke in chapter 15.

## THE LOST SHEEP
### Matthew 18
[12]What do you think? If a man has a hundred sheep, and one of them has gone astray, does he not leave the ninety-nine on the hills and go in search of the one that went astray? [13]And if he finds it, truly, I say to you, he rejoices over it more than over the ninety-nine that never went astray. [14]*So it is not the will of my Father who is in heaven that one of these little ones should perish.*

## Luke 15

**[4]"What man of you, having a hundred sheep, if he has lost one of them, does not leave the ninety-nine in the wilderness, and go after the one which is lost, until he finds it? [5]And when he has found it, he lays it on his shoulders, rejoicing. [6]And when he comes home, he calls together his friends and his neighbors, saying to them, 'Rejoice with me, for I have found my sheep which was lost.' [7]*Even so, I tell you, there will be more joy in heaven over one sinner who repents than over ninety-nine righteous persons who need no repentance.*"**

The combination of the three parables in Luke, the Lost Sheep, the Lost Coin, and the Prodigal Son, is so familiar and has proved so fruitful for preachers that it may seem rash to suggest that they came together and were assimilated to each other in the course of preaching, and that they did not originally belong together. The indications of this possibility are as follows. The introduction in Luke 15:1-3 closes with the words, "So he told them this parable." The singular, "parable," does not suggest a group of parables. Since the parable that follows has in Matthew another setting, the introduction here may well have belonged originally to the parable of the Prodigal Son, which deals more directly with the criticism in verse 2, "This man receives sinners, and eats with them." Secondly, the conclusion of the first parable (vs. 6-7) is parallel to the conclusion of the Lost Coin (vs. 9-10) and may have been assimilated from it. As a matter of fact, the gathering of friends and neighbors to rejoice is proper and likely in the case of the woman but rather unlikely in the case of the shepherd, who presumably takes the recovered sheep to rejoin the others which were left "in the wilderness" (v. 4). After the conclusions and applications became assimilated, the similarity of the two parables with the central interest of the third—the feast at the son's return and the father's joy—would logically draw them together. Whether this is to be attributed to Luke or to his special sources and the process of oral transmission it is difficult to determine.

The parable of the Lost Sheep has a different setting in Matthew and therefore a different application (cf. Matt. 18:14 and Luke 15:7). In Matthew this parable occurs in the passage on offenses (18:7-10), "See that you do not despise one of these little ones" (where "little ones" probably means not a child but a follower of Jesus from among the people at large). The interpretation given is, "So it is not the will of my Father who is in heaven that one of these little ones should perish (v. 14)"—an application more suitable, for the reason stated above, than that given in Luke 15:6-7.

Further, it may be noted that the shepherd's rejoicing more over the one recovered sheep than over the ninety-nine that are safe, as in Matthew, has less difficulties than its application in Luke, where there is more joy in heaven over one repented sinner than over ninety-nine righteous "who need no repentance." In the Matthaean version the joy is based on the activity of the shepherd in finding the sheep rather than, as in Luke, the activity of the sinner in repenting. It is clear that the former better fits the parable. The wording of Luke's version, where it departs from Matthew's, can be seen to be from assimilation to the parable of the Lost Coin. The sheep in Matthew goes astray, whereas in Luke it, like the coin, is lost by the owner. In Luke there is certainty of finding it (as with a coin lost in a room), whereas in Matthew we read, "And if he finds it" (v. 13).

I think we must say, then, that the two versions came down in the tradition separately, the Matthaean in a setting which preserved its form and interpretation, and the Lucan without setting or application, which permitted it to become attached to the other parable.[7]

If we accept, then, the version in Matthew as the more original, along with its setting, it appears to be a justification of Jesus' indiscriminate mission as a policy based on the will of God. The emphasis is on the search for the single sheep which has become separated and the added joy that attaches to its presence after it has been reunited with the flock. This joy is very natural and within our common experience. There is always something more dear about the child who has recovered from a dangerous illness than there is about the others who have enjoyed consistent health. They are not less beloved, but the love toward the other has an added quality of thankfulness. This consideration justifies Jesus' demand for an opinion, "What do you think?" (rather than Luke's "What man of you?" which parallels "What woman?" in v. 8). The meaning is clear from the context. There are none, no matter how far astray, whom it is proper to despise, but rather it is the will of God that just exactly these shall be sought out because their restoration gives a peculiar joy. In this form the parable is a direct response and challenge to those who called Jesus' policy into question. The transfer of the meaning to the higher realm is illuminated by the saying, "Of how much more value is a man than a sheep! (Matt. 12:12)." How perfectly this similitude caught the imagination of the early church is indicated by the allegorical treatment of the theme in John's Good Shepherd and in Christian art.

When the parable is seen not simply as an allegory of God and the sinner but as a justification of a mission, based on the very nature of God, its relevance to the church, handicapped constantly by financial, social, and racial exclusiveness, needs hardly to be pointed out. If this is the attitude of God, then the task of the church and the duty of the Christian are clear. It stands before us now as a continual reminder that the prime concern of the church must be with those who are "unattached" or unreached by Christian influence as much as, if not more than, with those who are "active members."

## THE LOST COIN
### Luke 15
**8"Or what woman, having ten silver coins, if she loses one coin, does not light a lamp and sweep the house and seek diligently until she finds it? 9And when she has found it, she calls together her friends and neighbors, saying, 'Rejoice with me, for I have found the coin which I had lost.'** *10Even so, I tell you, there is joy before the angels of God over one sinner who repents."*

On general grounds the application (v. 10) is to be regarded as secondary. The language is difficult and the "sinner who repents" is again not a true deduction from the parable, where the activities of the woman are the center of interest. We should expect from the introductory words a judgment on the simple and charming picture given. Of course she would so behave, is the answer expected.

Two differences between this similitude and the Lost Sheep might be noticed. In each case there is the same diligent search. In the case of the sheep it is a question whether it will be found. In the case of the coin, which is known to be in the room, only diligence is necessary. In the first case, therefore, we read (Matt. 18:13), "if he finds it." But in this case we read (v. 8), "until she finds it." Secondly, here the joy at finding the coin is appropriate, a joy to be shared with friends and neighbors, which, as we noted, did not fit so readily the situation of the shepherd.

In the form in which the two parables occur in Luke they appear as a pair, one designed to appeal to men in the audience, the other to women. Treated (as above) as independent parables, their emphasis is different. The Lost Sheep emphasizes the purpose of God to seek out even the hundredth—the one percent—so that not the least can be said to be despised or forgotten by God. Here that is assumed and the emphasis is on the diligent search which does not give up because it is certain to be rewarded and on the joy of the completed quest. There is no difficulty about its interpretation. If a woman will so act toward a coin, how much more diligent will be God's search for the lost soul and how real his joy in recovering it.

"But even the hairs of your head are all numbered (Matt. 10:30)."
"Are not two sparrows sold for a penny? And not one of them will
fall to the ground without your Father's will (v. 29)." There is no need
to ask (as Luke 15:10, with its angels, seems to have asked) who are
the "friends and neighbors," since this is a parable and not an allegory. It is another form of the justification of Jesus' mission, the
ground for which is found not only in God's will to seek the outcast
but also in the affirmation of God's pleasure in his recovery. The
contrast of that joy with the critical attitude of Jesus' opponents is
more fully and deeply treated in the remaining parable of Luke's
trilogy.

## THE PRODIGAL SON
### Luke 15
*¹Now the tax collectors and sinners were all drawing near to hear
him. ²And the Pharisees and the scribes murmured, saying, "This
man receives sinners and eats with them.". . .*

*¹¹And he said, "There was a man who had two sons; ¹²and the
younger of them said to his father, 'Father, give me the share of
property that falls to me.' And he divided his living between them.
¹³Not many days later, the younger son gathered all he had and took
his journey into a far country, and there he squandered his property
in loose living. ¹⁴And when he had spent everything, a great famine
arose in that country, and he began to be in want. ¹⁵So he went and
joined himself to one of the citizens of that country, who sent him
into his fields to feed swine. ¹⁶And he would gladly have fed on the
pods that the swine ate; and no one gave him anything. ¹⁷But when
he came to himself he said, 'How many of my father's hired servants
have bread enough and to spare, but I perish here with hunger! ¹⁸I
will arise and go to my father, and I will say to him, "Father, I have
sinned against heaven and before you; ¹⁹I am no longer worthy to be
called your son; treat me as one of your hired servants." ' ²⁰And he
arose and came to his father. But while he was yet at a distance, his
father saw him and had compassion, and ran and embraced him and
kissed him. ²¹And the son said to him, 'Father, I have sinned against
heaven and before you; I am no longer worthy to be called your son.'
²²But the father said to his servants, 'Bring quickly the best robe,
and put it on him; and put a ring on his hand, and shoes on his feet;
²³and bring the fatted calf and kill it, and let us eat and make merry;
²⁴for this my son was dead, and is alive again; he was lost, and is
found.' And they began to make merry.*

*²⁵"Now his elder son was in the field; and as he came and drew
near to the house, he heard music and dancing. ²⁶And he called one*

of the servants and asked what this meant. [27]And he said to him, 'Your brother has come, and your father has killed the fatted calf, because he has received him safe and sound.' [28]But he was angry and refused to go in. His father came out and entreated him, [29]but he answered his father, 'Lo, these many years I have served you, and I never disobeyed your command; yet you never gave me a kid, that I might make merry with my friends. [30]But when this son of yours came, who has devoured your living with harlots, you killed for him the fatted calf!' [31]And he said to him, 'Son, you are always with me, and all that is mine is yours. [32]It was fitting to make merry and be glad, for this your brother was dead, and is alive; he was lost, and is found.' "

The traditional title is too deeply embedded in the English tradition to be changed. For the purpose of study, however, it might well be modified to express the central contrast of the father and the older brother.

This similitude is so extended in its literary structure that we can hardly suppose, as with many shorter examples, that it was uttered on the spur of the moment in a polemical situation; rather, it was delivered in a more leisurely manner. It probably owes something of its finished form to Luke, who is known for his stylistic editorial work. But the narrative itself can be attributed only to Jesus, and it is polemic at its best.

The effort to divide the parable into two at verse 25 seems unnecessary and impossible. The place of the older son in the narrative is secured by the references in verses 11-13. There would be no point in this if the older son were to play no part in the story. The elder disappears temporarily from the account when interest is focused on the adventures of the absent brother and then on the father, but he reappears when needed to create the climax which provides the real point of the parable.[8]

It is unnecessary to deal here with the parable verse by verse, as reference may be made to the many commentaries. In these will be found adequate discussions of the Jewish property laws assumed by the situation. The legal situation at the son's departure and upon his return has been clarified by Derrett. The prodigal's "third" may not be accurate but, having taken his share, the prodigal would have no further claim on the estate. The rest would have been made over to his brother at the same time. The situation was that property could be given to his sons by a father, but the recipients, while owning the title, were required to keep it intact so that its income could be used by the father as long as he lived. The share received by the prodigal did not release him from either the obligation not to alienate it nor the obligation to use it for his father's support when needed. His failure to do this would be part of his shame, for to honor (support) one's parents was a "heavy duty."[9] There is nothing incongruous, e.g., in verses 17 and 19, where the hired servants are spoken of as "my father's." It should be noted, of course, that in verse 18, "I have sinned against heaven," means "against God."

The adventures of the "prodigal" are so well drawn and are so sound psychologically that much exposition has centered about them, to the neglect of the central point. The complete degradation of his situation as a Jew is depicted in verses 15-16, and most scholars quote the rabbinic saying, "When the Israelites have to eat of the carob tree, then only do they repent." Here the emphasis is not on the search, as in the previous parables, but on the son's response to a life he remembers so well that to have the most meager share in it appears preferable to his current situation. But the crux of the story lies in the activity of the father—not merely in his going to meet his son while "yet at a distance." The father's preparedness, which is implied in "while he was yet at a distance" he "saw him," his compelling compassion, his running,[10] his embrace, and his disregard of his son's prepared speech,[11] are all summed up and far exceeded by his instructions to the servants. These mean that the returned wanderer is not only treated as an honored guest but reinstated into the family circle, a son still; though once lost, found; though once dead to the family, now a living part of it. Here the skill of the narrative becomes apparent, for this is the important item in the father's attitude—his immediate and unquestioning purpose to restore his son—and it enables the succeeding contrast to be drawn for which the parable is designed.

We must not, in any parable, press details with too literal a demand. It is useless to speculate why the elder brother was not informed of the festivity or earlier aware of it. We might assume that he was too far afield or that he was certainly neither hoping for nor expecting his brother's return, as was his father. The elder's rather frigid dignity is well portrayed when he sends for a servant to explain the situation instead of making a personal investigation. The same concern shown for the younger son is shown by the father toward his other son in going out to plead with him. There is no reason to question the son's statements concerning his length of service or obedience, nor, on the whole, the contrast he draws. The point indeed rests on the acceptance of these things. His designation of the prodigal as "this son of yours," which is a refusal to accord him the name of brother, is the core of his objection, for it refuses the penitent a place in the same family with himself. His loyalty and diligence are not in debate, but his proud exclusiveness must be weighed against them.

The situation at the reunion was no longer as before. That the prodigal's leaving was not motivated by some unhappiness can hardly be the case, since, as Derrett suggests, his asking for his share was a desperate step, a "confession that he could not live in that home" (p. 106). That he knew he would be returning to a house under the ultimate control of his brother underlines his desperation. His father's response was a breakthrough he had no reason to expect, as his planned speech shows. The elder son could object to his father's squandering the income of the estate on this good-for-nothing, though the father had the right to do so. The elder may have felt his younger brother should get only what he could earn. This is the way the parable would be heard, and at every point it reinforces the choice demanded eventually, a choice between law and grace.[12]

The story in its entirety calls for an opinion. Which attitude toward the prodigal is to be commended and endorsed? The contrast drawn requires the hearer to choose between father and older brother. And to the question the detail and progress of the story, with its power to move and enlist sympathy, permits only one answer. Every instinct of the human heart draws it one way. Not that there might not be those present who would argue for the brother's position with some show of reason, but the story deals with fatherliness faced by an actual situation. Here the father is acting as nothing but father, faced with an instant decision to be made which, when made, determines the future. Hope is restored and the possibility of new life, and only after that has been made possible can the legalities in the case be dealt with. The older brother wants to reverse the order. The parable is addressed to fathers in the audience—and to prodigals or outcasts.

The transfer to another realm, once the judgment is made, becomes equally compelling. To reject the attitude of the older son in the story is to be forced to reject the attitude of Jesus' critics in his urgent campaign to restore hope and produce new life. Their integrity, like the elder brother's, cannot receive its due while it issues in hardheartedness. It is not so much wrong as out of place, mistimed. Only by being treated as a son can the penitent again become a son. Only by inclusion in his family life can he live again as one of the family. Then all things become possible that had not been possible while he was lost to the home in a far country. To treat him as a slave or a menial destroys his hope and limits the value of the family. Such treatment is impossible for those reasons, but more particularly because the father's heart prevents it. True, neither the prodigal nor anyone else can have what he has squandered, but he has learned that home life is all that matters and he may be content to leave the rest to his brother. The elder has this family truth to learn. The prodigal has to prove his gratitude by service in the fellowship to which he is restored.[13]

It will be observed that many of the details are so apt that, once the central point is grasped, many applications may be made and deductions drawn. The treatment of verses 14-20a as an anatomy of repentance, while not the principal interest or purpose of the story, reveals how suitably and skillfully the details are selected and used.[14] It is important to remember, however, that it is a parable and to treat it in the first instance as such. It is a well-nigh perfect example of the use of this method of teaching, touched at every point (even its most polemical) with Jesus' tact and consideration. It leaves no way of escape and deals firmly with the attitude condemned. Yet the first concern of the parable is not a negative one. The contrast is used only to draw attention to the attitude recommended. Jesus not only taught this attitude but exemplified it in his own practice.

The parable goes farther than this. By the use of a truly human comparison, it escapes from the captivity of time. It is as relevant now as then, and in exactly the same manner. The issue is no longer Pharisee versus outcast; the terms of the parable serve in any similar situation, for they are human and universal, not technical and provincial.[15] We often escape the impact intended by treating the parable as allegory. Much preaching, both good and bad, has been served by identification of the characters or details and will probably continue. Where this can be done without violence to the central purpose and meaning, perhaps it need not be unduly deprecated. But often preaching concentrates exclusively on one phase of the story (encouraging attempts to cut it in two) or becomes so involved in analysis that the judgment the parable demands and the application that judgment requires are lost sight of.

The contrast is essential to the parable and it is a contrast of attitude. The father is not to be identified as God, nor the elder brother as official Jewry or the Pharisees. This is a parable. Identification is not the clue, but the implicit demand, "What do you think?" The parallel attitudes are to be looked for in what Jesus clearly taught to be the attitude of God, required of all who would follow him, and the attitude exhibited by Jesus' critics to which the parable is the conclusive answer. The central elements of the one attitude are solicitude, expectation, compassion, and restoration with abounding joy. These are the elements of God's attitude toward the lost, which Jesus must himself follow, though it be at the expense of charges of heresy or excommunication and worse. The elements of the opposed attitude are calculation of merit, demand for reward, unfavorable comparison, and unrelenting exclusiveness. These Jesus felt must be condemned and opposed, *not because he felt them unworthy or unkind, but because they misunderstood or denied the true nature of God.*

A clear understanding of the purpose and scope of the parable is needed to prevent a mistaken use of it, and a double caution is probably necessary. It is not intended to be a complete exposition of God's nature, as is sometimes implied by the allegorical identification of the father with God. The parable is addressed to a particular situation and has a specific purpose. Since the point lies in the contrast between the attitude of the father and that of the older brother, on its own level it demands approval of the one attitude and, by contrast, refusal of the other. In this respect—in dealing with the returned wanderer, in accepting the lost son back into the family—how much more is God to be thought of as adopting an attitude of forgiveness leading to restoration than the strictly legalistic attitude of the older brother. It stands in contrast to the attitude of Jesus' critics, who must commend the father's response to his returned son but whose own attitude to the lost is akin to the less commendable attitude of the older son. To allegorize the parable and make the father stand for God immediately raises problems, because the father's whole course of action is not intended to draw attention, nor is his general character treated; only this particular response. The point turns upon the incident of the return and not at all on the initial departure from home. One might question the father's wisdom in allowing his son to realize his share of the estate and might criticize his training of the boy. But this is not the point; it is only the scenery of the story. To allegorize the parable produces an indulgent God. But it is not an allegory, and interpretation is guarded by its use as a parable in the limited situation to which it applies.

Neither must it be so read as to condone the behavior of the younger son.[16] The prodigal's adventure away from home is not justified, nor its shame lessened, by his restoration to the family. The restoration looks forward to an undetermined future to repair the loss and not backward to the past to excuse it. The prodigal received more than he dared hope for—like the latest hired in the parable of the Laborers in the Vineyard—out of his father's grace. But he was not the same person as he was when he left home, and never could be again. Whether he would become a more worthy member of the family because of his dual experience of loss and of grace is a question the parable does not answer, because that goes beyond its purpose. We look in vain in the parables for a completely developed theology, dogmatic or moral. What we can learn from the limited point with which each parable deals must take its place in a developed system, but the parable itself is not the instrument for developing a system. It is more spontaneous, more occasional, more dynamic.

To return to the parable, we are struck by the note of joy so constant in the first attitude as represented by the father and by the complete absence of it in the picture of the brother. This joy, the reasons for which are so well depicted here, appeared as an addition in the parable of the Lost Sheep and was planned as a celebration in the parable of the Lost Coin. Here it reaches its climax in a spontaneous demonstration about the actual person of the redeemed, who himself shares in it as, of course, neither coin nor sheep could do.

We may well ask, then: What was it about Jesus' opponents that kept them from sharing in this experience of joy or even admitting its validity? The rabbis taught repentance and accepted the repentant sinner. The issue did not center here. The point that Jesus made was the initiative of God in going out in diligent search for the lost; this was a characteristic and original note of his teaching. The possibility is that even this teaching might not have created much opposition. It was his persistent and open practice of the teaching and his inescapable justification of it in his parables that aroused his opponents and made them enemies capable of removing him. From their point of view he was heretical, and a menace to true Judaism.

The question asked above was dealt with by Jesus in a number of other parables. If the Prodigal Son deals effectively with the contrast between the right and the wrong attitude toward erring fellowmen, the next parable deals with the right and wrong attitude toward God.

## THE PHARISEE AND THE TAX COLLECTOR
### Luke 18

*[9]He also told this parable to some who trusted in themselves that they were righteous and despised others: [10]"Two men went up into the temple to pray, one a Pharisee and the other a tax collector. [11]The Pharisee stood and prayed thus with himself, 'God, I thank thee that I am not like other men, extortioners, unjust, adulterers, or even like this tax collector. [12]I fast twice a week, I give tithes of all that I get.' [13]But the tax collector, standing far off, would not even*

lift up his eyes to heaven, but beat his breast, saying, 'God, be merciful to me a sinner!' *¹⁴I tell you, this man went down to his house justified rather than the other; for every one who exalts himself will be humbled, but he who humbles himself will be exalted."*

We need not enter in detail into the discussion of the rabbinic attitude toward penitence or toward self-righteousness. In the parables of Jesus we must make allowance for the Oriental atmosphere and cast of thought which tended toward a hyperbole which we, with our literal minds, might be tempted to call caricature. Exaggeration is, nonetheless, an effective device of the teacher. In controversy over the teaching of the rabbis, we must bear in mind that it is possible to adduce evidence that many if not most of the ideals advanced by Jesus may be paralleled in the Jewish writings. At the same time, as Montefiore himself points out, they are scattered and the products of various minds, without the concentration, emphasis, or unity of authorship found in the Gospels.[17] It is possible also for a religious system to hold together a great many truths, yet its genius is more properly determined by those beliefs to which it gives constant emphasis by habitual practice.

Hence in this parable we find an element of exaggeration which creates an indelible impression. The Evangelist has recorded that it was aimed not at the system as a whole but at a tendency to be observed among certain exponents of it, whose very accomplishments led them into dangerous attitudes and tempted them to look for redemption in the wrong direction. I see no reason for rejecting the setting of the parable: "He also told this parable to some who trusted in themselves that they were righteous and despised others (v. 9)."

The interpretation of the parable is to be determined by this purpose which, in turn, is to be read in connection with verse 14a: "I tell you, this man went down to his house justified rather than the other." These words are attributed to Jesus—a case where our Lord gives his own interpretation of the parable. There is no reason in the parable itself to question the introduction or application, for it yields the same sense. Ultimately, decisions as to either must be determined where possible by the form and natural meaning of the similitude.

The same reasons, however, lead to the rejection of the second half of verse 14: "For every one who exalts himself will be humbled, but he who humbles himself will be exalted." This can be said to follow from the parable only in a derivative sense. The point is not humility and exaltation but justification before God. The saying is found also in Matthew 23:12 and Luke 14:11 and is another of the floating logia, or "morals," that tended to become attached to parables in the course of preaching. As a result of uncritical deference to the text of the Gospels and of an uncritical homiletic use of the parables, the preaching of these moralisms, with the parables used as illustrations, has become one of the weaknesses of the Christian pulpit.[18]

The fact that this parable follows the Widow and the Judge (vs. 1-8) is probably explained when we note that each parable has a similar introduction. In each case the parable is said to have been spoken for a specific reason. Apart from the fact that both parables deal in some sense with prayer, there seems to be nothing more than an editorial reason for their juxtaposition.

The opening contrast of the parable is broadly drawn, and the point throughout is one of contrast: on the one hand a Pharisee, dedicated to the full observance of the Law and guided therein by the traditions of the scribes; on the other hand a tax collector, the very nature of whose employment made it impossible for him even to attempt the way of life the Pharisee felt to be essential. There can be no question of the sincerity of either party.

A textual difficulty in verse 11 has exercised scholars, and we are tempted to increase the contrast by accepting the minority reading of D and other sources[19]: "The Pharisee stood by himself and prayed thus." Probably the text is a simple description of the usual practice: "The Pharisee stood [the recommended attitude] and prayed thus with himself [i.e., silently, his lips moving but no sound audible; cf. 1 Sam. 1:13]."

To begin prayer with thanksgiving was the proper procedure, but the character succeeds in setting himself apart from other men by his own estimate, assuming it to coincide with God's because outwardly he has conformed to the Law. It is right to give thanks for deliverance from the gross sins mentioned, but the tone is not one of deliverance; it is one of achievement. Neither can we question the fact of his freedom from usury and the like. The words translated "or even" ($\bar{e}$ *kai*) have caused difficulty. To read "or for that matter" is probably better than to understand it as though it read, "and certainly not like this fellow." It is probably a thanksgiving for deliverance from unavoidable defilement, necessarily attendant upon the functions of a tax collector. This is supported by the Pharisee's concluding assertion (v. 12), which in turn is not to be questioned. This claim to recognition arises from the fact that he is one of those who have voluntarily agreed to undertake certain extra religious duties. The double weekly fast was assumed as a "work of supererogation" and was not required. The meaning of "all that I get" is "all that I acquire," and the point of it is that by tithing everything he purchased the devotee avoided the use of produce that had not been tithed at the source. It is similarly an assertion of scrupulosity, admirable in its way, the validity of which is not in doubt.

It can therefore be seen where the Pharisee puts his trust. For him justification is secured negatively by freedom from notable sins and accidental defilement and positively by freely assumed extra duties and disciplines. The judge in the matter is his own conscience, which is formed by the Law as elucidated and applied by the scribes. The element of caricature, if it exists, does not lie in the accurately drawn picture of the finest type of practicing Pharisee but in the attitude of self-righteousness engendered by the system and the temptation to scorn others.

The tax collector provides a clear contrast at every point. He barely enters the sacred precincts; he adopts a pose of utmost humility, fearful even to look toward God; he emphasizes his words by an act of penitence; he offers no thanksgiving; he stands alone in the Presence, with no thought of comparison with other men (unless we find in the marginal reading of verse 13, "*the* sinner," a sense that he is guilty above all others). If we do not question the sincerity of the Pharisee, neither may we question the sincerity of the tax collector. His approach to God, with whom alone is his concern, is uncalculated and subject to no assessment but that of God's holiness. Penitent, he throws himself on God's mercy, trusting only in the nature of God, "who desireth not the death of a sinner" (cf. Ezek. 18:32).

The concluding words, "this man went down to his house justified," have extreme force because the direct objective of this man was not justification, whereas it was precisely this that the Pharisee sought and claimed. The Pharisee was seeking to *justify himself,* and it was in just this respect that he went away empty. This is not Paul speaking but Jesus, and yet there can be no doubt that the apostle's theologically elaborated doctrine of justification by grace through faith has a firm basis in Jesus' teaching. The immediate point, however, is that it was this effort to achieve justification "by the works of the law," and the tendency to believe that not only could God's demands be met but that merit might in addition be achieved, which led to the inability to see and feel the joy of God over the repentant sinner and the failure actively to seek those without.

The gulf between Jesus' view of God and that which he attacks by these parables is clear. It is a gulf so wide as to involve a rejection of the most cherished dreams of his critics—dreams that involved ultimately the question of the kingdom of God and the Messiah. For the Pharisee, the kingdom would be the reward of repentance and of the practice of the Law. For Jesus, the kingdom was a gift of God, the presence of which constituted a demand for repentance. "Repent, for the kingdom of heaven is at hand," was an inversion that lay at the basis of all Jesus' teaching. It is not difficult to see, after studying this particular parable, why the opposition to Jesus continued to grow in intensity until it produced the inevitable result. If the parable had been simply a counsel to humility, he would have been applauded.

In another parable the same problem is treated with an emphasis that falls rather on the attitude of God, though it is, in itself, a further criticism of men's attitude on this matter.

## THE SLAVE IN FIELD AND HOUSE
### Luke 17

**[7]"Will any one of you, who has a servant plowing or keeping sheep, say to him when he has come in from the field, 'Come at once and sit down at table'? [8]Will he not rather say to him, 'Prepare supper for me, and gird yourself and serve me, till I eat and drink; and afterward you shall eat and drink'? [9]Does he thank the servant because he did what was commanded? [10]So you also, when you have done all that is commanded you, say, 'We are unworthy servants; we have only done what was our duty.' "**

The servant portrayed here is the highest in the three grades employed by the Jews. The "bondman" (*doulos*) was protected by the law and was in a superior position to "menservants and maidservants" (*paides*) and to the hired "laborers" (*misthoi*). On larger estates or in wealthy homes there were more elevated functionaries known as "stewards" (*oikonomoi*) and "household servants" (*oiketai*). The situation here depicted, with the intimate realism of so many of the parables, seems to be an unpretentious home which provides only one servant who cares for all the work of the farm, within and without.[20]

It may well be that the rabbis and other Oriental teachers looked on men as slaves of God or the gods. Certainly Paul did not hesitate to call himself the slave of Jesus Christ (Rom. 1:1; Phil. 1:1). But it is not a necessary deduction from this parable or any other that Jesus had this in mind or was consciously teaching it. Treated as a parable it is not necessary to identify the master and slave respectively with God and his servants. This is indicated by the introductory formula

(v. 7), "Will any one of you . . . ?" A judgment is expected, confirming that the situation exists and is normal. The same deduction is to be made as to the situation between man and God, a deduction which the Pharisee in the preceding parable did not make. The assertion, "We are unworthy servants," is one expected to be compelled from the lips of him who understands what God's demands and man's capacity are, not a status assigned by God who as Father, in Jesus' teaching, waits to treat men as sons.

Indeed, this is the point of the similitude. The servant might, in view of his daylong work in the fields, assume that he had a claim against his master at least for rest. Rather, he finds that he has by no means finished his task. Household duties are yet to be faced. Not until everything has been completed may he even satisfy his hunger. At the very end he receives and probably expects no thanks, for he has but done the duty that his situation requires. There is no opportunity to do more and so earn approbation.

Clearly the attitude of the master, with its undertone of inconsiderateness, is not meant to be a picture of God. The meaning of the parable is clearly indicated in verse 10: "So you also, when you have done all that is commanded you, say, 'We are unworthy servants; we have only done what was our duty.'" The adjective can scarcely mean "unworthy" in the usual sense of that word, for the master derives the benefit of the slave's services. The servant is not worthless but simply a servant, or only a servant; the word *achreioi* may be interpreted as "poor." We are to say, "We are simply servants, happy if only we can do our duty."[21] The question of whether Jesus here assumes we can do all that God commands seems to be somewhat beside the point, since in the previous parable we understood him to say that even works of supererogation were ineffective to plead our righteousness before God; even if we could do all our duty and more, the situation is not changed.

The parable is a further warning against presuming that we can press any claim to God's favor or reward. God's love is not engendered by our service, nor aroused by our merits. It is his nature to love. If we may trust the story of the washing of the disciples' feet (John 13:1-14), we may add that, though God cannot recognize any humanly compelled obligation to reward us, he may out of his freely given love take our places—not because of our achievements but because he is self-moved to do so.

Since this parable and that of the Pharisee and the Tax Collector cut so sharply against the attitude of Jesus' contemporaries, it is worthwhile to quote Montefiore:

We have responsibilities and duties, but no right to, or claim upon, reward. Whatever good a man does, he cannot do more than he owes to God. For to him he owes all that he is capable of doing. . . . That was not quite original teaching, but it was so relatively. The tilt against exaggerations and perversions of the doctrine of tit-for-tat is a prominent and characteristic feature of the teaching of Jesus. What we receive from God is grace and goodness, and not reward.[22]

Nothing further need be said except to note again here that the attitude attacked is that which makes it difficult for the critics of Jesus to see why the nature of God determines his open mission. The parable must not be thought to banish the idea of God's goodness or giving of reward, for in a sense the interpretation leads directly to a more correct view of God's relationship with men and the basis upon which he deals with them. That basis is the subject of the next parable.

### THE LABORERS IN THE VINEYARD
Matthew 20

[1]"For the kingdom of heaven is like a householder who went out early in the morning to hire laborers for his vineyard. [2]After agreeing with the laborers for a denarius a day, he sent them into his vineyard. [3]And going out about the third hour he saw others standing idle in the market place; [4]and to them he said, 'You go into the vineyard too, and whatever is right I will give you.' So they went. [5]Going out again about the sixth hour and the ninth hour, he did the same. [6]And about the eleventh hour he went out and found others standing; and he said to them, 'Why do you stand here idle all day?' [7]They said to him, 'Because no one has hired us.' He said to them, 'You go into the vineyard too.' [8]And when the evening came, the owner of the vineyard said to his steward, 'Call the laborers and pay them their wages, beginning with the last, up to the first.' [9]And when those hired about the eleventh hour came, each of them received a denarius. [10]Now when the first came, they thought they would receive more; but each of them also received a denarius. [11]And on receiving it they grumbled at the householder, [12]saying, 'These last worked only one hour, and you have made them equal to us who have borne the burden of the day and the scorching heat.' [13]But he replied to one of them, 'Friend, I am doing you no wrong; did you not agree with me for a denarius? [14]Take what belongs to you, and go; I choose to give to this last as I give to you. [15]Am I not allowed to do what I choose with what belongs to me? Or do you begrudge my generosity?' [16]So the last will be first, and the first last."

At the point in Mark where the discourse on the rewards of the disciples closes with the words, "But many that are first will be last, and the last first (10:31)," Matthew has inserted this parable. The point at which it is introduced and the moral appended to it, "So the last will be first, and the first last (v. 16)," which is a modification of Mark's verse, reveal the meaning the Evangelist found in the story. It is to be noted that there are signs of the independence of the parable and the setting. Whereas Mark starts with the "first," the saying in verse 16 has been changed to mention "the last" first, in order to bring it into line with verses 8-12 of the parable, where the latest hired are the first paid. The concluding verse of the Marcan material (Mark 10:31) has been brought into conformity in Matthew's parallel section before the parable (Matt. 19:30). Thus the interpretation of the parable is based upon what is at best an incidental detail at the expense of the central theme, no matter how necessary the detail is to the story.

Further, we detect in this appended moral the interpretation given the parable by the church tradition from which Matthew received it, and this is borne out by its insertion at this point. In Mark 10:28ff. (followed by Matt. 19:27ff.) Jesus has dealt with Peter's question concerning the reward to be expected by those who have left all to follow Christ. The reply ends with the warning that the first shall be last, and the last first. The insertion of the parable at this point is doubtless intended as an illustration of this truth, the implication being that the priority of the apostles in following Christ does not give them precedence of reward. Even those who become workers in the latter days shall receive an equal recompense. The traditional interpretation of the parable has, of course, followed these lines. We must question whether this is its original meaning and whether it would necessarily bear that meaning apart from its context and added moral.[23]

Modern homiletical exposition has done more violence to it by allegorizing details. Attention focused on verses 6-7, "Why do you stand here idle all day? . . . Because no one has hired us," has prompted sermons on social security and full employment, and the payment of all alike has been used as an argument for "a living wage." On the other hand, attention focused on verse 15, "Am I not allowed to do what I choose with what belongs to me?" has produced arguments for laissez-faire economics or free enterprise in the capitalistic sense. Nothing could have been farther from Jesus' mind or purpose.

The Matthaean flow of argument arises in the story of the "rich young ruler," which may be interpreted as another example of the discussion on works and grace (Matt. 19:16-22).[24] The question, "What good deed must I do?" and the assertion, "All these I have observed," lead to Jesus' demand for a decision which is *clearly* beyond the young man's capacity: "Sell what you possess and give to the poor (v. 21)." This need not be interpreted as a general rule but as a demand designed for the individual case facing Jesus. But Mark, followed by the other Synoptics, has made it the text for a discussion of riches (Mark 10:23-27; Matt. 19:23-26; Luke 18:24-26) and of rewards (Mark 10:28-31; Matt. 19:27-30). While it is to illustrate this discussion that the parable is here introduced, we shall come nearer the original meaning if we associate it with the rich man rather than with Peter's question.

Once again difficulties encountered by some in the eccentricity of the farmer disappear if the story is taken as a parable rather than as an allegory. The eccentricity of the man—which consists in his instruction to the steward to pay the last first (v. 8) rather than in the scale of payments—cannot be ignored, since it is the point of the story, but it is not to be taken literally as a picture of God. The payment of the latest-hired laborers in the presence of all the rest is essential to the point.[25]

The parable is one of those designated as of the kingdom of heaven (God). Not that the kingdom is like the man, but the state of affairs in the kingdom is like the state of affairs here depicted. The man, at daybreak, hires laborers from the market place, where it was customary for casual laborers to congregate for this purpose. With them he makes an agreement—to pay them a denarius for a day's work. A denarius was considered a normal day's pay. From the way in which verses 3 and 4 are expressed ("And he . . . saw others standing idle . . . and to them he said, 'You go into the vineyard too . . .' "), and more particularly verses 6 and 7 ("Why do you stand here idle all day? . . . You go into the vineyard too . . ."), we are probably intended to understand that the farmer at the successive later hours did not need additional help, or needed it less and less urgently, but was willing, until the eleventh hour, to give work to any he found, not alone perhaps out of compassion but partly to expedite the vintage.

His compassion is more clearly exercised when he pays everyone the same wage. The amount of work achieved and the hours and conditions of labor are alike ignored. Some other consideration evidently determines what to the last-employed might have seemed a whimsy and what to the first-employed seemed an outright injustice. The complaint (v. 12) that the recently employed had been made equal with all the others is really a charge of injustice, since to make them equal is to give the last hired not equality but a definite advantage. We note that only the first and last groups are mentioned, and those hired at the third, sixth, and ninth hours do not take part in the discussion. That is what the story demands for the sake of a clear contrast, particularly since only those first hired received a contract for a specific sum. At the beginning of the day they could bargain with the farmer and he must needs promise them a fair wage. Later he was under no such urgency or necessity. The others were willing to trust him to deal fairly with them.

The point is that he deals not simply *fairly* but *generously* with them. With the first he deals according to the terms of the contract, and this is his defense when challenged. Neither his contract nor his generosity is a proper subject for argument. Contention is based on envy and a desire to weigh merit and reward in nicely adjusted scales. To treat all in terms of the agreement with those first employed would mean a miserable pittance for the last, scarcely worth their trouble any more than hiring and paying them would be worth the farmer's trouble. The treatment of those whose efforts were worth scarcely anything afforded an opportunity to act with generosity and to exercise a freedom that none could deny was the farmer's right.[26] The fault lay not with him but in the carping spirit of those who murmured at his exercise of gracious consideration for those who were unfortunate through no fault of their own.

The contrast is inescapable and, again, balances free grace against the bargaining spirit which expects (and, as here represented, demands) something over and above on the basis of comparative merit. After raising the question of whether the rabbinic teaching is an out-and-out seeking for reward, Dr. Montefiore says of this parable:

> Such criticism is greatly exaggerated. But it cannot be denied that both in the Old Testament and in the Rabbinical literature the principle of measured retribution and reward is very prominent. That the Rabbis had a peculiar "lust for reward" is false. . . . But the doctrine of the parables does supply a corrective to a frequent element of their teaching. It emphasizes that, in addition to the principle of retribution (which Jesus by no means denies), there is also the principle of grace.[27]

The interpretation suggested by these words of Montefiore is clearly more original than the traditional Christian application that incommensurate service, either in amount or in quality, receives equal reward from God (making the last first, etc.), which is to press a detail of the parable as it should not be pressed. The sort of judgment expected (on what might well have been considered a humorous story) would certainly be that, though eccentric, the farmer had the right to be generous and to ignore calculation if he wished. On the spiritual plane it reminds us that God's dealings with man are independent of man's carefully calculated achievement.

The parable uses a well-worn theme, but the rabbinic parallels stand in clear contrast. The one most frequently quoted deals with the laborer who was so efficient that the king removed him from among the many others after two hours, walked with him at leisure, and paid him his full wage *on the ground that* "This man has done more in two hours than you have done in the whole day."[28] The teaching in Jesus' parable is the exact opposite of this rabbinism, which preserves the very attitude Jesus is attacking. The contrast vividly illuminates Jesus' genius—in this case his ability to rework a theme and give it new glory.

On the other hand we are not to think that the parable teaches that God is capricious. The parable, like the others, was used to meet a definite situation, and, though the situation is not stated, we find it in that predominating misinterpretation of the Law with which Jesus elsewhere deals in other ways. The tendency that made generosity to the sinner difficult here appears as a complaint based on concern for one's own deserts. The very fact that it was adapted to the needs of the church serves to indicate not only its original necessity but the appearance of a like spirit in the new fellowship. It stands as a perpetual warning to the Christian against forgetfulness of God's grace and against spiritual pride. Once again the parable would lead us to say, "We are but servants."

However, to believe firmly in God's goodness, grace, or generosity might lead us to forget another principle of the spiritual life. That principle is based, essentially, on the same doctrine, but serves to notify us that even God's grace cannot be operative under all conditions.

## THE UNMERCIFUL SERVANT
### Matthew 18

[23]"Therefore the kingdom of heaven may be compared to a king who wished to settle accounts with his servants. [24]When he began the reckoning, one was brought to him who owed him ten thousand talents; [25]and as he could not pay, his lord ordered him to be sold, with his wife and children and all that he had, and payment to be made. [26]So the servant fell on his knees, imploring him, 'Lord, have patience with me, and I will pay you everything.' [27]And out of pity for him the lord of the servant released him and forgave him the debt. [28]But that same servant, as he went out, came upon one of his fellow servants who owed him a hundred denarii; and seizing him by the

throat he said, 'Pay what you owe.' ²⁹So his fellow servant fell down and besought him, 'Have patience with me, and I will pay you.' ³⁰He refused and went and put him in prison till he should pay the debt. ³¹When his fellow servants saw what had taken place, they were greatly distressed, and they went and reported to their lord all that had taken place. ³²Then his lord summoned him and said to him, 'You wicked servant! I forgave you all that debt because you besought me; ³³and should not you have had mercy on your fellow servant, as I had mercy on you?' ³⁴And in anger his lord delivered him to the jailers, till he should pay all his debt. *So also my heavenly Father will do to every one of you, if you do not forgive your brother from your heart."*

Matthew, who alone has this parable, presents it as an illustration of the teaching expressed in Jesus' answer to Peter's question (v. 21), "As many as seven times?" The answer goes as far beyond the *lex talionis* as that law of equal satisfaction went beyond the unlimited blood revenge of Genesis 4:24: "If Cain is avenged sevenfold, truly Lamech seventy-sevenfold." "But seventy times seven" in Jesus' reply (v. 22) clearly implies unlimited forgiveness. It expresses the best of Old Testament, pre-Christian, and rabbinic teaching.²⁹

The parable, however, turns, not on repeated forgiveness but on unlimited forgiveness, i.e., forgiveness for a debt so great that it cannot be repaid. It is perhaps to introduce this note that the sum in verse 24, "ten thousand talents," is made so huge. Some critics think it has become multiplied in the course of transmission or by the editor. The sum mentioned, approaching the modern equivalent of ten million dollars, was many times the usual revenue of a number of provinces. Thereby appears the seeming incongruity of verse 25 ("and payment to be made") and verse 34 ("till he should pay all his debt"). If the sum stands, the punishment must carry beyond death! If the sum be reduced to something very large but still within reason, the point of the parable remains unimpaired, though its logical connection with the preceding dialogue is lessened.

We are helped to understand the situation envisaged if we suppose the servant to be not a slave in our ordinary understanding of the term but an official of an Oriental despot. Perhaps, like the servants in the parable of the Talents and the Pounds, he is given charge over some share of his master's affairs. Or we may conceive of him as a tax farmer who is to collect the revenue of a province. The possibility of restoring a large sum would then depend on its collection rather than on its being earned. Or, again, we may note that in verse 27 the debt is referred to as a loan (*daneion*), and this again suggests a share in the master's capital or estate turned over to his servant for exploitation.[30]

Apart from these difficulties, the meaning is inescapable. When, as we would say, the audit is made, an enormous deficiency is revealed in the affairs of one servant. The master determines to follow the customary practice of selling servant and family in the slave market, along with all their possessions, in order to recoup himself as far as possible. In this he is acting in the accepted fashion. But he is not just a despot. Moved by the debtor's plea for patience, he does far more than accede to the plea or trust the promise—which was not very likely to be fulfilled. He entirely forgives the whole debt.

At this point it is worth while to note the instructive comment of Cadoux:

> The big debtor had not troubled about the little debt due to him, knowing that whatever came to him belonged to his creditor, but when his debt was forgiven, whatever he could squeeze out of the little debtor became his own. The forgiveness which he had received, not moving his spirit in like kind, became a positive incentive in the opposite direction.[31]

It is not characteristic of these simple stories to enter into such subtleties, but the observation is just and heightens the very impression the parable creates.

By contrast the sum owed to the forgiven debtor is trifling, amounting to scarcely an equivalent of twenty dollars—trifling whether we accept the original figure as ten thousand or ten talents. The unmerciful servant again acts as was customary. The plea made by the small debtor is in the same terms his creditor had earlier used, "Have patience with me, and I will pay you," except that here the promise is one that it is possible to carry out. But while the debtor is willing to emulate his lord in one respect, in the demand for payment and the application of rigid penalty, he is indifferent to the example from which he has himself benefited and still benefits. It was not permitted to sell debtors into slavery unless the debt was as large as the sum likely to be realized, which here is manifestly not the case.[32]

The fellow servants of verse 31 may be assumed to have witnessed the mercy extended by the lord, and the contrast in every respect moves them, not only to compassion but to indignation. If it were only compassion, they might easily have paid the small sum owing and bailed out the unfortunate debtor. The lord's response is decisive. He explains that the original debt was forgiven because of the debtor's plea, but it had the further grounds, implicit though not expressed, that the recipient of mercy be also, in turn, merciful.

"And should not you have had mercy on your fellow-servant, even as I had mercy on you?" (v. 33). The lord's mercy is now turned to anger and the punishment is apparently more stringent than that proposed before. Mercy that does not stimulate mercy turns into the same rigorous demand for justice exhibited by the one who, forgiven, could not forgive.

The moral added in verse 35, "So also my heavenly Father will do to every one of you," which appears in a more simple form in Matthew 6:15 (cf. Mark 11:25-26), refers the meaning to the personal relationship between God and men in place of the parable's, "Therefore the kingdom of heaven may be compared to," and speaks of the necessary inward depth of sincerity necessary to human forgiveness if God is to forgive us.

The point of the parable, avoiding any unnecessary insistence on details, is clearly that the only hope we can have of God's grace, operating to remove the heavy load of debt to him which we cannot expect to meet, must lie in our being willing, in our sphere, to show the same spirit to those whose injuries against us are, by comparison, negligible. Once again Jesus appeals to the nature of God. To deny the validity of the principles of mercy, forgiveness, and patience in our human affairs is to deny the nature of God himself and to shut ourselves off from the operation of his love. His grace is uncalculated as in previous parables, and only our own unrelenting spirit can prevent its apprehension. Just as we cannot earn our way into God's favor, neither can we appropriate his mercy if we insist upon calculation in our dealings with others. And when all is said and done, the parable itself speaks more clearly than any words we may use in an effort to draw out its meaning.

The cumulative effect of these parables, if the interpretations offered be justified, leads us to observe the true basis for Jesus' compassion. They were, we believe, offered as vindications of his mission. Justification of his teaching and practice is not based on the needs of men, strongly though these must appeal to a sensitive nature, but on the purpose of God and his nature. If, as we observed earlier, the temptation represents Jesus' rejection of the traditional hopes for the kingdom and of the usual conceptions of the messianic function, we find here an echo of Jesus' refusal to turn stones into bread. Jesus must have been moved by the sad economic plight of men, but his mercy was not compelled by sympathy for that condition in which he himself shared, for "man shall not live by bread alone." We know from the Gospels that Jesus was frequently "moved with compassion." He could not resist the appeal of the sick and crippled (Matt. 14:14; Mark 1:34), and to the plea of the leper he responded by reaching out and touching the unclean as no one else was likely to do (Mark 1:41). For the multitudes he was moved with "compassion . . . , because they were like sheep without a shepherd" (Mark 6:34). His anger was aroused by the officious attempt of the apostles to keep the little children from him (Mark 10:14). Even on the cross his mercy was directed toward his enemies (Luke 23:34) and the wretch who shared his fate (Luke 23:43). All the sources record compassion as characteristic of Jesus. But the same Gospels contain the parables which justify his mission and base that justification on the character and will of God and not on the human situation.

In other words, the mercy and love of God, uncalculated, unrestricted, seeking and outreaching, is not conditioned, is not aroused by the plight of men. It is, as Nygren put it, "uncaused"[33]; or, as we might better phrase it, God himself is the only effective cause of the love which he exercises and which Jesus teaches and demonstrates.[34]

Here there is no ground for expediency or resort to the argument of sound practicality, true as that argument may be. The sentimental appeal made by modern preaching, in an effort to play upon the natural pity of the hearers, is a long way from this element of the Gospel. An attempt to stir people is valid, but it is woefully ineffective in the long run because it does not reach deep enough. Pity itself, as the revelations of atrocities in Europe in 1945 or of the starving legions of 1946 demonstrated, may become numbed into indifference by a sort of satiation. The same has been reinforced by the even more colossal examples of genocide, starvation, and displacement of peoples in various countries of Africa and in Southeast Asia during the sixties and seventies. The demands of God's own nature and his revealed will do not suffer from this weakness, and they must again be presented as an effective cause. The argument that brotherhood or love works, ensures peace—is, in effect, good policy—is even less fundamental. The preacher, like Jesus in his parables, must speak to people in terms they can understand, but the Gospel itself must not be reduced along with the terms in which it is expressed. It stands firmly on the ground where its ultimate appeal must always rest, on the revealed nature and purpose of God.

Further, the mercy and grace of God are not stimulated or increased by the virtues or service of men, self-originated and self-achieved, even when inspired by the effort to keep the Law. It was this which Paul found true in his own experience, and it led him to the knowledge of salvation by faith. Man's achievement as well as man's incapacity failed to close the gap between God and man. He not only found that "I do not do the good I want, but the evil I do not want is what I do (Rom. 7:19)." He realized that "no human being will be justified in his sight by works of the law (Rom. 3:20)." If "a man is justified by faith apart from works of law" (Rom. 3:28), it is because God is known in Christ to be the God of grace and not the God of calculations, a God whose love is so great that no powers of earth or heaven may separate us from it (Rom. 8:38-39).

Paul is often accused of distorting and complicating the "simple religion of Jesus." This charge fails to take account of the teaching in these parables. Jesus' situation was utterly different from that of Paul. His audience was not the same, nor was his mission. Much that Jesus necessarily assumed in addressing his fellow countrymen, his great apostle could not assume in writing to "mixed" congregations of hellenized Jews and converted gentiles. The fundamental human problem faced in the parables considered in this chapter is essentially the same as that with which Paul dealt in his great theological passages. To suppose that there is a fundamental gulf between what Jesus and Paul taught is one result of the failure to seek the primary meaning of the parables and to understand their place in the work of Jesus. The essential difference and notable exception is that Paul believed in and taught a risen Lord. The religion of Jesus (which could not be ours in any case) and the religion concerning Jesus must necessarily stand each on opposite sides of the age-transforming events of crucifixion and resurrection. The faith Paul held he received and transmitted (1 Cor. 15:3), and his anathemas were hurled at those who had, as it seemed to him, the temerity to change it (Gal. 1:6-12). In the parables, and in particular in those considered in this chapter, we find the true sources of the theology that Paul found to be essential to one who had faced human failure and had discovered the goodness of God revealed in the face of the Lord Jesus Christ.

# FIVE THE CRISIS OF GOD'S CHOSEN

The mercy of God which Jesus expressed by his mission to all Israelites and vindicated in the parables just studied is the true basis upon which the universalism of Christianity rests. It is not simply an addition made by the Evangelists in the interest of the gentile mission. The outreach beyond Israel doubtless accounts in part for the preservation of the parables, but the authority for the church's practice rests on Jesus' justification of his own work. In transmission the records have undergone a shift from the national to the individual and universal point of view. The Gospels, we must remember, are later than Paul. Jesus' first appeal was not directed primarily to the individual but to the nation, to the people as a whole. We cannot ignore the sense of corporate identity possessed by the Jew.

Certain sayings in the Gospels imply a universalist view on the part of Jesus. When they stand alone they are not so strong as they are with the parables as background. "The tax collectors and the harlots go into the kingdom of God before you (Matt. 21:31b)." "Truly, I say to you, not even in Israel have I found such faith. I tell you, many will come from east and west and sit at table with Abraham, Isaac, and Jacob in the kingdom of heaven" (Matt. 8:10b-11; cf. Luke 13:28f.). The passages concerning the widow to whom Elijah was sent and the Syrian leper cleansed by Elisha (Luke 4:25-29) may also be mentioned. The parables are limited in the first instance to the topic that was under discussion and do not raise the question of authenticity as do the words "from east and west."

On the other hand, Jesus elsewhere seems to represent particularism when he says, "I was sent only to the lost sheep of the house of Israel (Matt. 15:24)," and instructs his disciples, "Go nowhere among the Gentiles, and enter no town of the Samaritans, but go rather to the lost sheep of the house of Israel (Matt. 10:5-6)." His dealings with non-Israelites are few and fortuitous. Universalism, as at earlier times, is again qualified. But there was in the scriptures what might be called a *prophetic particularism,* and its ultimate aim was universalistic. It conceived of Israel as an instrument prepared and fashioned by God (Isa. 49:2) to be "a light to the nations, that my salvation may reach to the end of the earth (Isa. 49:6)." President Morgenstern has found in this "God-appointed destiny" the very reason for Israel's failure to undertake a universal mission.

> This feeling of peoplehood, this consciousness of uniqueness and separateness in the world, narrowed, but at the same time deepened, the application of the principle of universalism in Judaism. It held Judaism back from a world-wide proselytizing program of absolute universalism, and thus actually called Christianity into being, as its daughter-religion, and gave to it its mission to become the proselytizing religion of the western world, transcending all differences of peoplehood and nationhood.[1]

Jesus appealed to his people for the lifting up of their burden, for the realization of their mission. This, if any, was his solution for the political dilemma—not a political but a religious solution.

On the view that Jesus spoke to his people as to a church with a missionary task, and limited his own mission primarily to calling it to that task and equipping it to carry it out, we can understand why his appeal was limited to Israel. His mission was to call Israel to be God's servant indeed. His purpose was to call the people as a whole to undertake the universal task for which it was ordained. If this be so, we should expect to find Jesus' criticism of those who held his people back from their true destiny. Since the parable was his most effective weapon, we are not surprised to find that both his appeal and his attack are expressed in parabolic form. The relevant parables sound a note of urgency and of warning that is not explained simply by an appeal to the nation to work out its destiny but strikes the hour of destiny itself.

The appeal to Israel as something more than just another nation, free to pursue the path of any political entity or to embrace any worldly expedient, is shown clearly in Jesus' demand for a standard not asked of others. In his temptation, he himself had rejected the worldly hopes of Jewish nationalism. He asked the people to follow him in that renunciation and to be truly unique among the peoples of the earth. "If you love those who love you, what reward have you? Do not even the tax collectors do the same? And if you salute only your brethren, what more are you doing than others? Do not even the Gentiles do the same?" (Matt: 5:46-47; see Matt. 6:7, 32 for other references to "the Gentiles"). The God-given function of Israel explains this insistence on a standard demanded of this nation above others or required of those within the nation who would be true Israelites. Jesus' complaint was that they refused to read the signs of the times and to sense the jeopardy in which they stood. His own sensitivity to the urgent danger aroused his irony. It also moved him to tears and led him finally to the agony of the cross.

Such an appeal to his people must be incomplete and inconclusive unless it be tested in the Holy City. It must be addressed finally to the hierarchy that controlled the course of the nation, though an appeal to the people for popular support would be a necessary preliminary. Jesus' reaction to opposition was to withdraw, but he withdrew only to prepare an advance. In the face of a "falling away" which seems to have prompted the secular authority at last to move, he retreated beyond the borders of Galilee. But it was there that he formed his decision to proceed to Jerusalem, a decision represented (though obscured by later interests) in the story of the transfiguration. It is no accident, then, that those parables which, when stripped of later accretions, reveal his urgent appeal are associated with his approach to Jerusalem.

From a brief parable concerning the doing of God's will we discern that Jesus thought of his people as standing in a special relation to that will.

## THE TWO SONS
### Matthew 21
28"What do you think? A man had two sons; and he went to the first and said, 'Son, go and work in the vineyard today.' 29And he answered, 'I will not'; but afterward he repented and went. 30And he went to the second and said the same; and he answered, 'I go, sir,' but did not go. 31Which of the two did the will of his father?" They said, "The first." Jesus said to them, "Truly, I say to you, the tax collectors and the harlots go into the kingdom of God before you. 32For John came to you in the way of righteousness, and you did not believe him, but the tax collectors and the harlots believed him; and even when you saw it, you did not afterward repent and believe him."

The parable is introduced by Matthew into a section of Marcan material to follow the challenge of Jesus' authority in the temple (Mark 11:27ff.; Matt. 21:23ff.; Luke 20:1ff.). It is placed before the parable of the Tenants of the Vineyard, which in Mark and Luke follows immediately. To judge by Matthew's methods, the parable seemed to him to have to do with the hierarchy (cf. v. 23). The point of contact is the discussion of the authority of John the Baptist (vs. 25ff.). Matthew adds to the parable (ending at v. 31a) and its first application ("the tax collectors and the harlots," etc., v. 31b) the interpretation which deals with attitudes toward John (v. 32).

"What do you think?" is typical of the parable method, since it calls for a judgment. The question is asked in more specific terms at the end: "Which of the two did the will of his father?" It is a question posed on the level of human experience by the situation of the father and the two sons, the first of whom, unwilling, changed his mind and acted, the second of whom expressed his consent but did not act. The question is, Which did what was required to obey the father's will? The expected answer ("The first") is given, i.e., the one whose unwillingness was changed to action.

The available texts of the parable cause some confusion. Those followed by the *King James Version* and the *Revised Standard Version* are represented above. There are other texts that reverse the order in which the sons are approached but, by producing the answer, "The last," do not change the sense. This order has the virtue of final emphasis but is of no necessary importance. The third reading presents a difficulty that would affect the interpretation of the parable. The order in which the sons are approached is as above (RSV), but the answer given is, "The second"; that is, the son who *said* he would go but did not.

With the majority of scholars we should be wise to reject the third variant. The Jewish doctrine of repentance makes it likely that Jesus' hearers would approve of the son who went after he had first refused.[2] To give any other answer would be to put verbal conformity above practice, and it is difficult to believe that Jesus' opponents would have adopted that position. It is sufficient for Jesus' purposes if they agree that, in the situation presented, the son who refused verbal but yielded actual compliance was the one who obeyed his father. It seems to me that the answer would be the one in the usual text, but that Jesus' opponents would refuse to accept either alternative as a picture of their own situation. It is around this point that interpretation revolves. In what sense are they like the second son who promised but did not give obedience?

Jesus here is distinguishing, in the language of the parable, between verbal obedience and practical obedience. In the realm to which the parable applies this would appear as outward conformity, on the one hand, and actual work, on the other; formal, legal, and ritual observance of God's requirements as against repentance which leads to due service of God among and for men. This is the prophetic doctrine: "I desire steadfast love [*chesed*, loving loyalty?] and not sacrifice" (Hos. 6:6; cf. Matt. 9:13; 12:7).

All this is clear, but it does not explain the tradition which places the parable in the context of conflict with the authorities (even though we reject as editorial the application Matthew gives in 21:31b-32). The main point of the parable is not the repentance of the first son but the contrast between the sons. As a characterization, the leaders would have to reject it, because they would feel they had responded to God by both will and deed. They would see no need to repent, as they had seen no need to respond to John's baptism. Reliance on their race and their orthodoxy would preclude any such acceptance of the charge. But Jesus had responded to John's call and had been baptized. Those who had joined him in the movement had that much authority to question the sincerity of their challengers. This valid connection we may see in the setting. And it is here, in the actual situation rather than in the simple application of the prophetic demand, that the parable becomes a charge. Jesus' opponents say "Yes" to God in the traditional way and do not see that their response is not inclusive enough. It is probably not accidental that the work suggested in the parable is in a vineyard. There was a tradition behind the figure. It is the term used for Israel's special vocation. The extent of God's call and the meaning of the task presented to Israel is what its leaders do not see. Their response does not go the full length of God's requirements. What they have done, necessary as it is, is in effect a verbal response only and does not amount to real obedience. It is necessary for them first to see that loyalty is lacking in some vital aspect before they will realize the true extent of their calling. "Not every one who says to me, 'Lord, Lord,' shall enter the kingdom of heaven, but he who does the will of my Father who is in heaven (Matt. 7:21)."[3]

It is Jesus' method, as a good teacher, to bring people to teach themselves, to persuade them to see the real meaning and extent of their own religious ideas and to answer them out of their own mouths. It is the method of this parable as of others, notably of the Prodigal Son and of the Rich Man and Lazarus (see Chapter Seven). The parable of the Two Sons is an attempt to make the nation see its failure, to comprehend that it needed the teaching and example of Jesus—and more. What he attacks is not the refusal to obey God but the refusal to see the full implications of God's call and the urgency of the need to implement the resulting vocation. But Jesus does not allow the nature of the call and the failure to implement it to remain a generalization. He brings against the national leaders in at least one parable a specific charge of failure. At the same time he clearly enunciates the primary task in a trenchant criticism of the attempt to evade it by casuistry. The parable of the Good Samaritan, it seems to me, must be so interpreted. It is a well-known parable, but difficult for all its familiarity. The difficulty is revealed by the way it is usually treated in preaching and by the critical debate which arises around its setting.

## THE "GOOD" SAMARITAN
### Luke 10

*25And behold, a lawyer stood up to put him to the test, saying, "Teacher, what shall I do to inherit eternal life?" 26He said to him, "What is written in the law? How do you read?" 27And he answered, "You shall love the Lord your God with all your heart, and with all your soul, and with all your strength, and with all your mind; and your neighbor as yourself." 28And he said to him, "You have answered right; do this, and you will live."*

*29But he, desiring to justify himself, said to Jesus, "And who is my neighbor?" 30Jesus replied, "A man was going down from Jerusalem to Jericho, and he fell among robbers, who stripped and beat him, and departed, leaving him half dead. 31Now by chance a priest was going down that road; and when he saw him he passed by on the other side. 32So likewise a Levite, when he came to the place and saw him, passed by on the other side. 33But a Samaritan, as he journeyed, came to where he was; and when he saw him, he had compassion, 34and went to him and bound up his wounds, pouring on oil and wine; then he set him on his own beast and brought him to an inn, and took care of him. 35And the next day he took out two denarii and gave them to the innkeeper, saying, 'Take care of him; and whatever more you spend, I will repay you when I come back.' 36Which of these three, do you think, proved neighbor to the man who fell among the robbers?" 37He said, "The one who showed mercy on him." And Jesus said to him, "Go and do likewise."*

Critical exegesis here has recently proceeded to eliminate the question asked by the lawyer in verse 29, on the ground that it is out of harmony with the question asked by Jesus in verse 36 after telling the story. The debate centers on the setting and its relation to the parable, with the usual result that the setting is classed as secondary. In particular, the lawyer's question is considered an awkward transition introduced by the Evangelist. Frequently little attention is given to the parable itself.

The preliminary story into which Luke has set the parable seems to be his version of the discussion found in Mark 12:28-31 (cf. Matt. 22:34-39), where it occurs in a series of debates—the question of the tribute money (Mark 12:13-17), the question about the seven husbands and the resurrection (12:18-27), and the question about the first commandment (12:28-31). Luke has followed Mark in reproducing the first two debates (Luke 20:20-26, 27-38) but has omitted the third. He uses it here as an introduction to this parable (or rather as an introduction to the question that prompts the parable), following a section from Q with which it has no apparent connection, being joined simply by the word "and" (Luke 10:25). The section is part of the longer section headed, "He set his face to go to Jerusalem" (Luke 9:51). After the parable the "travel" is resumed with the words, "Now as they went on their way (10:38)." We shall see that one scholar has argued from this editorial work the rejection of the parable along with the setting. At the moment we note that the story as it appears here reverses the situation found at Mark 12:29. There the scribe asks the question and it is Jesus who, in his reply, makes the famous combination of the laws to love God and to love one's neighbor (Deut. 6:5; Lev. 19:18). Here, however, the combination is quoted *by the lawyer* in response to Jesus' demand: "What is written in the law? how do you read? (Luke 10:26)." The whole discussion, arising from the question of the lawyer, "What shall I do to inherit eternal life? (v. 25)" reminds us of the question of the rich man in Mark 10:17.

The scholars treat this passage, then, as Luke's version of the story he has omitted at a later point—omitted there because already used here to introduce the parable. There are difficulties either way when it is treated as a literary problem. The usual solution does not seem necessarily final. In the nature of the case the likelihood is that both the question about eternal life and the question about the commandment of first importance would be asked more than once. It is not beyond reason that a scribe might answer as he answers here with the twofold summary. Jesus' unique contribution is not based exclusively on this combination! Neither does it seem essential to say that Luke omitted the story at the Marcan point in order to use it here. It is possible that he omitted the Marcan story because he had already one like it. As a matter of fact the omission of the story at the later point provides a rather better climax to the series of debates in Luke 20:38 ("He is not the God of the dead, but of the living; for all live to him") and makes more fitting the statement (v. 40), "For they no longer dared to ask him any question," than the interchange with the scribe in Mark 12:28-34a provides.[4]

This discussion would be somewhat irrelevant except that it is usually presented as part of the argument that the connection of the parable with the setting is purely editorial—and rather ineptly so, at that. The lawyer's answer in Luke 10:27 is commended by Jesus:

"You have answered right; do this, and you will live (v. 28)." But the lawyer, "desiring to justify himself (v. 29)," asks a further question concerning the extent of the obligation to love one's neighbor. This reflects the effort to define "neighbor" and perhaps to confine the meaning of the term to fellow members of the race and nation, an effort characterized in Matthew 5:43 as issuing in the dictum, "You shall love your neighbor and hate your enemy."[5] Hence the question, "Who is my neighbor?" which, it is said, the parable does not answer, thereby revealing the whole setting to be secondary.

To this we might reply that two considerations must be weighed against the literary analysis. The first is that the Law itself is not usually called in question by Jesus or his opponents; the debate concerns its relevance as interpreted by accepted tradition. Thus the two typical test questions: Which is the most weighty commandment? and, How far does this obligation extend? To attempt to live by a book produced questions of this type and made essential their specific application to every conceivable situation, affording the scribes their proper function. There is nothing conclusive about the twofold law of love. It brilliantly answers one question, but for practical living it gives rise to innumerable others, of which the one asked in verse 29, "Who is my neighbor?" is of supreme importance. In this respect, then, we may be permitted to argue that Luke's treatment of the matter is more vital than the treatment in Mark, which ends with a rather pious interchange (Mark 12:32-34). Further, without the setting, the parable is indeed an "example story," as it has often been called; it lacks the force of a parable and deserves the treatment it usually receives in preaching. In its setting it has, instead, far greater force and is more in keeping with Jesus' usual method of carrying the fight to the enemy and of penetrating convenient confusions to reach down to weightier matters.

This brings us to the second consideration mentioned and, at length, to the parable itself. The second consideration to be weighed is the content of the parable and the structure of the story. As Cadoux says, "attention to the form of the story is the first essential to understanding."[6]

The parable begins, *anthrōpos tis,* "A man." The assumption may be that this is a Jew, but travel on the road was not limited to Jews, and it is therefore only an assumption. We note the vagueness with which this character is introduced and the complete neglect of further definition. He is one of a class, and the class simply that of travelers on that road. No note is made of his purpose in so traveling, which otherwise might have afforded commentators at least a clue to his business. Nothing, obviously, is said of his race, color, nationality, position, or faith. He is completely anonymous, a lay figure.[7]

This featureless feature has been taken up by the preachers, and very usefully, homiletically speaking. Since the traveler is not further described but may be considered simply a human being who falls into desperate need, the parable teaches—so argues the pulpit—that anyone in need, in any sense in need, is to be considered in the category "neighbor." That would be justifiable exegesis *if the story were designed to answer the lawyer's question,* which, as many have pointed out, it palpably does not. As a matter of fact this is precisely *not* the point.

B. T. D. Smith notes "that the traveller is unidentified only because the popular story omits all irrelevant detail,"[8] and thus disposes of the homiletic capital made of this lack of description. It is true, rather, that the omitted detail is irrelevant precisely because the story has another purpose and is following the laws, not only of the folk tale but of its own inherent plan. Details that would attract attention to the unfortunate wayfarer are omitted in order to draw attention elsewhere. The sufferer is anonymous and vaguely drawn because he is not the central actor or one of the principal actors but, excepting only the innkeeper and the donkey, the least important actor. He should not even be allegorized. The purpose of the story defeats the modern preacher no less than the traditional interpreter. More clearly drawn, "this man" would be a distraction. The attention is directed away from him to others. His wounds which are to be bound up, his naked state and destitution, are remarked only as occasions for the functions performed by the Samaritan.

Literary attention and dramatic interest are focused on the subsequent travelers.[9] True, equally few words are used, but few are necessary to produce in the minds of the audience a clear and distinct impression. Priest and Levite are types well known—perhaps too well known—to the hearers. They can readily supply the details for themselves, as they are not invited to do with the victim.

The "rule-of-three," as B. T. D. Smith again notes, is invoked, and dramatic skill quickly supplies the expected third figure. The hearers "would probably have been prepared to identify him beforehand. Priest, Levite, *Israelite:* so ran the familiar classification of society within the Jewish Church."[10] The substitution of a Samaritan is a master stroke. He, likewise, needs in this connection no further introduction. Since he is the surprise element, it would be difficult, as well as gratuitous, to attempt a portrait. His inner nature is amply revealed by his activities—which, it need hardly be said, have no further purpose or meaning than this. The fact that he is a Samaritan serves the purpose. The contrast as it stands is overwhelming: as against the sacred obligation of the hierarchy, the generosity of a heretic; as against noblesse oblige, the instinct of a mongrel or alien; as against a son of Abraham, a child neither of faith nor promise.

Here we must pause to observe that the French scholar Halévy, followed by Montefiore and others, has questioned whether the Samaritan is original to the story or a later addition. In fact, Dr. Enslin, starting from the use of Samaritan incidents in Luke, argues that the parable is to be attributed to the Evangelist rather than to Jesus.[11] The objection to the Samaritan is based on the unlikelihood of a Samaritan's traveling frequently on that road and being apparently well known to the innkeeper (v. 35), and on the incongruity of the trilogy (priest, Levite, Samaritan) which, Halévy argued, was like saying, "Priest, deacon, Frenchman"—the first two being orders of ministry, the third a nationality. The third term should read "layman," i.e., in this case, "Israelite." It might be answered that Jesus' parables, while notable for their verisimilitude, are under no necessity to be naturalistic at all points. The behavior of the farmer in the Laborers in the Vineyard was not exactly normal, but it was effective in making the point. Also, we could say that while Samaritan might suggest to us a foreigner and not a true third to two members of castes, for the Jew the Samaritan was not simply a foreigner but a religious sectarian, definitely heretical. To be a member of the Jewish church, one had to be by birth—or become, by the initiation of circumcision—a member of the Jewish race. So that the case is not quite so clear-cut as Halévy presented it. Not all scholars have accepted the rejection of the Samaritan.

All the same, we may ask whether the meaning of the parable would be essentially changed if it could be proved that it originally read, "Priest, Levite, Israelite," as would be expected. In effect the contrast would then be between the members of religious orders and the layman—and it would still be a contrast, though not so startling or so original. One thing we must be clear about, which many preachers and nearly all lay people are not clear about: the question of whether the merciful one was a Samaritan has nothing whatever to do with Jewish compassion to Samaritans. It is not the Samaritan who is in need; neither do we know that it is a Jew who is aided by the "Samaritan." Eliminating the Samaritan does nothing to help make the parable a simple answer to the scribe's question. This the structure of the story does not permit, no matter who the rescuer may be. The vagueness of the victim, contrasted (in its received form) with the startling and vivid introduction of an alien heretic (or at the least a layman who might even be "a sinner"), serves its purpose and must not be left out of account. The structure of the story makes the victim the *object* and the Samaritan cannot be made other than the *subject*. The impact of the story is not the mundane suggestion that one ought to be as thoughtful as the character in the story—which would be its meaning apart from the question it does not *directly* answer—but is a more telling thrust, more offensive in its purpose.

Attention is centered on the three who travel the road, who themselves, as far as the story is concerned, stand in no need of a neighbor to help them. Were a Samaritan *the victim*, one might well argue that his presence there was to be attributed to the universalizing tendency of Luke. The Samaritan is, however, not the *object* but the *subject,* who reads the Law better than the lawyer, who is more truly a member of Israel than one of the hierarchy, if to be an Israelite is to do God's will. Is not this a dictum which bears, one might almost say, a signature?[12]

From the technique employed it is clear that the focus of attention has been shifted adroitly from the question, "Who is my neighbor?" to another question, "Who proves himself neighborly?"—or, in accord with the laws of the folk tale and the suspense the "rule-of-three" provides, "Who is this third who will offer himself as neighbor?" Attention is directed, with charm and skill, away from the man who needs a neighbor to those to whom is presented an opportunity to show the initiative of a neighbor. Here the focus of attention rests, and here it remains while the emphasis is built up.

The parable prepares for the question that follows it and for no other: "Which of these three, do you think, proved neighbor to the man who fell among the robbers?" Yet the parable is unduly involved and of needless artifice unless preceded by some such situation as that of verse 29. The question to which it leads is not the question asked; nor, as far as I know, is the final question one likely to have been asked. The debate had usually taken the direction, "Who may be considered within the scope of the obligation?" That is what is *asked*. The transition to the other question, i.e., from object to subject, is effected by the story—a story that, it would seem to me, is designed to make such a transition and for Jesus could serve no other purpose. Its essential structure provides no clue whatsoever to the answering of the first question, but deliberately draws attention away from it to another question which, without the story, would not be asked.

To attempt to force the attention of the story on to the victim is to provide to the question, "Who is my neighbor?" the answer, "Anyone." I am not persuaded that Luke would consider this appropriate to the setting. It would then indeed be artificial—but it would not be the setting that would be artificial or secondary but the parable. The text as we have it is better Greek than is usually found where an Aramaic original has been translated. The tradition most probably reached Luke in translation, and Luke was likely to improve the style.[13] If the story itself is secondary, we find ourselves in the position of being asked to whom we may attribute it. In its setting an answer becomes even more difficult, for its author, asked a question debated but never settled for generations, supplies, by a method distinguished alike for finesse, courage, and suspense, not to say audacity, the answer *that the wrong question has been asked.* There can be no final answer to "Who is my neighbor?" and, as a matter of fact, the debate rages currently. But to the question, "To whom am I prepared to be a neighbor?" there must be answer made, and the answer is daily made, not in theory or discussion but in act and life. If the parable assumes and requires the setting, to whom can we attribute it but to Jesus?

The parable is a true parable, leading to a question the answer to which cannot be avoided.[14] In it the Samaritan (or Israelite) achieves the will of God where the priest and the Levite, Israelites par excellence, fail. Rather, they deliberately ignore their obligation. There might be many grounds on which, by deliberation, the members of the hierarchy in the story might justify their indifference. To stop might lead them to the same fate or involve them in uncleanness— and the service of the temple was more important. The victim was unidentified and perhaps unidentifiable and the category of neighbor therefore did not necessarily apply. To attempt thus to carry on the debate on the part of the hierarchy reveals more clearly, if it were necessary, the purpose of the parable. As was implied in the parable of the Two Sons, something more than the usually accepted function of Israel (exemplified by the hierarchy) was needed, and the essence of it was *to be a neighbor*, with no questions asked about the object of neighborliness. Thus an ordinary Israelite (even a Samaritan) might better understand the will of God than a priest or a Levite. This is not simply anticlerical in its motive. The hierarchy represents the quintessence of Judaism. The charge lies against the leaders as leaders, a charge against Israel.

When the parable is thus interpreted in relation to its immediate setting, we see features characteristic of Jesus' work. Once again he cleaves through the verbal confusion and traditional thinking to the fundamental and essential crux of the situation. He is not here the advocate of purely pedestrian morality or goodwill, for he is addressing Israel with its special vocation, and, in its setting, this is not a matter of simple compassion but a much more important matter of obeying the fundamental will of God. This is how Luke presents it, not as an example story, and it seems likely that the tradition he received is accurate. Once again Jesus is fearless and does not hesitate to incur enmity. Whether the Samaritan was part of the original story or no, the attack on the hierarchy remains. And, like all Jesus' attacks, it is based on a consideration that does not admit of counterattack. The only possible response is that Jesus has no authority—the perennial refuge of officeholders under attack —and we shall see that Jesus was subject to exactly that criticism. It becomes apparent in this parable and still more in those that follow that he was an offense and a stumbling block to the leaders of the Jews. Thus interpreted, this parable may lose some of its surface homiletic value, but it gains in providing a clearer understanding of Jesus and of why he was crucified. This in itself seems a valid, if secondary, canon of criticism.

The next parables show that he did not hesitate to carry his attack farther, to a limit where his opponents could not long ignore him but must find him much more than a disturbing factor.

## THE BARREN FIG TREE
### Luke 13

*¹There were some present at that very time who told him of the Galileans whose blood Pilate had mingled with their sacrifices. ²And he answered them, "Do you think that these Galileans were worse sinners than all the other Galileans, because they suffered thus? ³I tell you, No; but unless you repent you will all likewise perish. ⁴Or those eighteen upon whom the tower in Siloam fell and killed them, do you think that they were worse offenders than all the others who dwelt in Jerusalem? ⁵I tell you, No; but unless you repent you will all likewise perish."*

*⁶And he told this parable: "A man had a fig tree planted in his vineyard; and he came seeking fruit on it and found none. ⁷And he said to the vinedresser, 'Lo, these three years I have come seeking fruit on this fig tree, and I find none. Cut it down; why should it use up the ground?' ⁸And he answered him, 'Let it alone, sir, this year also, till I dig about it and put on manure. ⁹And if it bears fruit next year, well and good; but if not, you can cut it down.' "*

The number of parables in The Gospel According to Luke is larger than in the other Synoptics, and the proportion of polemic is higher.[15] The facts are related. The parable was very valuable in Jesus' form of polemic, and much of his case was stated in this way. The use of parables is fortunate because they are easily remembered apart from the discourses in which they appeared, while this very fact makes their interpretation difficult until we see them in Jesus' time and situation. In the case of the present parable, the Evangelist has done this for us. We can hardly suppose, however, that the parable illustrated only the saying called forth by this particular incident, "Unless you repent you will all likewise perish" (vs. 3, 5). It is rather an incident and saying typical of the sort of situation in which Jesus would use the similitude of the fig tree. Once again the teaching is directed in the text to a small group, but, as the parable indicates, the meaning is for all Israel.

The same charge of failure is made here, but a new note now enters, the note of impending crisis. While the critical nature of the situation may be deduced from the parable as its prime meaning, it is heightened by the setting. Jesus is informed of an incident—"the Galileans whose blood Pilate had mingled with their sacrifices (v. 1)" —of which there is no historical record and which Josephus does not mention. It implies a ruthless massacre during a festival, probably in the courts of the temple—"mingled with their sacrifices" need not be taken to mean anything more literal. The term "Galileans" may imply the victims were Zealots involved in some nationalistic demonstration. There is likewise no record of the calamity Jesus uses as a parallel—"those eighteen upon whom the tower in Siloam fell and killed them (v. 4)." The historicity of the two events does not affect the point. In any case they provide two types of calamity—one political, the other natural ("an act of God") or accidental. Jesus' treatment of the implications is "modern" and runs counter to the traditional concept of retribution (vs. 2, 5). People on every hand in our own time treat war or loss, sickness or accident, in the same questioning and querulous manner that Jesus here rejects. The victims were not guilty beyond the rest of their compatriots, not worse offenders than the rest of the inhabitants of the city. Events in their relation to the individual are fortuitous and are not related by measure to virtues or faults. Jesus draws from it rather the danger of judgment under which all stand who do not repent (vs. 3, 5): "Unless you repent you will all likewise perish." ("Likewise" does not mean "by the same means" but in the sense of "as certainly" or "as inevitably.")

It is against this background of Jesus' note of warning and denial of the traditional treatment of the problem of suffering that Luke has set the parable. The note of crisis unmistakably emerges. Judgment is inevitable; though postponed, it is delayed only for a definite season and still threatens. The points of the story that determine its meaning are: the seeking for fruit; the resolve to cut the tree down for a double reason—that it does not bear and that the ground may be freed for more productive use; the response to the plea for mercy; and the limit set of one season before the final decision is to be made. The story occasions no difficulty, and it is hard to see how the meaning of it can be escaped.[16]

To the Jews the fig tree, along with the vine, suggested the bliss of prosperity and peace characteristic of their land at its best and holding promise of fulfillment in the age of blessedness to come. In the Old Testament the combination "the vine and the fig tree" symbolized peace (1 Kings 4:25), security (Micah 4:4), and hospitality (Zech. 3:10), and the loss of fruit was a symbol of complete destruction (Jer. 8:12-13). The vine became the symbol of Israel—of Judah in particular—and while the fig tree acquired no such allegorical value, it was closely associated in the ways suggested with the special blessings of God's people. We must resist the attempt to allegorize it here, where it has only a suggestive value. A *fruit* tree is necessary to the story. The fig tree, because of its associations, was the most useful and was familiar on every hand in Judea. Commentators have attempted to see in the vineyard in which it is planted a symbol of Israel and therefore try to identify the tree either as the individual (probably with Ps. 1:3 in mind) or as the Holy City. After the fall of Jerusalem it may well have acquired this interpretation, particularly in view of the incident in Mark 11:12-14, 20-21; Matthew 21:18-19. There is no need thus to allegorize the parable, in which, apart from its connotations, the fig tree has the general reference of John the Baptist's saying, "Even now the axe is laid to the root of the trees (Matt. 3:10)."

The occasion of judgment represented is the repeated disappointment of the owner in finding, after three seasons or more, no fruit on the tree.[17] Fruit is the purpose for which it exists and the only justification for its being allowed the use of the ground. Without fruit it is using space that can be put to better use (v. 7). The decision is natural, and we see here implied the principle "how much more." We can hardly resist the suggestion that, if it is proper for a farmer so to decide with regard to a fruit tree, how much more certain is it that God will place a term upon his indulgence of a people likewise designed to produce results but likewise unproductive? The hearers are expected to form an opinion of this kind, and here we see again the parabolic method at work.

The point is reinforced by the plea of the vinedresser (v. 8). He asks for a chance to do what can be done to ensure fruit bearing. A strong feature of the parable is that the vinedresser himself admits the justice of drastic action if these final measures fail. This is the last attempt. Even he agrees that a limit must be set. The abrupt conclusion on a note of doom issuing from his lips rather than those of the owner makes an artistic and powerful climax, and the Evangelist has wisely resisted any pressure of tradition (if such existed) to add a "moral."

These words of Jesus cannot but have reference to the immediate situation. The destiny of Israel was under hot debate, and for our Lord it was a question to be decided by Israel's function in God's purposes. Like the fig tree, Israel was neither fulfilling its own purpose nor allowing the space and care involved to serve their best use. The times, however, though they have not yet run their course, have entered their last phase. The present attempt is the last. What is implicit in this later becomes explicit—that is, Jesus' presence and work afford the last chance. The introductory incidents add to the sense of crisis. Some, like the victims there, are suddenly removed from the scene. But, because the rest seem in no immediate danger, the very state of affairs that exists ought to put them on their guard against a false feeling of security. If we were tempted at all to allegorize the fig tree, we should say that it (on the Old Testament analogy) represents Israel's feeling of secure blessedness. The juxtaposition of fig tree and vineyard suggests this connotation and, at the very least, shows how extremely apt is Jesus' choice of material. He had a sense of the "overtones" of his people's tradition. But, like the great prophets, Jesus cannot see in this apparent security a reason for ease. He sees the very opposite, the warning of judgment. The delay is due to God's grace, and the very safety and escape from calamities into which others accidentally fall should lead the safe to repentance and every effort to produce the "fruits" for which they have been spared and blessed. The time is short. The last effort is afoot. The doom approaches.

The incident recorded in Mark 11:12-14, 20-21 (the cursing of the fig tree), which Luke omits, may be explained in part as later reflection on the parable. It is probably not to be explained as a parable become miracle but as an incident (whether with some basis in actuality or not) which was included because events that had recently taken place when Mark compiled his Gospel confirmed the judgment Jesus envisaged in the parable.[18] The same major points appear. Jesus, like the owner in the parable, looks for fruit; when he finds none, the tree is doomed. The further step is recorded when (vs. 20-21) the fig tree is found to be withered away. It reads like a confirmation of Jesus' parabolic warning in the light of events that must lead (in the fall of Jerusalem) to disaster for Israel. It is placed near the close of Jesus' career when, so to speak, the period of grace represented by his presence and call to repentance had come also to an end. In my article I propose a clue to the origin of the passage and an explanation of the "miracle," by which we can hardly fail to see in it an underlining of the interpretation of the parable. The fact that Luke omits the incident but includes the parable may not constitute a deliberate correction but may suggest that at this point he was nearer the authentic tradition than Mark, who was influenced by the tragic events afoot when he wrote or, conceivably, by preaching that had expanded the parable in the light of the Jewish refusal of Jesus. In each passage we cannot escape the realization that Jesus is claiming that a critical period is present, and in strong terms which the hearers could scarcely dissociate from the speaker.

This note is strengthened with each further parable, for this is not the only one that deals with expected results that have not appeared and with a radical imminent judgment. In another parable the note of critical urgency which demands response comes out in spite of an uncertainty about its setting which makes interpretation difficult.

## THE APPROACH TO COURT

### Matthew 5
25"Make friends quickly with your accuser, while you are going with him to court, lest your accuser hand you over to the judge, and the judge to the guard, and you be put in prison; 26truly, I say to you, you will never get out till you have paid the last penny."

### Luke 12
58"As you go with your accuser before the magistrate, make an effort to settle with him on the way, lest he drag you to the judge, and the judge hand you over to the officer, and the officer put you in prison. 59I tell you, you will never get out till you have paid the very last copper."

Luke's version of this parable is more nearly a similitude and Matthew's a counsel. Matthew has associated it with the section of the Sermon on the Mount on reconciliation (Matt. 5:21-24), finding obvious connections in the legal phraseology and with approaching the altar in a state of unresolved enmity. Luke's setting is very different. The parable follows the discussion of inability to discern the signs of the times (Luke 12:54-56) and the passage on divisions (vs. 49-53), in which Jesus speaks of the urgency that constrains him (v. 50: "How I am constrained until it is accomplished!"). Following it (13:1-9) is the parable of the Barren Fig Tree, with its introductory discourse which, as we have seen, dealt with the false sense of security and the judgment not indefinitely postponed. The transition from the discussion of signs to this similitude is made by the words (v. 57): "And why do you not judge for yourselves what is right?"

The situation depicts the steadily nearer approach of a crisis. If the man and his adversary arrive at court without a settlement, the process of justice and retribution will take its inevitable, relentless course. Two things are obvious: the case is one of debt (v. 59) and the debtor is liable and unable to pay. Judgment, if once entered into, will take its full course. In this case it is worldly wisdom to settle the case, to sue for mercy, to come to some agreement with him who is leading one to judgment, before matters are put into other hands.

We get into trouble at once if we try to allegorize this. There are four parties—the debtor, the creditor, the judge, and the officer, and they cannot be identified. If it is a parable, the difficulty is overcome and the question is to what the *relationship* here suggested is to be compared. The emphasis falls upon the need for action on one's own part before matters are taken completely out of one's own hands. Hence the significance of verse 57, asking why they ("the multitudes," v. 54) do not judge themselves rather than drift into the inexorable judgment of God. Here too is the significance of its connection with the signs. For Jesus it was essential that his people understand from what was happening in their midst that they were rapidly approaching the judgment and only their own action could prevent their paying the last full price of neglect and refusal. It says that if you were being taken to a law court by your creditor you would see the urgent need of settling with him before becoming involved in the processes of the law. The same situation exists with regard to the nation, and the same deduction will be made by those who have perception.

This sense of a critical moment in history in which it is essential that there be readiness to respond when the hour strikes is the clue to two parables which, in their present form, provide a certain amount of difficulty. The probability that each had as its original background the idea of the messianic banquet makes it necessary to treat them here.

## THE TEN VIRGINS
### Matthew 25
[1]"Then the kingdom of heaven shall be compared to ten maidens who took their lamps and went to meet the bridegroom. [2]Five of

them were foolish, and five were wise. ³For when the foolish took their lamps, they took no oil with them; ⁴but the wise took flasks of oil with their lamps. ⁵As the bridegroom was delayed, they all slumbered and slept. ⁶But at midnight there was a cry, 'Behold, the bridegroom! Come out to meet him.' ⁷Then all those maidens rose and trimmed their lamps. ⁸And the foolish said to the wise, 'Give us of your oil, for our lamps are going out.' ⁹But the wise replied, 'Perhaps there will not be enough for us and for you; go rather to the dealers and buy for yourselves.' ¹⁰And while they went to buy, the bridegroom came, and those who were ready went in with him to the marriage feast; and the door was shut. *¹¹Afterward the other maidens came also, saying, 'Lord, Lord, open to us.' ¹²But he replied, 'Truly, I say to you, I do not know you.' ¹³Watch therefore, for you know neither the day nor the hour."*

As a parable this bristles with difficulties. Any mention of "the bridegroom" is suspect by many scholars as suggesting the usage of the Christian church.[19] It is therefore decided that we have here not a parable but an allegory developed to advocate a certain attitude during the period of waiting for a delayed Parousia. The difficulty then arises that in the usual text no bride appears, though some texts add the words, "and the bride," to verse 1. The ten virgins would, in an allegorical sense, represent the church. We have seen already Matthew's interest in the "mixed" state of the church's membership, which may be again reflected here in, "Five of them were foolish, and five were wise (v. 2)." To treat it as an allegory, however, sets other problems. Apart from the question of what the oil represents (since all had oil to start with), the theological problem presented by verse 9, where the "wise" refuse to share, can lead only to casuistry. In short, an allegorical treatment raises more difficulties than it solves.[20]

On the other hand, to treat it as a parable based on village life has its difficulties. The virgins go to meet the bridegroom—presumably to escort him to the bride's house. But the feast was normally held in the bridegroom's home, to which he brought his bride from her own home. Were the virgins perhaps not assigned attendants but casual villagers? The virgins, further, "went to meet" in verse 1, whereas in verse 6 they are called to "come out to meet him." Among the variety of suggestions made, none seems entirely satisfactory. We may make one or both of two assumptions. It may be that we are not sufficiently acquainted with the folk customs of those days and that neither sources nor analogy from present Eastern custom serve sufficiently to enlighten us. Or we may assume the confusion to be in the tradition or text. A combination of both may prove the solution. The suggestion that it is a clumsily constructed allegory clears up the difficulty only to create others more central and insoluble.[21]

Are the difficulties sufficient, however, to obscure the point of a possible parable here preserved? To answer the question we must first decide what the essential story is. It has frequently been suggested that it should end with verse 10 in the climactic phrase, "And the door was shut." The remainder falls into two parts, verses 11-12 and verse 13. The last verse, "Watch therefore, for you know neither the day nor the hour," fits the unexpected hour of the bridegroom's arrival but seems hardly appropriate when it is recalled that each group of virgins went to sleep and had to be awakened. The wise did not succeed by staying watchfully awake! This exhortation has doubtless strayed from another context. The words: " 'Lord, Lord, open to us.' But he replied, 'Truly, I say to you, I do not know you,' " do no more than diminish the climactic value of verse 10 without adding to its meaning. Indeed, it raises an unnecessary question: In what sense did the bridegroom know any of the attendants? A similar situation is given in Luke 13:25ff., where the "householder" has shut the door and to those who knock replies (v. 25b), "I do not know where you come from." In its Lucan context it answers the question of whether there be few saved. It seems very likely that these verses have been added to the parable either intact or adapted from the Lucan saying. It seems unnecessary to suppose that Luke knew of the parable or that the parable is an allegorical expansion of Luke's scene.

The next step is to examine the essential structure of the story. The introductory words which point to the future, "Then . . . shall be compared," may be accounted for on the grounds of the distant future envisaged by the church and may owe something to the apocalyptic passages that precede them in chapter 24. The whole tenor of the story indicates that the essentials of the situation are that a lighted escort should be provided for the bridegroom when he arrived and that those who participated in the procession would also participate in the feast; the one was the necessary preliminary to the other. The designation of five as "wise" and five as "foolish" has no absolute meaning; they were wise or foolish in relation to the situation only. All came equipped for the objective they had in mind, but only half of them were prepared for instant response at any time. The suggestion is that the torches were kept burning, ready for instant use, even while they slept (hence "trimmed their lamps" in v. 7 and "our lamps are going out" in v. 8). No blame attaches to their sleeping, for all alike went to sleep in the interval. It was apparently not their function to watch but to be instantly prepared when called. The midnight arrival in the midst of their sleep emphasizes the unexpected and sudden demand for activity. The refusal of the wise to share their supply of oil causes no difficulty if it be taken as a parable and not as an allegory. The girls are concerned about the procession rather than about themselves, fearful that a sharing of the oil that remains will mean no light at all before the ceremony is completed. In other words, they argue that it is better to have five torches all the way than ten part of the way. We are under no obligation, in a parable, to justify their viewpoint. The inability of the other five to repair their omission and to participate in the procession means that they have no further share in the feast. They have excluded themselves.[22]

We shall see this again in the parable of the Banquet, where those invited exclude themselves because their real interests lie elsewhere. Several of Jesus' parables deal with the importance of understanding and doing what one (or a nation) has been designed to do. Here the two themes are knit together in an atmosphere of crisis, and a distinction is made between those who enter and those who do not. The emphasis is on those who respond when the instant call comes. They are prepared, and they are concerned above all about the purpose that is in hand. Certainly we should be right to see here an emphasis on the discriminating power of a crisis which comes no man can say when. Two types are distinguished, not alone, or most significantly, by their preparation but by their sense of the import of the occasion. From the beginning the "wise" are fully committed to the cause in hand. An instant response is demanded and it is met. The others awake to the situation unable to meet it except by reliance on the others, a state of affairs that would defeat the whole project.

It seems to me that we have here, perhaps in a mutilated form, an authentic parable of Jesus. He warned his disciples elsewhere that the coming of the kingdom would give a man foes even in his own household (Matt. 10:34-36); that loyalty to lesser causes and loyalty to himself were not compatible (Matt. 10:37-38; Luke 9:57-62); that discriminations would be inevitable in "that night" and one would "be taken" and another "left" (Luke 17:33-35). It is probably the church that sees in it an application only to the Last Judgment; its original relevance was probably to a situation in which some could see what the occasion demanded and others would neither see nor commit themselves completely. Its lesson is not so much "Watch" but "When the call comes, be wholly committed to do what is demanded." Only instant response finds the door open. The emphasis is here on the two types and two responses, rather than upon the delay, for the delay was not entirely unexpected (the wise took extra oil) and "As the bridegroom was delayed," is quite casually introduced to provide the explanation of their going to sleep (vs. 4-5). There is, in short, every indication that men's response to the crisis precipitated by Jesus' own presence and their response to the crisis to be presented by "the days of the Son of man" are not essentially different in character and that the one has a bearing on the other. Jesus' own loss of popularity, the confused attitudes of the last days in Jerusalem, the test of the crucifixion and even of the resurrection ("for some doubted"), all testify to the fact.

When the denouement of Jesus' career was past, what was more natural than that the church should place this teaching in the eschatological setting? And yet every age in the church's history and even the crises of personal life reveal that the final judgment has its immediate intimations, and they are not different in character. Jesus seems here to be calling for decision. He requires constant vigilance in the face of critical emergencies so that their demands may not be missed. Several parables or similitudes to be briefly referred to later convey the same impression. The desire for a sign, which must be kept in mind with many of the parables, is illustrated by apocalyptic passages concerning the "signs of the end." Jesus was not at all what was expected. The complaint was made that he was merely a carpenter (Mark 6:3), and the unexpected nature of the demand of which Jesus speaks is perhaps found not so much in its timing as in its apparent incongruity or even irrelevance to the Jewish mind of the times. We recall that Jesus, according to Matthew, attributed Peter's insight in naming him Messiah to no native ability but to divine revelation (Matt. 16:17) and in response to Peter's rebuke, which expressed the normal Jewish viewpoint, charged his apostle with deserting inspiration in favor of human opinion (Mark 8:33; Matt. 16:23).

The celebration from which the foolish virgins were excluded probably belongs in the category of the messianic banquet, which was one form in which Israel's final hope was expressed. In a parable extant in double form we see under the same figure another treatment of the crisis that faced Israel.

## THE BANQUET

### Matthew 22

¹*And again Jesus spoke to them in parables, saying,* ²"The kingdom of heaven may be compared to a king who gave a marriage feast for

his son, ³and sent his servants to call those who were invited to the marriage feast; but they would not come. ⁴Again he sent other servants, saying, 'Tell those who are invited, Behold, I have made ready my dinner, my oxen and my fat calves are killed, and everything is ready; come to the marriage feast.' ⁵But they made light of it and went off, one to his farm, another to his business, *⁶while the rest seized his servants, treated them shamefully, and killed them. ⁷The king was angry, and he sent his troops and destroyed those murderers and burned their city.* ⁸Then he said to his servants, 'The wedding is ready, but those invited were not worthy. ⁹Go therefore to the thoroughfares, and invite to the marriage feast as many as you find.' ¹⁰And those servants went out into the streets and gathered all whom they found, *both bad and good*; so the wedding hall was filled with guests.

*¹¹"But when the king came in to look at the guests, he saw there a man who had no wedding garment; ¹²and he said to him 'Friend, how did you get in here without a wedding garment?' And he was speechless. ¹³Then the king said to the attendants, 'Bind him hand and foot, and cast him into the outer darkness; there men will weep and gnash their teeth.' "*

## Luke 14

*¹⁵When one of those who sat at table with him heard this, he said to him, "Blessed is he who shall eat bread in the kingdom of God!"* *¹⁶But he said to him, "A man once gave a great banquet, and invited many;* ¹⁷and at the time for the banquet he sent his servant to those who had been invited, 'Come; for all is now ready.' ¹⁸But they all alike began to make excuses. The first said to him, 'I have bought a field, and I must go out and see it; I pray you, have me excused.' ¹⁹And another said, 'I have bought five yoke of oxen, and I go to examine them; I pray you, have me excused.' ²⁰And another said, 'I have married a wife, and therefore I cannot come.' ²¹So the servant came and reported this to his master. Then the householder in anger said to his servant, 'Go out quickly to the streets and lanes of the city, and bring in the poor and maimed and blind and lame.' ²²And the servant said, 'Sir, what you commanded has been done, and still there is room.' ²³And the master said to the servant, 'Go out to the highways and hedges, and compel people to come in, that my house may be filled. *²⁴For I tell you, none of those men who were invited shall taste my banquet.' "*

Here are two parables which, while they are similar in the general plot, have considerable differences and little verbal conformity.

Luke's version (in spite of objections that will be dealt with) is the more consistent and is free from the intrusive element that can be seen in Matthew's. It is unlikely that they arise from a common written source, and the endeavor to make them do so involves, among other things, the unnecessary assumption that Jesus used each theme only once.[23]

By comparing the two stories, we see that in Matthew "a man" of Luke 14:16 has become a king, who prepares a banquet for the marriage of his son (v. 2). In Matthew 22:7 the angry king sends armies to destroy the reluctant guests who ill-treated his envoys and to burn "their city." The discussion of the ruler in the intrusive element in Luke 19 (the parable of the Talents and the Pounds), will remind us of this incident. The regal element fits into the parable with difficulty. The man giving a supper seems to become a king in order to accommodate the element of destruction; the guests would necessarily be very brave to have "made light" (v. 5) of the invitation which, being royal, is virtually a command, not to say to treat the heralds brutally; in verse 5 their occupations are those of ordinary citizens rather than officials or princes; and, finally, verse 8 allows no sufficient time to elapse for an expeditionary force to do its work as in verse 7. The sending of "other servants" (v. 4) after the first messengers (v. 3), and their being treated "shamefully" and killed (v. 6), seems to owe something to the similar passages in Mark 12:4b and Luke 20:11b (the parable of the Tenants of the Vineyard), which suggest the succession of prophets sent to Israel.

This theme does not seriously affect the story, except to complicate it at verses 6-7, and the general plot is the same as in Luke. We can see here again the result of the developing thought forms of the church, which came to think of Jesus as the heavenly Bridegroom and of itself as the Bride of Christ. In fact it became difficult for the church *not* to think in this way. The messianic banquet— which is probably the more original background of the parable— became the marriage banquet of the Christ, and we saw the theme appearing in the parable of the Ten Bridesmaids. The fact that the basic material of the parable does not readily conform to adaptation to this later material is testimony that there is an original core with which both parables deal.[24]

Other elements of expansion are detected in the double sending of servants to notify the guests in verses 3-4; "the rest" of verse 6, who ill-treated the second set of envoys; and the phrase "both bad and good" in verse 10. This phrase reminds us that it is in Matthew we find the difficulty of the early church with "mixed" congregations reflected in the parable of the Tares Among the Wheat, the expanded parable of the Dragnet, and the parable of the Ten Virgins. The same interest is reflected here, along with the succession of the prophets and the fall of Jerusalem. The final addition is found in the incident of the man who comes as guest without a wedding garment (vs. 11-12), the punishment for which (v. 13) is expressed in terms of binding and burning, again reminiscent of the parables just mentioned (Matt. 13:40-42, 49-50), and reflecting the same concern. It finds its link with the parable proper in the intrusive words in verse 10, "both bad and good." It can doubtless be explained as another similitude originating in the early church, either as an expansion of this parable or separately, and then attached to it.[25] To this same interest we can credit the addition of verse 14, "For many are called, but few are chosen," which does not really arise out of the parable but only out of the wedding-garment extension. The parable proper ends in both Matthew and Luke when the banquet is filled with guests.

In one particular the Lucan version has an expansion not found in Matthew. While Matthew has two expeditions to notify the guests —which serves to accommodate elements suggested above—Luke has instead two expeditions to seek substitute guests. Of the two versions, again the Lucan seems more original; the double expedition at the end, though it has been severely criticized, has its place for reasons suggested below. We can come nearer the original in the Matthew version if we read verses 1-3 to the words "marriage feast" and resume at the word "saying" in verse 4. This provides the original set of messengers with a message to deliver and eliminates the others. If we then read the rest of verses 4 and 5 and verses 8-10 (except for the words "both bad and good"), we have a reasonable parable (omitting vs. 6-7). In this form we find Matthew has a more condensed account of the response of the original guests than Luke, who, in verses 18-20, quotes their excuses. This Lucan variation has suffered attack on several grounds, as, for instance, that a man would not have bought land or oxen without inspecting or testing them, or that the invited guests would not be undertaking these projects at suppertime. But this is to take the words too literally and to refuse to Jesus some delightful flashes of humor. The phrase (v. 18), "They all alike began to make excuses," suggests what the excuses illustrate, that their mutual concern is to stay away and they do not much care how reasonable the excuses sound. Further, while a shorter form is often on critical grounds to be preferred, as an integral part of the story the longer form is sometimes more likely to be original where it has a characteristic function in the popular Eastern tale. The direct discourse here represented, with its playful humor, is more characteristic than the vague condensed summary of verse 5: "But they made light of it and went off, one to his farm, another to his business." We can see that Matthew might condense this part of the story in order to introduce the cruel treatment and the king's angry response. In Luke the emphasis on the common effort to avoid the supper has a dramatic value which, for the parable as parable, focuses attention on the real issue. In spite of much learned opposition, it seems to me to be original, or more original than the Matthew version. Moreover, business, acquisition of wealth, and marriage are elsewhere in the Gospels set forth as obstacles to the doing of the will of God (e.g., Luke 12:13-21; 18:24; 14:26; Matt. 19:12). While they were no doubt obstacles to discipleship encountered by the church, I think we cannot question that they also represent an original element in Jesus' teaching in face of a critical emergency.

In Luke 14:17, the host sends out only one servant, and it has been asked whether this is allegorical and represents Christ himself. But this does not seem a necessary deduction, as the prestige of Matthew's king would require more than one servant, and Jesus (in the parable of the Slave in Field and House) elsewhere visualizes a simple establishment of this kind (Luke 17:7ff.). The single servant is also more likely to have to make a second expedition to find enough guests than a group capable of searching more thoroughly.

While on these grounds we may find the version in Luke more original, it has been attacked and frequently rejected as an allegorical construction on the very ground of the double expedition to fill the seats (vs. 21b-23). From the point of view of the church the guests first invited would be Israel; the haunters of the city streets, the outcasts in Israel; the denizens of the "highways and hedges," the gentiles. This works out very neatly, and scholars like Montefiore attack the whole parable as an example of apologetic concerning the universal mission designed by the church. It is true that this must be the point of view of the church, and there can be no doubt at all that the parable was so understood and used. But did it necessarily have this meaning when first spoken, and would it, if spoken by Jesus, have been understood so completely as an allegory? It is the *allegorical* treatment of it that forces this construction on it.[26]

To examine the verses in detail: In Matthew 22:9, the servants are sent out to invite "as many as you find." In Luke 14:21b, this becomes, more specifically, "the poor and maimed and blind and lame." This is the same terminology as in verse 13, whence it is suggested it came into the parable, the parable representing the church's actual implementation of Jesus' advice in the earlier passage. But while we may admit the assimilation of language, it does not invalidate the whole parable, for this is but a minor detail and, as we shall see, does not really affect the main point. Also, it is just possible that the previous saying may, instead, be dependent on the parable. The word "compel" in verse 23 is also suspect as suggesting the extra effort needed to win gentiles to the new faith. But when the parable is read as parable and not as allegory, this may also be seen as necessary to the main point and not an artificial construction to meet a historical situation. The whole criticism meets with difficulty because if the story is pressed as allegory some heavy theological weather is encountered. Are those first invited—i.e., the Jews—now completely excluded, and have those of the countryside—i.e., the gentiles—not before been invited by God? This would seem rather to be Matthew's meaning in verse 8 where he says, "but those invited were not worthy." These difficulties beset the attempt to treat it mechanically as an allegory but are somewhat irrelevant if the story is treated as a parable.

The answer to the objections raised lies in seeking the meaning of the parable that lies behind both forms and that seems more clearly preserved in Luke. A host prepares a feast to which he has previously invited certain guests. When the day arrives and the feast is ready he, in the customary Oriental manner, sends a servant to remind them that the day has come. At the critical moment (when it is too late to cancel the arrangements), the guests find other matters of more interest or for some reason are disinclined to come and invent excuses. The host is understandably annoyed and, with the double intention of holding the party and securing that, should the original guests again change their minds, they shall not be able to find room, scours the neighborhood to find substitutes. If we treat this simply as a story, not without a whimsical humor, the excuses of the guests and the deliberateness of the redoubled effort to fill the places both serve to heighten the drama and reinforce the point. The elaboration of the general desire to be excused establishes the point that the declination at the critical juncture is of central importance. The failure of the first effort made in the town to find enough substitutes and the order to go farther afield establishes the climactic point (which Luke expresses in 14:24) that the aim of the host is to fill every place and leave no room for another change of mind on the part of the unreliable recipients of the original invitation. If they reject their priority it is a final rejection! "For I tell you, none of those men who were invited shall taste my banquet." To press the search farther afield is natural if more were needed than could be found in the streets, and it is essential to the point if it is to be made inescapable, whether the church later uses it as an allegory or not. The compulsion used is simply that of urgent hospitality —in the East, hospitality cannot be treated lightly—and this darkens the picture of those who declined to come and explains the anger of the host.[27]

The concluding verse (v. 24) just quoted reads at first sight as part of the parable. The opening phrase, however, as noted elsewhere, is characteristically used by Luke to introduce an application. The plural pronoun "you," identified as the audience, supports this view. Its difficulty lies then in the pronoun "my" applied to "supper," which apparently would then be read as though Jesus spoke as Messiah, host at the messianic banquet. On the other hand it may be taken as part of the parable when the pronoun in the second person plural ("you") constitutes the difficulty. It must then be read as a comment addressed by the host, not to the single servant but to others present. In either case one of the two pronouns causes difficulty, and perhaps the real solution is that this verse has become modified in transmission as a result of the allegorical use of the parable by the preacher. In any case it quite clearly brings out the meaning of the parable, which is complete in all necessary features at verse 23.

When we begin to consider the meaning of this perfectly charming and yet extremely strong parable, we realize it might have been treated with the series that applied to the mission to the outcasts (see Chapter Four). The element, however, of finality, as of a last chance refused, which the structure of the tale shows to be central, determines its place here. If taken allegorically, the parable in this respect raises more problems than it answers and decidedly loses the charm which seems, when one becomes familiar with Jesus' method, to be the mark of its originality and the hallmark of its authorship.[28]

As parable, the story prompts the judgment that under the circumstances depicted the host would be within his rights to act as he did and the negligent and decidedly impolite guests would deserve the situation that would face them if they should change their minds. We are not expected to press the details. It is those who were invited and accepted but found other interests or their own convenience more to be consulted—and these only—who are excluded. The exclusion arises from no vagary of the host but from their own fickleness, just as the fate of the Unmerciful Servant was the result of his own failure to pass on the mercy he had received. It is clearly a parable of warning and has in it a distinct element of crisis such as we have seen is associated with the other parables of this group. The messianic banquet was bound to be suggested to the Jewish audience; without making an allegory of it, the parable says clearly that when the time comes they may find that they themselves have excluded themselves from the joys of the kingdom. The "foolish" virgins likewise found themselves shut out by their own neglect. Places are not kept open indefinitely at the messianic table, and those who assume, because of national priority, that there will always be room for them are likely to receive a rude shock. "Do not begin to say to yourselves, 'We have Abraham as our father'; for I tell you, God is able from these stones to raise up children to Abraham (Luke 3:8)." We may refer again to passages like Matthew 8:11-12 (note especially "sit at table with Abraham," etc.), Luke 13:29, and Mark 14:25, for other uses of the banquet theme. It was this pride in and reliance on birth that Jesus' great apostle found it necessary to reject. "Are they Hebrews? so am I. Are they Israelites? so am I. Are they descendants of Abraham? so am I (2 Cor. 11:22)." "For we are the true circumcision, who worship God in spirit. . . . Though I myself have reason for confidence in the flesh also . . . of the people of Israel, of the tribe of Benjamin, a Hebrew born of Hebrews. . . . I count everything as loss . . . that I may gain Christ (Phil. 3:3-8)." The initial invitation belongs to the Jews, but as an act of grace and as a call to service and not by the assured priority of birth.

It is interesting that Luke has set this parable in and as the climax to a passage that describes Jesus at the table of a Pharisee, a passage that has apparently gathered to itself at least two extraneous elements which break the continuity. We cannot, unless they seem essential to the sense or structure, place great reliance on these settings, which are often the work of the Evangelists. Here, while the parable can stand alone, the setting gives further evidence that its original meaning in the tradition was that indicated above. Luke 14:1 sets the scene. Then an incident is included (Jesus' questions when confronted on the sabbath with a sick man to be healed, vs. 2-6) which is like the story set in Mark 3:1-6 (and parallels) in a synagogue. The supper setting is resumed in verse 7, where Jesus marks with disfavor the scramble for places of honor. His response to this is the discourse of verses 8-10. This passage has occasioned a good deal of difficulty. It can be paralleled from other sources, and the advice given seems to be "worldly" and not in keeping with Jesus' teaching or practice. It forms a reasonable illustration of the saying in verse 11, "For every one who exalts himself will be humbled," but this does little to improve matters. A further item for a collection of "table sayings" is given in verses 12-14, a phrase of which is connected with a phrase in the parable, as we noted. Then, verse 15, follows the pious remark of one of the guests at table, "Blessed is he who shall eat bread in the kingdom of God!"

Whether we accept the introductory setting as in part at least an actual meal or as a collection, a traditionally pietistic saying like this might well be used by one of Jesus' fellow guests to distract Jesus when his discourse began to press too close for comfort. We can well imagine it or similar remarks being made to Jesus as a conventional response (cf. Luke 11:27). People still behave in this fashion. It breathes all the self-confidence of a privileged member of the chosen race. It assumes that the speaker, with becoming modesty but with assurance, is counting on being among the blessed. It is, then, in reply to this attitude that Luke represents the parable as being spoken, as if Jesus had turned to his sanctimonious neighbor and said ,"Yes, but let me tell you a story." In this context it is not merely effective but well-nigh devastating. If the interpretation thus indicated by the Evangelist be correct, reinforced by the structure of the story itself as suggested in the foregoing analysis, then once again we can understand why the opposition to Jesus continued to increase to the point where removal could be the only solution short of acceptance of Jesus and his message.

For this parable too is clearly an indictment of the prevailing attitude of Jesus' people, particularly exemplified in the religious leaders. There is an inescapable logic developed in this group of stories. They teach that the people of Israel must give more than external conformity to God's call. They must realize that it requires attention to the primary task of being a neighbor. To fail to bear the fruit God intends means early removal as an unproductive obstruction. The time is not unlimited, and to procrastinate is to be caught in the toils of judgment or to be excluded from the fruition of the age to come. To count on the priority of race and blood is to fail to grasp the last opportunity when the hour strikes. This judgment Jesus sets forth in other parables, and its basis is the very nature of Israel. Upon this people judgment must fall with more immediacy because of its vocation. The blessedness upon which Israel counts as a safeguard is the very occasion for the critical nature of the situation.

# SIX THE JUDGMENT OF GOD'S CALL

The crisis of which Jesus speaks in the parables was a crisis peculiar to the life of Israel. It arose out of its very nature as the "chosen people." There was an exclusiveness which continually tempted people to pride. And while Jesus does not deny the uniqueness of his people, he does reject the pride inspired by a wrong attitude toward it. Consequently, he fastens upon Israel's uniqueness as the occasion and the basis of God's judgment. Here he stands in the line of Israel's authentic prophets. Amos, speaking for God, had said, "You only have I known of all the families of the earth; therefore I will punish you for all your iniquities (Amos 3:2)." He may have been the first but not the last to take this position. Jesus stands in the same line, but not upon the same plane. Where the prophets speak under the compulsion of "Thus says Yahweh," Jesus speaks as if his words were self-authenticating and says, "But I say unto you . . ." The Jerusalem of his day could not ignore this presumption and knew how to meet it.[1]

We see this final clash coming to a head in the next parables. Jesus, like Amos, found Israel's greatest gift to be its greatest danger. The crisis of judgment which his parables illustrate and drive home is the imminent danger that the life of Israel will lose all meaning if the nation does not live to further God's purposes. Its divine calling, which might be its greatest glory, may weigh it down to its doom. Its uniqueness was a uniqueness of function rather than of privilege. If, then, its highest privilege is service, to refuse to serve is to be without privilege. And Israel without a function, without distinction, without privilege could be a tragic thing—for itself and for the world. A function ordained of God cannot be abrogated. God's will is God's will and must be done. If Israel rejects it, it must and will be done by some other servants—or servant. His call cannot go unheeded; his work cannot go by default. Behind the parables that

127

follow lies this final conviction. And beyond them begins to take shape the cross.

In the parable of the Barren Fig Tree we saw the prospect of judgment which threatened unfruitfulness. In the parable of the Tenants of the Vineyard the issue is more clearly drawn, because in it the fruits are there but they are withheld by a deliberate act of will.

## THE TENANTS OF THE VINEYARD

### Matthew 21

[33]*"Hear another parable.* There was a householder who planted a vineyard, and set a hedge around it, and dug a wine press in it, and built a tower, and let it out to tenants, and went into another country. [34]When the season of fruit drew near, he sent his servants to the tenants, to get his fruit; [35]and the tenants took his servants and beat one, killed another, and stoned another. [36]Again he sent other servants, more than the first; and they did the same to them. [37]Afterward he sent his son to them, saying, 'They will respect my son.' [38]But when the tenants saw the son, they said to themselves, 'This is the heir; come, let us kill him and have his inheritance.' [39]And they took him and cast him out of the vineyard, and killed him. [40]When therefore the owner of the vineyard comes, what will he do to those tenants?" [41]*They said to him, "He will put those wretches to a miserable death, and let out the vineyard to other tenants who will give him the fruits in their seasons.".* . .

[45]*When the chief priests and the Pharisees heard his parables, they perceived that he was speaking about them. [46]But when they tried to arrest him, they feared the multitudes, because they held him to be a prophet.*

### Mark 12

[1]*And he began to speak to them in parables.* "A man planted a vineyard, and set a hedge around it, and dug a pit for the wine press, and built a tower, and let it out to tenants, and went into another country. [2]When the time came, he sent a servant to the tenants, to get from them some of the fruit of the vineyard. [3]And they took him and beat him, and sent him away empty-handed. [4]Again he sent to them another servant, and they wounded him in the head, and treated him shamefully. [5]And he sent another, and him they killed; and so with many others, some they beat and some they killed. [6]He had still one other, a beloved son; finally he sent him to them, saying, 'They will respect my son.' [7]But those tenants said to one another, 'This is the heir; come, let us kill him, and the inheritance

will be ours.' [8]And they took him and killed him, and cast him out of the vineyard. [9]*What will the owner of the vineyard do? He will come and destroy the tenants, and give the vineyard to others. . . ."*

[12]*And they tried to arrest him, but feared the multitude, for they perceived that he had told the parable against them; so they left him and went away.*

## Luke 20

[9]*And he began to tell the people this parable:* "A man planted a vineyard, and let it out to tenants, and went into another country for a long while. [10]When the time came, he sent a servant to the tenants, that they should give him some of the fruit of the vineyard; but the tenants beat him, and sent him away empty-handed. [11]And he sent another servant; him also they beat and treated shamefully, and sent him away empty-handed. [12]And he sent yet a third; this one they wounded and cast out. [13]Then the owner of the vineyard said, 'What shall I do? I will send my beloved son; it may be they will respect him.' [14]But when the tenants saw him, they said to themselves, 'This is the heir; let us kill him, that the inheritance may be ours.' [15]And they cast him out of the vineyard and killed him. What then will the owner of the vineyard do to them? [16]*He will come and destroy those tenants, and give the vineyard to others."*. . .

[19]*The scribes and the chief priests tried to lay hands on him at that very hour, but they feared the people; for they perceived that he had told this parable against them.*

The Evangelists assert that the authorities knew this parable was directed against them and desired, therefore, to get Jesus into their power. Mark and Luke connect it with the debate about Jesus' authority. Matthew inserts the parable of the Two Sons (see Chapter Five) before introducing this parable. We cannot accept the arrangement as it stands until we examine the parable proper and determine its meaning. And here we run into initial difficulties.

A majority of scholars class the passage as secondary, on the ground that it is full of allegorical material which shows signs of construction "after the event."[2] The difficulties suggested are real and become apparent by comparing the three versions. The form is rather clearly that developed in the preaching of the church. The aspects thought to be allegorical are as follows (taking Mark's version).

In Mark 12:1 there is a definite reminiscence of Isaiah 5, in which the vineyard is similarly described and is identified as Israel.[3] The version in Luke (20:9) says simply, "A man planted a vineyard," and omits the detail. This objection does not seem serious because the Jews were familiar with the figure of the vineyard, especially as it appears in the Old Testament. If Jesus' words had been simply those of Luke's version, the likelihood is that the hearers would have found the traditional treatment suggested to them. In all probability, Jesus would have allowed for this, expected it, and, perhaps, desired it.[4] So that if the description was added later, borrowed from Isaiah, it is a legitimate addition and necessary to the sense. The description as a matter of fact is part of the story, for it tells simply what was customarily done to establish a vineyard for permanent production and to protect and equip it as a going concern. This adds force to the expectations of the absent owner, for he has left it in a workable state and has every reason to look for results. It is conceivable that Luke's omission is deliberate, as the phrases might not bear the necessary connotation for his readers.

There is little difficulty with verses 2-4, which tell of the sending in succession of two servants to collect the appropriate share of the proceeds (Mark and Luke have, "*some of* the fruit"; Matthew, "*his* fruit," with the same meaning). The refusal to surrender a share of the crop, the rough treatment of the first servant, and the shameful handling of the second also cause little trouble. In verse 5 another servant is sent and is killed. In Luke this one is wounded and cast out; in Matthew "other servants" are treated like their predecessors. In verse 5b difficulties again arise with the phrase "many others," some of whom are beaten, some killed. The trouble here is that if it is taken allegorically the servants of verses 2-4 must represent prophets and the "many others" of verse 5 represent the long succession of prophets in Israel's past. More reasonably *this* phrase (v. 5b) suggests the long succession of the prophets and so prompts us to treat the first two servants allegorically. The words, "And so with many others, some they beat and some they killed," are summary, and for that reason unlike the style of Jesus' parables. We can see here an effort to bring the passage into line with the facts by an allegorical treatment, but if verse 5b is omitted as an expansion used in preaching, the need to treat verses 2-4 as allegory is not so obvious.

The difficulties accumulate in verses 6-8. The "one other, a beloved son" (v. 6),[5] who is sent as the last messenger on the ground that he will be reverenced, presupposes, the critics say, the Christology of the early church. The phrase is reminiscent of language used of the Davidic kingly expectation reflected in Mark 1:11 and 9:7 and is unlikely on Jesus' lips. The point is pressed in the study of Matthew's and Luke's revision of verse 8. In Mark, the son and heir is killed and cast out of the vineyard, while in Matthew 21:39 and

Luke 20:15 he is *first* cast out and *then* killed—in which scholars see an all-too-clear reference to the crucifixion outside the walls of Jerusalem. It is true that the reference to the son reads as a definite claim that Jesus is not only the last messenger (as implied in the Barren Fig Tree) but also the Messiah or Son of God or both. The whole passage seems to be an allegory of the crucifixion of the Christ. It is so read by the Christian. If it is not itself the product of the church, it would not fail to be so interpreted by the post-resurrection community and the language so modified. This, however, is not finally conclusive. There is still the possibility that Jesus in the parable may have made the heir the climactic figure, heightening the drama by the expectation of the impression he would create, without the hearers' *necessarily* supposing that he was speaking of himself or taking it as a messianic claim. It is difficult for us to put ourselves in the place of the audience or to read the passage free of the associations that Jesus and his words have for us. It is certain that the language has been modified by those who accepted the words as a claim, whether they were so understood in the first instance or not (assuming that we are here dealing with a parable). As *allegory* the words must be taken as a claim. The question at issue is whether the passage is all allegory or a parable that has suffered allegorical treatment.

The reasoning of the tenants in verse 7 has been attacked on the ground that tenants would not suppose that murder of the son would secure them the property. But to this it has been answered that the appearance of the heir may well have suggested to the tenants an opportunity to secure the property for themselves, as we shall see below. Here the treatment of the parable as allegory seems even more difficult, since in what sense could destruction of the Messiah be expected (by Jews) to ensure them the kingdom?

The ultimate difficulty arises in the second half of verse 9, where Jesus answers his own question, "What will the owner of the vine-yard do?" with the words, "He will come and destroy the tenants, and give the vineyard to others." Here again the objection is that this all too clearly implies the fall of Jerusalem and the inheritance of Israel's mission by the church. The objection is also made that Jesus does not normally answer his own question (a difficulty avoided in Matthew 21:41, where the reply is made by the audience, "They said to him"). When this is taken not as allegory but as par-able, the difficulty seems to disappear. The question Jesus asks, given something of the circumstances, would be answered in roughly Mark's terms by any person of business acumen. The thing to do would be to get tenants who would pay the rent or surrender a proper share of the crops. Destruction of the first tenants is not essential, and this may well be a modification of the language of the original in the light of later events.

The passage cannot be taken in its present form as original, but can we discern behind it an actual parable overlaid with allegorical modifications in the course of transmission and in the light of events?

First of all, the state of the times and the repetition of the theme of the absent owner and his unexpected return suggest that a story of this kind has nothing unlikely about it. The frequency with which Jesus used the theme suggests that personal attention to affairs of property was rather the exception than the rule. The employment of agents was sufficiently well-known and understood, along with the laws governing their representative function (notably in the parables of the Unmerciful Servant, the Dishonest Steward, and the Talents and the Pounds). The idea of a foreign landlord, suggested by Dodd and supported by Jeremias, is not essential, and their discussion has been superseded by that of Derrett, as far as his elucidation of the basic concepts of the contractual arrangement and maneuvers goes, to show what might well have been understood by Jesus' hearers.[6] We have seen how familiar was the material Jesus used in parables, and there is no reason to reject this example on the ground of lack of reality.

It has seemed possible to reach beyond the present form of the passage and recover a text characteristic of the parable form rather than of allegory. This (as I suggested) might be done by combining Mark 12:1-3 with verses 4a and c (omitting "wounded him in the head, and"), 5a ("And they sent another, and him they killed"), and 9a ("What will the owner of the vineyard do?"). Here verse 1 is retained as necessary to indicate a project designed as an investment justifying the hope of eventual returns. The wounding in the head of verse 4, the succession of prophets implied by verse 5b (Heilsgeschichte), and the incident of the son are eliminated as allegorical expansions of postresurrection preaching. This leaves the folk tale "rule-of-three," ending with murder as the climax, and leads naturally to the question posed. It has seemed to some to derive support from the versions of Luke and of the Gospel of Thomas (Logion 65).

Previously I also suggested that the above might be taken through 4a and c, omitting verse 5 entirely, to find the third and climactic point in the mission of the son, as follows:

> [1b]A man planted a vineyard, and set a hedge around it, and dug a pit for the wine press, and built a tower, and let it out to tenants, and went into another country. [2]When the time came, he sent a

servant to the tenants, to get from them some of the fruit of the vineyard. [3]And they took him and beat him, and sent him away empty-handed. [4a]Again he sent to them another servant and they . . . [4c]treated him shamefully. [6]He had still . . . a beloved son; finally he sent him to them, saying, 'They will respect my son.' [7]But those tenants said to one another, 'This is the heir; come, let us kill him, and the inheritance will be ours.' [8]And they took him and killed him, and cast him out of the vineyard. [9a]What will the owner of the vineyard do?

Here again the form is threefold and climactic, the soliloquy and colloquy characteristic of folk tale and parable. We would have to assume that the audience heard it simply as a parable without treating it as an allegorical claim to messiahship—indeed, how could an audience possibly have thought it to apply to Jesus himself?[7]

The hazards of reconstructing this parable by literary formulas, however, are suggested by Derrett's more recent treatment of the possibility, under the conditions and legal understanding of the time, that the audience would have recognized the story of three agents followed by a son as a reasonable and not unlikely story, a dramatic parable. This does not, of course, deny that it was used by the church as an allegory, as some of the turns of expression show.

The opening (reminiscent of Isaiah or not), envisages a vineyard which, as Derrett points out, would have to be tended for four years before, under Jewish law, the fruit of the vines could be profitably exploited by owner or tenants. In the first three years, when little or no profit could be expected, the owner had obligations, rights to which the tenants were entitled. They may have been trying to enforce these rights and to establish a claim for themselves by their treatment of the servants who came annually. Only after three rejections of the owner's claim (most clearly in Luke) could the tenants attempt to take the vineyard for their own. "The fourth year was therefore the vital year" (Derrett, p. 302).

Derrett also argues that the sending of the son would be essential, as one who bore the full right of the owner, if the claims of the tenants to possession were to be denied. The rejection of the heir would be a complete and unmistakable rejection of the owner's claim. The argument of the tenants as to the advantage of killing the heir makes sense under the law of the time and place and is not, as many commentators have argued, nonsense and hence purely allegorical.[8] According to Derrett the tenants might well assume the owner had already transferred ownership in whole or in part to his son while still alive to reinforce his son's authority. They would still have the owner to deal with, and the owner retained the right and power to deal with them. This makes an answer to the question in verse 9 unnecessary. The solution would be obvious to any hearer. So, while the parable most probably ended with the question, and the reaction of the owner is only later spelled out in view of the events of A.D. 70, we cannot categorically deny the son a place in the original parable and we need not attribute the allegorical aspects to Jesus. The phrasing of verse 6a in Mark ("still one other, a be-loved son") probably betrays Christian influence. The adjective is omitted in Matthew. In Luke it occurs in the form of the owner's expanded soliloquy, also a later development. If Derrett's arguments are well-founded, we can accept the structure and plot while being aware that transmission has made it more obviously applicable to the preaching of the "mission of the Son of God."[9]

We find, then, that we can detect here an original parable spoken by Jesus in which the due returns of an investment are called for and met in each successive case by deliberate refusal, accompanied by increased violence. When refusal does not produce punishment but only further requests, the tenants begin to feel secure. They forget that they are tenants and make plans to use the vineyard as their own property. The parable is strengthened, since the "wickedness" of the tenants consists not only in keeping for themselves any produce or profit but in claiming the whole enterprise as their own.[10]

In the realm of religious history, the principle "how much more" will apply. If this is the case with the owner of a vineyard where only vintage, rent, or profit is involved, how much more true will it be of God's grant of stewardship to a race or nation? Since a vineyard inevitably has the power to suggest Israel, and is spoken where it can easily be reported to the hierarchy (if not addressed directly to their representatives), the meaning can hardly be escaped. To reject the appeals of God's messengers, to develop a false sense of security, and to appropriate to private use what belongs to another must in the end mean the loss of all rights and privileges of stewardship. The inheritance cannot be treated as Israel's own, no matter if judgment does seem to be deferred. God must achieve his purpose, he must receive what he installed Israel to render, or his people will discover that they are only tenants and be turned out in favor of others who will render to God what is his. It is not by accident that this parable is followed in Mark and Luke by the story of the tribute money, in which the pronouncement is made, "Render to Caesar the things that are Caesar's, and to God the things that are God's (Mark 12:17)." The claim made on Israel, and refused, is not primarily a claim for fruit but for recognition of ownership and of *the right to ask for fruits.* We noted that the parable follows the debate about

Jesus' authority and here again we can see its relevance: not that Jesus is necessarily claiming messiahship but that the true Israel, the Israel of God's design, could recognize his appeal as a proper claim having the authority of Israel's own history, situation, and nature. The relation of this parable (as seen in the form suggested above) to the Barren Fig Tree is clear. God, like the vineyard owner, will not continue to take no for an answer any more than he will, like the farmer, suffer a useless tree to "use up the ground." Neither delay prompted by mercy nor the sending of messengers in succession is to be taken for granted as continuing indefinitely. The last measures are the last, and the final messenger someday appears. Perhaps he is not seen to be the last until his rejection has brought judgment upon those who fail to recognize him as such.

Similar teaching, with emphasis on the rejection of the prophetic messengers, is explicitly set forth in Matthew 23:31-32, 34-38:

> Thus you witness against yourselves, that you are sons of those who murdered the prophets. Fill up, then, the measure of your fathers. . . . Therefore I send you prophets and wise men and scribes, some of whom you will kill and crucify, and some you will scourge in your synagogues and persecute from town to town, that upon you may come all the righteous blood shed on earth, from the blood of innocent Abel to the blood of Zechariah the son of Barachiah, whom you murdered between the sanctuary and the altar. Truly, I say to you, all this will come upon this generation.
>
> O Jerusalem, Jerusalem, killing the prophets and stoning those who are sent to you! How often would I have gathered your children together as a hen gathers her brood under her wings, and you would not! Behold, your house is forsaken and desolate.

This passage in its present form owes, like the parable, a good deal to later development, particularly in Matthew's use of the Wisdom genre.[11] The address to Jerusalem is not an address to the literal city but to it as the leader, representative, and quintessence of Judaism: an address to Israel. It is an extension and sharpening of the thought inherent in the parables of this group, of which the present one, in its original form, is a typical example. The note of urgent crisis as a warning against the complacency of apparent security is clear in the parable.

Following the parable, at Mark 12:10-11, Matthew 21:42, 44, and Luke 20:17-18, the Evangelists insert the passage concerning the "stone," which may be considered as a conventional Christian proof text and may be eliminated from consideration as part of the parable. In Matthew 21:43 the meaning of the parable has been brought out by a gloss, "Therefore I tell you, the kingdom of God will be taken away from you, and given to a nation producing the fruits of it." This sounds rather like a phrase from a Christian sermon legitimately based on the parable. Further study shows the whole context, Mark 11:1—12:12, to be based on a series of themes associated with *Succoth*, the Feast of Tabernacles.[12]

Mark 12:12 and Luke 20:19 credit the leaders with understanding that this parable was spoken against them, i.e., they accepted it as allegory and identified themselves with the tenants. We had best not assume as Cadoux did that they resolved to remove Jesus because they recognized in him an authority higher than their own.[13] In fact it was their refusal of him as an unapproved authority that led them to plan his removal. The passage is an editor's note introduced as part of the explanation of the Passion. Matthew 21:45 makes it refer to all Jesus' parables of this kind or of this period. As we proceed we can see that the authorities could not continue to ignore the Jesus who taught in this fashion, though we need not assume that they admitted allegorical interpretations that identified themselves. The meaning of the parables, applied in the broadest way to all Israel or to national policy or party politics (whatever they found most impinged upon, whatever they were most sensitive to), demanded action or reply on their part. If it had been one parable, it might have been overlooked, but parable followed parable with insistence. The question must arise, On what authority does this itinerant provincial say these things? Jesus is invading sacred precincts, not only in the literal sense of putting his feet within the temple courts or even using his hands to change arrangements there as in the "cleansing," but by means of—as we have learned to say— a confrontation. In the terms of the parable, he is raising the questions, when challenged: Whose is this field? To whom does the vineyard belong? Is this a possession or a trust? Are you owners or tenants? "You will know them by their fruits"! There can be no doubt that the Evangelists are right and that the parables, as perhaps the clearest and most popular part of Jesus' teaching, contributed to his fate.

It is not surprising that in the group of parables we are concerned with we should find much evidence of subsequent expansion and modification when the events had shown in what form the judgment, which appears here as a contingency, had become a reality, when the spiritual dangers Jesus foresaw in quite general and parabolic terms had issued in specific results. The temptation to point the moral would be overwhelming; the very charter of the church's life is written here. The general and parabolic terms then become specific, reminiscent, and allegorical. As Dibelius says (and it applies with much the greatest force to this group of parables), "But in any case we must reckon that the tendency of the Churches to derive *as much exhortation as possible from the words* of Jesus must have affected the handing down of the parables."[14] Or as Dodd says of this particular parable, "The Church is dotting the i's and crossing the t's of the original application. . . . All this progressive elaboration indicates that the Church held the parable to be of peculiar importance, and was anxious to put its interpretation beyond doubt."[15]

The "peculiar importance" has prompted us to deal at some length with the problems that arise from the present text. But behind it we find a teaching in which Jesus proceeds to drive his charge and his urgent appeal more firmly home. Israel exists only for a purpose, and the purpose must be achieved even though Israel be lost. As I shall hope to show later, Jesus could not say this except with a breaking heart, for he too was a Jew. Jesus, in the parable of the Sower, stated the need to persist in his God-given vocation in spite of opposition or failure; here we find him following in practice in more dangerous places the logical necessities of his own teaching. And while we detect the early church triumphantly turning to the parable as useful apologetic against the Jews, we who stand in the church at this distance should be guilty of the very thing against which the parable is directed if we treated it simply as of historical interest. For with all the certainty of the church's inheritance of Israel's place, it inherits also the danger of this judgment. What is here directed against Israel must in every age be directed against the church, against ourselves, and be received in penitent humility. To refer to it only as a factor in the crucifixion of Jesus does not exempt us. It is still true. God has made us tenants only, and he still looks for "his fruits."

The expectation of use that will bring advantage to the owner as a vitally important part of the parable and a clue to Jesus' thought is made even more clear in the next parable, which has come down to us in two quite divergent forms.

## THE TALENTS AND THE POUNDS

### Matthew 25
[14]"For it will be as when a man going on a journey called his servants and entrusted to them his property; [15]to one he gave five talents, to another two, to another one, to each according to his ability. Then he went away. [16]He who had received the five talents went at once and traded with them; and he made five talents more. [17]So too, he

who had the two talents made two talents more. ¹⁸But he who had received the one talent went and dug in the ground and hid his master's money. ¹⁹Now after a long time the master of those servants came and settled accounts with them. ²⁰And he who had received the five talents came forward, bringing five talents more, saying, 'Master, you delivered to me five talents; here I have made five talents more.' ²¹His master said to him, 'Well done, good and faithful servant; you have been faithful over a little, I will set you over much; enter into the joy of your master.' ²²And he also who had the two talents came forward, saying, 'Master, you delivered to me two talents; here I have made two talents more.' ²³His master said to him, 'Well done, good and faithful servant; you have been faithful over a little, I will set you over much; enter into the joy of your master.' ²⁴He also who had received the one talent came forward, saying, 'Master, I knew you to be a hard man, reaping where you did not sow, and gathering where you did not winnow; ²⁵so I was afraid, and I went and hid your talent in the ground. Here you have what is yours.' ²⁶But his master answered him, 'You wicked and slothful servant! You knew that I reap where I have not sowed, and gather where I have not winnowed? ²⁷Then you ought to have invested my money with the bankers, and at my coming should have received what was my own with interest. ²⁸So take the talent from him, and give it to him who has the ten talents. ²⁹*For to every one who has will more be given, and he will have abundance; but from him who has not, even what he has will be taken away. ³⁰And cast the worthless servant into the outer darkness; there men will weep and gnash their teeth.'* "

## Luke 19
¹¹*As they heard these things, he proceeded to tell a parable, because he was near to Jerusalem, and because they supposed that the kingdom of God was to appear immediately.* ¹²He said therefore, "A nobleman went into a far country to receive kingly power and then return. ¹³Calling ten of his servants, he gave them ten pounds, and said to them, 'Trade with these till I come.' ¹⁴But his citizens hated him and sent an embassy after him, saying, *'We do not want this man to reign over us.'* ¹⁵When he returned, having received the kingly power, he commanded these servants, to whom he had given the money, to be called to him, that he might know what they had gained by trading. ¹⁶The first came before him, saying, 'Lord, your pound has made ten pounds more.' ¹⁷And he said to him, 'Well done, good servant! Because you have been faithful in a very little, you shall have authority *over ten cities.*' ¹⁸And the second came, saying, 'Lord, your pound has made five pounds.' ¹⁹And he said to him, 'And you are to be *over five cities.*' ²⁰Then another came, saying, 'Lord,

here is your pound, which I kept laid away in a napkin, <sup>21</sup>for I was afraid of you, because you are a severe man; you take up what you did not lay down, and reap what you did not sow.' <sup>22</sup>He said to him, 'I will condemn you out of your own mouth, you wicked servant! You knew that I was a severe man, taking up what I did not lay down, and reaping what I did not sow? <sup>23</sup>Why then did you not put my money into the bank, and at my coming I should have collected it with interest?' <sup>24</sup>And he said to those who stood by, 'Take the pound from him, and give it to him who has the ten pounds.' <sup>25</sup>(And they said to him, 'Lord, he has ten pounds!') <sup>26</sup>I tell you, that to everyone who has will more be given; but from him who has not, even what he has will be taken away. <sup>27</sup>But as for these enemies of mine, who did not want me to reign over them, bring them here and slay them before me.' "

Here again are two parables which, while similar in plot, have material differences. Luke's is, by general consent, the more secondary, and the reasons for this opinion can be seen by comparing the two. Like the two versions of the parable of the Banquet, it is unlikely that they are versions of a single written source. At the same time they may go back through divergent oral traditions to the same original parable.

The chief thing the two versions have in common is the theme of property left by an absent lord to the care of servants from whom he takes a reckoning upon his return. Dodd, therefore, has called these parables "Money in Trust," and B. T. D. Smith, "Entrusted Wealth." The point of the trust, it is to be noted, lies not in the safekeeping of the money but in the use of it to produce results. When these parables are read in connection with the Barren Fig Tree and the Tenants of the Vineyard, it becomes apparent that Jesus is insisting upon a principle which for him is of great importance.

The theme of the absent lord which appeared in the previous parable here goes a stage farther because it develops the situation that·arises when the absent lord returns. At this point we note that the primitive church would certainly fasten upon this aspect and find in it a reference to its own situation and proceed to develop it. This, however, need not be taken to mean that the theme itself is a construction of the church, for absentee ownership was an observable fact and the original connotation to the hearers was no doubt limited to this primary parabolic sense. It has been shown by Derrett that the essential theme is consonant with Eastern law, and the situation of the participants would be understood.

The eye of the Christian sees in it a prophecy of the ascended Lord's return, a legitimate homiletic extension but not originally or necessarily vital to the sense.[16] The early church, disappointed that Jesus or the "Son of man" did not immediately appear in glory, was exercised about the Parousia. The traces of this concern are apparent in the text. In Matthew's version (v. 19) the lord returns, "after a long time," and the twice-repeated phrase (vs. 21, 23), "Enter into the joy of your master," is to be attributed to this interest. The apocalyptic addition in verse 30 ("And cast the worthless servant into the outer darkness: there men will weep and gnash their teeth") shows the sense in which the parable was used.[17] In Luke's version the lord had departed "to receive kingly power and then return" (v. 12; cf. v. 15). The church understood this to be the case with Jesus' ascension. But, apart from the text of the parable, Luke's introduction points out that the central interest is found in the prolonged absence when he says (v. 11), that "he proceeded to tell a parable, because he was near to Jerusalem, and because *they supposed that the kingdom of God was to appear immediately.*" The parable occurs in the long Lucan section of the approach to Jerusalem (cf. v. 28), and certainly its original relevance is illuminated if, like the others in this series, it belongs to the later Judean phase of Jesus' ministry.[18]

Increasingly, toward the end, Jesus' parables take on the tone of impending judgment and bear a note of expectancy. In Matthew (25:31) the parable is followed by the discourse on the judgment of the nations which begins with the phrase, "But when the Son of man comes," a phrase that does not necessarily identify Jesus with the Son of man. It reminds us of the distinction which appears on the surface in Luke 9:26 (cf. Mark 8:38): "For whoever is ashamed of me and of my words, of him will the Son of man be ashamed when he comes in his glory and the glory of the Father and of the holy angels." The parables themselves, seen in the setting of Jesus' own time (rather than in the life situation of the Christian community), disclose that the urgency is connected with his appeal to Israel in its historical situation. They constitute the main element in his warning. The question of his own place in the scheme of things does not arise with any directness from the parables—for this is not their central theme—but indirectly, when it is asked on what authority or by what right Jesus adopts this attitude and issues warnings of this kind.

It is necessary, then, to examine the parables as we have them to discover what might have been their original form and meaning.

Into Luke's parable there is woven what seems to be an intrusive theme which, far from being essential to the story, appears as a distracting and confusing element. It is observed in verses 12b, 14, 15a, 17c, 19b, and 27. It can be extracted to provide in itself the nucleus of a separate story:

¹²ᵇ"A nobleman went into a far country to receive kingly power and then return. . . . ¹⁴But his citizens hated him and sent an embassy after him, saying, 'We do not want this man to reign over us.' ¹⁵ᵃWhen he returned, having received the kingly power . . . [he said?] ²⁷'But as for these enemies of mine, who did not want me to reign over them, bring them here and slay them before me.' "

The intrusion of this theme into what we may suppose to be a story more like Matthew's accounts for the modifications at verses 17 and 19. There the reward given to the faithful servants is authority over cities—presumably a share in the kingdom the lord has received. It is barely possible that another and now lost parable is here partially preserved which may have some connections with similarly intrusive elements in Matthew's parable of the marriage feast for the king's son. It has a parallel in the historical incident of Archelaus' journey to Rome to confirm his inheritance of a part of Herod's empire. A delegation of Jews followed him to argue against his claims. It is plausible that the incident has been applied to the early church. The only help the intrusion provides to the parable (and that from the church's point of view) is that it explains the reason for the nobleman's absence and affords opportunity to introduce the element of destruction. His absence, however, requires no explanation in the parable, but only from the viewpoint of a delayed Parousia. The vengeance incident probably reflects the fall of Jerusalem.[19]

In other respects Luke's parable specifies ten servants, to each of whom an equal sum (one pound, i.e., one mina) is given, whereas in Matthew only three servants are specified, and the amounts given (five, two, and one talents) are varied according to their ability. Matthew's is likely to be the more original version, since there are indications in Luke that there were originally only three servants, and to them also graduated responsibilities were given. In verse 20 the Greek reads, "Then another came," as though he were the third and last, and in verses 16 and 18 the results of trading are varied, as in Matthew, in a decreasing scale.

The "talent" of Matthew represents a large sum; the "pound" of Luke a much smaller sum. It is precarious to argue that the smaller sum is original on the ground that it fits better Luke's "faithful in a very little" (v. 17) and Matthew's "faithful over a little," though it is true that five talents is no insignificant sum unless the lord be wealthy or a ruler. I suspect that the matter is unimportant, except that it originally suggested the kind of transaction which Derrett is able to explain as familiar to the time. The principle taught remains unaffected.

The essentials of the tale in each case are that a holder of property departed, leaving his affairs in the hands of his servants, and on his return made an accounting with them. He expected profit to accrue to himself through their use of his resources. This was clear when he commended those who exercised the trust to his advantage by active employment of the means at their disposal. The reward, where this had been done, was further responsibility, a greater trust. The condemnation fell on the servant who made *no use* of the money left to his care, in spite of the fact that it was still intact.

It is difficult to see anything in this but a further explication of Jesus' challenge to his people. It is true, a perfectly general moral lesson may be drawn from it, and the fact that "talent" has come to mean an individual "gift" or aptitude is a result. In ordinary preaching the inequality of personal endowment is illustrated by the varying sums given (in Matthew) to the servants in turn. But as a matter of fact the various amounts are so given *because* of differences in ability and are not themselves the differing abilities. Commonplace references to the "one-talent man" are an unconscious resort to allegory, since the term implies that his lack of ability was the point. One should say, "the man to whom only one talent was given." Derrett (p. 26) shows that the small trust might easily tempt him to feel the relationship was not worth entering into (by trading), and even the bank would provide so little interest that it would all go to his lord. Derrett says, "Since the smallest and most secure business would offer him nothing, he declined to do business at all." At first sight the personal application seems indicated by the three characters and the separate dealings with each. But it is characteristic of the folk tale that there should be three characters or incidents and direct discourse or conversation. The literary function of the two successful traders is to form a background for the unsuccessful third. They provide the contrast which shows wherein the last has failed. It is properly the case of the third servant upon which the interpretation depends.

The church interpretation involved the delayed return of Jesus and counseled active Christian service in the interim. The "joy of your master" probably has some affinity with the messianic banquet, but here acquires a more specifically Christian connotation. The saying added in Matthew 25:29 and Luke 19:26, "to every one who has will more be given," is a floating saying which we have come across before and probably was a text that the parable could be made to illustrate in preaching. Its connection with the parable is general, growing immediately out of the command to take away the money held by the unprofitable servant and give it to one of the others (Matt.

25:28; Luke 19:24). This command has been attacked on the ground that it is unnecessary to the story (which would then end in Matthew at v. 27 and in Luke at v. 23, in each case with the words "with interest"). It is said that the one thing the unprofitable servant would wish for is to be relieved of his trust. But actually the story is incomplete without it, for it does not tell what treatment was accorded the unprofitable servant. On the analogy of the others, who were rewarded by additional trust, he would be punished by being deprived of a trust (granting he had shown no evidence of wanting it). To decide whether the taking away of the talent is irrelevant to the parable as parable it is necessary to seek its meaning in the actual situation.[20]

It would be dangerous and irrelevant to seek to allegorize it, for that would involve making the absent lord Christ and make it necessary then to identify what the money and each of the servants represented. If, on the other hand, we take it as simply a story of normal happenings, we find that a man who entrusts others with valuable property expects some return from the trust reposed in them. His expectation will determine his treatment of the trustees and the nature of the reward or punishment. This is what we find in the parable. We have to think of the unsuccessful servant as a servant. Like his fellows, he would want a share with them in the control of affairs, and in the end to be deprived of any trust at all means to be no longer a servant—at least in that class of servants who are stewards. His unfitness to hold office is shown, rather cleverly, by the wrong deduction he makes from his master's character (Matt. 25:25; Luke 19:21). In effect he refused the trust the moment he laid the money safely away. We should see here, incidentally, the danger of allegorizing the story, since to do so would leave us with the character description as applying either to Jesus or to God.[21] When his lord answers him out of his "own mouth" (Luke 19:22), he is not endorsing the description but merely showing the servant that on his own grounds his deduction is at fault. The taking away of the money completes his own rejection of the trust of which money is the outward form, and the giving it to the one who best understands the purpose of the trust is logical and underlines the central point. Without the money the servant has no longer any evidence that he is in the same class with the others.[22]

It will not do to lift the parable bodily from the Gospels and its organic place in Jesus' campaign. To do so has made it seem possible, as was said above, to apply it to everyday moralizings about the use of personal endowments. This again leads us into the trap of "salvation by works," and Jesus becomes another pundit. It is manifestly true that those who are endowed with gifts above the average have a responsibility to their fellows and in community. But this is a very distant use of the parable. The original hearers would not be likely to have taken it in this sense. They would have understood Jesus to be talking about God's call to Israel.[23] And we should understand it to apply to God's commission to the church. Only in that context, as the individual is a sharer in the endowment of the church, can the usual application be justified. The Epistle to the Ephesians correctly indicates the true line of development: "I . . . beg you to lead a life worthy of the calling to which you have been called. . . . There is one body and one Spirit, just as you were called to the one hope that belongs to your call. . . . But grace was given to each of us according to the measure of Christ's gift" (Eph. 4:1, 4, 7; cf. vs. 11-13). As Paul observed, there are diversities of gifts, of administrations, and of operations, but "To each is given the manifestation of the Spirit for the common good," and though a body have many members and each its own function, it remains one body (1 Cor. 12:4–13:13).

The burning issue of Jesus' day was the function and future of Israel. We see here another parable bearing upon this issue. In essence it has the same meaning as the previous parable. It is likewise based on natural procedure at the level of ordinary worldly affairs. If an absent landowner or businessman will so judge and so decide, *how much more* likely is it that God will so act with reference to his purposes in history? The aptness of the story may, I think, be made clear without danger of allegory. Some nations have many interests, and doubtless God requires an accounting from them. But Israel has only one concern, to make God known, and to neglect it means to lose any meaning in history at all. This, I think, is a logical extension of the meaning, and a proper one. The original was more broad and simple—that God expects from his trust employment which will produce results, and that merely to safeguard what is entrusted is virtually to ask that it be taken away. "Use or lose!" would be a crude summary. How could a people then—or a church now—whose besetting problem for centuries was the safeguarding of their religion and culture by exclusion, withdrawal, and rejection, out of fear of its contamination in the hurly-burly of history—how could this people fail to see the meaning of the parable? And how, we may ask, could the leaders of this people fail very soon to see in the man who spoke such parables a dangerous threat? They must challenge his authority to speak in this manner and discredit him with the people. If this failed and he persisted (and could not convince them by an acceptable "sign"), they must remove him. This would not be true if the parable (as it is usually preached) had reference merely to individual "talents," and it would contribute nothing to our understanding of Jesus' eventual fate.

We need not, like the early church, dwell upon the historic fulfillment of Jesus' warnings, but we should rather recognize that *the church* now stands where Israel once stood, faced by the same Lord, faced by the same divine demands. The lesson of the parable can have individual application within the church. Even more strikingly, all history testifies that it has application to nations, and the nations of our own time may well take heed. But above and beyond all this, and justifying these other applications, stands the awe-inspiring meaning for God's church in its temporal, institutional embodiments. "Trade with these till I come" is still the mandate. It needs to be reiterated ever and anon when ecclesiastical and institutional considerations block "the witness" of the Christian folk to a struggling world.

One is tempted to ask, What, then, becomes of the servant who has been relieved of his trust? A good deal of morbid apocalyptic thought may be expended here, but I am not convinced that Jesus was interested in it. Yet to ask this question leads to the suggestion of a possible clue to what is in some ways the most difficult parable of all. We may, therefore, here treat the parable of the Dishonest Steward as a reflection of the same concern.

## THE DISHONEST STEWARD
### Luke 16

**[1]He also said to the disciples, "There was a rich man who had a steward, and charges were brought to him that this man was wasting his goods. [2]And he called him and said to him, 'What is this that I hear about you? Turn in the account of your stewardship, for you can no longer be steward.' [3]And the steward said to himself, 'What shall I do since my master is taking the stewardship away from me? I am not strong enough to dig, and I am ashamed to beg. [4]I have decided what to do, so that people may receive me into their houses when I am put out of the stewardship.' [5]So, summoning his master's debtors one by one, he said to the first, 'How much do you owe my master?' [6]He said, 'A hundred measures of oil.' And he said to him, 'Take your bill, and sit down quickly and write fifty.' [7]Then he said to another, 'And how much do you owe?' He said, 'A hundred measures of wheat.' He said to him, 'Take your bill, and write eighty.' [8]*The master commended the dishonest steward for his prudence; for the sons of this world are wiser in their own generation than the sons of light.*"**

This baffling story belongs with the present series of parables by reason of its theme—the steward left in charge and the day of reckoning. The essential difference arises from the fact that here the steward is dismissed and the story deals with the problem that arises from the dismissal. This parable occurs only in Luke, and with no indication of occasion other than (v. 1) that it is addressed to the disciples. As a parable, it suffers more than any other from this lack of context, and the interpretation is likely to suffer more than most from not being taken as a parable.

This difficulty was evidently felt early in the history of its use and transmission, for appended to it are what seem to be several applications. The story proper may be taken to end with verse 7, or with 8a, the commendation of the steward by his master. The next verse observes, "The sons of this world are wiser in their own generation than the sons of light." This, as application, may be deduced from the story, though we are not told how we are to judge the wisdom or otherwise of "the sons of light." Verse 9 starts with the words, "And I tell you," which in Luke seems to mark the application of a parable (11:8; 15:7; 15:10; 18:14) and may well represent the words of the Christian preacher rather than the words of Jesus. On this ground both parts of verse 8 are by some taken to be part of the parable. The application then given is: "Make friends for yourselves by means of unrighteous mammon, so that when it fails they may receive you into the eternal habitations." This advice means the giving of alms to the poor with the hope of eternal reward, but, as has been pointed out, the difficulty with it is that the money used to give alms belongs to someone else. The third application occupies verses 10-12 and concerns faithfulness—faithfulness which is tested in small things, in the use of the unrighteous mammon, and to a trust. These verses seem to have about them a note of caution against the misinterpretation of the parable. Each of the three applications may be said to have some connection with the parable, but the difficulty with all of them is that they miss some essential point and do not seem of sufficient importance to justify a parable of this kind. Dodd's note is well justified: "We can almost see here notes for three separate sermons on the text."[24] It is rather obvious that by the time the parable reached the Evangelist its meaning had been lost and it had acquired these variant interpretations from different expositors. It is a testimony to the fidelity of the record that this material is included. A fourth saying added in verse 13, "no servant can serve two masters. . . . You cannot serve God and mammon," is parallel to Matthew 6:24 and would seem to have a closer connection with the basic theme. It might be said to apply to both characters alike. ("Mammon" occurs in three of the applications, verses 9, 11, and 13, so that it appears to be the overall theme of the editor.)

The first difficulty in seeking to recover the meaning arises from verse 8a: "And his lord commended the unrighteous steward because he had done wisely (RV)." Read in this way, it is apparently part of the parable and "his lord" (RV) or "the lord" (KJV) refers to the lord by whom the steward is employed and who has by now been twice taken advantage of (v. 1 and vs. 5-7). It has always seemed difficult to take it in this sense unless it can be shown that what the steward did was of present advantage to his lord as well as of prospective advantage to himself. It may be read, however, as "*the* lord*," (KJV) referring to Jesus. The difficulty here is greater, for it seems to give Jesus' approval to the reasoning that the way to get out of a difficulty into which one has got by neglect or fraud is to aggravate the offense. The vagueness of the reference may be taken as a sign that verse 8a is an editorial or preaching link which makes possible the first (v. 8b) and the second (v. 9) applications.[25] Many have so taken it. The difficulty is that the text says, "*his* lord"—that is, the steward's lord—and it is necessary first to see if there is any sense in which it might have been possible that the master would indeed commend his discharged steward.

We are dealing in the parables with the people of the Near East, and the Western ear is not the best means for catching the nuances of their stories. In this area Derrett has brought some help, and we must gratefully draw on his knowledge of Eastern law and custom.[26] His suggestion in effect is that the steward was not further depriving his master but cutting down the amount of the usurious (and religiously illegal) interest he, in his lord's name, had charged. (Such interest is on a scale beyond our normal credence but is still one of the roots of the constant disturbances and distress in Eastern lands.) This reduction would bring relief to the clients, for which they would be grateful to the steward, and they would be prepared in some way "to return the favor"—which was his purpose. But the clients would also attribute the rebate to his master, since the steward (though fired) was acting as his agent in their sight, and hence the lord would not only "save face" but be admired as a generous and considerate man with whom to deal. The master would not lose anything except his share of the exorbitant interest originally stipulated. The steward would lose his share, but it would be a calculated loss, accepted with an eye to the position it would give him with the clients for whom he had been the effective agent of their relief. We can see then that "his lord commended the dishonest steward" (the RSV has changed "his lord" to "the master") would make sense when taken literally and would be part of the parable. The steward is still, no doubt, "dishonest" as regards his previous actions, but they too were in line

147

with the master's practice, though presumably carried out previously more to the steward's advantage than to the master's. The steward's sharp and shrewd response to his dismissal might well appeal to his former master, given a sense of humor on his part, since his own reputation was now enhanced. It would certainly appeal to the sense of humor of Jesus' listeners. The steward evidently remains discharged, but both would have made some gain. As Via observes,[27] neither character is enhanced by this suggestion (from our point of view), since a shrewdness is in each case exhibited from which we shrink—in profession if not always in practice!

If this is nearer the reality of the time and place than previous attempts to deal with the problem, what are we to make of the interpretation and application? Via treats the parable as a "comedy" in that there is an "upward movement"; the steward retrieves some hope out of the prospect of a threatening future.[28] Perrin treats it as a parable of decision in the face of crisis,[29] which would put it in the class with those in our previous chapter. The question is whether this is the extent of what would be "heard." Verse 8b would still be application (perhaps pre-Lucan but postresurrection) involving the application of the principle "how much more." That is, if a rascal like the steward, faced with personal disaster, can act with such decisiveness and shrewd calculation in what is, after all, a fairly sordid business, how much more should we in affairs of the kingdom of God use no less powers of decision and well-calculated foresight? One of the reasons for being slightly uneasy with this is that, as has been said, we feel reluctant to attribute to Jesus a sense of humor—for that is what is implied here. The humor is both a sign that we may be in touch with a real person (how little understood as such!) and certainly with an aspect of his skill in communication where the involvement of the hearers is the primary aim and where the good teacher (or preacher) knows that humor and tragedy, a wry smile and a step toward change, are not far apart. In 1948 I suggested that there is something ironic, yet tragic, about this parable if the "how much more" principle applies and if its relevance to Israel's situation in Jesus' time is felt. I think it must have been. We have an advance here on the previous parable where the tenants would be put out of the vineyard and lose all, even what they might legitimately have claimed. Here the steward, having also lost his position, takes care to secure some kind of future by using the kind of shrewdness which has been the source of his trouble, now not to his own advantage alone, but to bring some credit also to his lord.

The one function of tenants is to produce and render their share. The one requirement of a steward is, as Paul says, to "be found trustworthy (1 Cor. 4:2)." What if a person—or a church, or a nation

—rejects its function, fails its trust, is there any prospect but to continue in its own preferred mode of life? The introduction to the parable (v. 1) in which it is addressed to the disciples is most likely editorial and prepares for the series of applications that follow it, adapting the parable to the situation of the Christian and the church in various ways. If, however, it was spoken openly, as we must assume, Jesus' audience would be more likely to apply it to their own case. Without allegorical identification, we can see how the situation of the steward might be seen as parallel to the situation in which the people were, or were soon to find themselves to be. It is not necessary, as Cadoux did, to pinpoint one group. He suggested the high-priestly caste as "inclined to barter the national ideal and the interests of a spiritual trust in order to get Roman favor and secure themselves in an office."[30] This, taken more generally, is close to the theme of the parable. It conforms generally to Jesus' stress on the judgment that those who reject their sole calling or appropriate to themselves its benefits have no further hope than to continue their own chosen way. It appears that for Jesus the critical time had come when such a decision faced his people (of course it would devolve most heavily on its leaders), and two things were necessary. First required was an awareness of the crisis as impending judgment, and second a resolve to respond before it should be too late. If Jesus could, even in this case, be not without humor, we are also to be reminded that he himself was one of the people and, in the Gethsemane scene (Mark 14:32ff. and parallels; cf. John 12:27f.), may be understood to be facing the same issue himself and with distress, distress for his people rather than, or as much as, for himself. In this sense the last of Luke's applications, the placing here of the saying in verse 13, "no servant can serve two masters . . . God and mammon," may be the most inclusive and germane of them all. The histories of nations and of human institutions (not excluding churches), no less than of individuals, are sufficient comment on Jesus' simply presented but penetrating analysis.

The next parable carries the discussion a stage farther, since it may be interpreted as a warning that a negative decision means to refuse an opportunity and leads to a worse disaster.

## THE EMPTY HOUSE

### Matthew 12
[43]"When the unclean spirit has gone out of a man, he passes through waterless places seeking rest, but he finds none. [44]Then he says, 'I will return to my house from which I came.' And when he comes he finds it empty, swept, and put in order. [45]Then he goes and brings

149

with him seven other spirits more evil than himself, and they enter and dwell there; and the last state of that man becomes worse than the first. *So shall it be also with this evil generation."*

## Luke 11

[23]*"He who is not with me is against me; and he who does not gather with me scatters.*

[24]**"When the unclean spirit has gone out of a man, he passes through waterless places seeking rest; and finding none he says, 'I will return to my house from which I came.' [25]And when he comes he finds it swept and put in order. [26]Then he goes and brings seven other spirits more evil than himself, and they enter and dwell there; and the last state of that man becomes worse than the first."**

This material, which has been variously interpreted, appears to come from Q. In Luke it stands in the discussion of exorcism following the parable of the Strong Man (vs. 20-23; see Chapter Seven). It is separated from the discussion of the generation that seeks a sign (vs. 29ff.) by Jesus' reply to the woman who commended his mother (v. 27): "Blessed rather are those who hear the word of God and keep it! (v. 28)." This may be taken as Q's parallel to the Marcan passage concerning the family of Jesus, copied by Matthew and Luke (Mark 3:31-35; Matt. 12:46-50; Luke 8:19-21), which in Matthew follows the passage with which we are concerned. The discussion of the generation that seeks a sign occurs in Matthew as the prelude (Matt. 12:38-42) instead of, as in Luke, the sequel.

It seems fair to say that while the occasion for the saying is, super-ficially, the dispute about casting out demons, the more immediate connection in each Gospel is the discussion of signs and the true kindred of Jesus. In Luke the exorcisms are treated as a sign of the presence of the kingdom (v. 20). We shall see how the parable of the Strong Man interprets and is interpreted by this saying. If the present passage is interpreted in the same connection, the verses concerning Jesus' mother and those who hear and keep the word of God appear as an interruption only, since the sayings concerning signs follow immediately. And yet the interruption is more apparent than real, for it is the *repentance* of the Ninevites at the word of Jonah and the *response* of the queen of the south to the wisdom of Solomon upon which the passage turns, just as the true brethren of Jesus are those who *respond* to the word of God. In reverse order, the same connec-tion is found in Matthew with one significant addition at the end of Matthew 12:45: "So shall it be also with this evil generation." These words have been treated as an addition by the Evangelist. The question, however, is whether they properly interpret the saying and, by linking it with the mention of "this generation" in the preceding passage (vs. 39, 41-42), correctly refer the saying to the discussion of signs, of which the casting out of demons is the chief.

Without the setting and Matthew's note it would be difficult to tell what the parable means, because the verse that precedes it in Luke (11:23), "He who is not with me is against me," has been given a personal interpretation. The parable's meaning for the church is found in passages that deal with backsliding as, for example, 1 Corinthians 3:10-17; Hebrews 6:4-6; 10:36-39; 2 Peter 2:20-22 (note especially the words, "the last state has become worse for them than the first"); and Revelation 2:4-5. But the place the parable holds in the Gospels indicates that it was originally taken to have had, when first spoken, a broader application in the situation of Jesus. It is this that moves us to treat it as a parable rather than as a literal analysis of demon treatment (true psychologically though the analysis be).

The saying, of course, assumes the then-current Jewish lore concerning evil spirits—that they are unclean, that they defile the person they possess, that they have no bodies of their own, and that since they are afraid of water they inhabit waste places reluctantly but of necessity when no other habitation offers itself (cf. Mark 5:10-12). There is also clear indication that exorcism was not of itself a cure, but that some positive infusion of a more "holy" spirit must take place to occupy the personality against a renewed and aggravated attack.[31] We may, on this basis, assume that Jesus is characteristically drawing his material from ordinary life and appealing again to the experience of men on the human level. The expulsion of demons was suggested by him as evidence of a new age. He is using a personal illustration to illuminate a corporate situation. The meaning of the parable would then be that those who experienced the powers of the new age, if they ignored it, refused to commit themselves wholly to it, would not allow themselves to be possessed by it, would be wholly subject to the passing age and its doom. To have known the kingdom of God and to have failed to profit from it would be a last state worse than the first. It then becomes a further warning of the danger to Israel in refusing the opportunity that is presented by his presence. The family sayings, which are closely associated with the parable and which concern doing the will of God, then represent the positive attitude and hold out the promise, under the figure of the family, of a new life open to those who respond. As a warning addressed to the people as a whole, it suggests again the line of thought that the parable of the Dishonest Steward indicated was not foreign to Jesus' viewpoint. The man out of whom the evil spirit has gone but who remains "empty," unoccupied, is in no worse case than an Israel that has renounced the sins of uncleanness and found a champion able to command the evil spirits but has found no vocation worthy of its calling or of God's grace in providing a new opportunity.

The juxtaposition here of the words, "He who is not with me is against me" (Luke 11:23), like the association of "No servant can serve two masters" with the previous parable discussed, seems to indicate that the question of loyalty was at stake in each case. In Luke the present parable offers the picture of the man in his "last state . . . worse than the first" as a comment on the assertion, "He who does not gather with me scatters." The parable shows that an individual cannot remain empty—that is, undecided, uncommitted; he either makes a new commitment or he becomes a worse slave to an evil master than before. The parallel may be drawn for the nation or church. Verse 23 now, it is true, appears in an individualized form like the parable, but the likelihood is that it originally had a wider and more historical application. Matthew's "So shall it be also with this evil generation" is probably the trace of an earlier stage in the interpretation. Though Bultmann (p. 164) feels its original meaning is hard to discern, this may preserve the original application. He does not think the parable is a community construction because of its lack of specific Christian features.

The similarity of the problem of "What then?" with which these two parables deal under different figures suggests their parallel treatment. Together they constitute a solemn warning of the serious result of Israel's refusal to accept Jesus' urgent challenge. The parable of the Empty House has, of course, a perennial meaning for the individual's religious experience which needs no further comment. It is its possible original bearing on the climax of Jesus' struggle that has been neglected. We shall see when we come to discuss the scene in Gethsemane that the prospect of a last state worse than the first for his own people was not something that Jesus faced with composure. The possibility that the Christian church in the dawning of every new era in history may also fail to go beyond self-cleansing to seize new opportunities should cause us serious concern.

This series of parables may well be closed with two little similitudes in multiple form which cap the argument that Israel is worthless and useless apart from its primary vocation.

## THE SALT

### Matthew 5
[13]"You are the salt of the earth; but if salt has lost its taste, how

can its saltness be restored? It is no longer good for anything except to be thrown out and trodden under foot by men."

## Mark 9
⁴⁹*"For every one will be salted with fire.* ⁵⁰Salt is good; but if the salt has lost its saltness, how will you season it? *Have salt in yourselves, and be at peace with one another."*

## Luke 14
³⁴"Salt is good; but if salt has lost its taste, how shall its saltness be restored? ³⁵It is fit neither for the land nor for the dunghill; men throw it away. He who has ears to hear, let him hear."

Here is an example of a small similitude which, separated from the context of its original use, has found several applications in the Gospel tradition. What would appear to be a simple comparison becomes confused by its several uses in Mark. If Matthew and Luke had both Mark and Q as sources for the saying, they have followed Q and ignored two applications of the metaphor in Mark, verses 49 and 50b.

In the Marcan set of sayings we can see that the only real connection is that each (vs. 49, 50a, and 50b) has to do with salt, and they are drawn together on that basis. It is a useless strain on the imagination to seek a connection. In verse 49, "Every one will be salted with fire," we are probably intended to think of the purifying, astringent qualities of salt. Thus follows the section that recommends the elimination of bodily members when they obstruct the religious life. The fire of sacrifice must purify the disciple. In some manuscripts a gloss from Leviticus 2:13 has been added as if to help this meaning: "And every sacrifice will be salted with salt," but it succeeds only in confusing the metaphor. In the third saying, in verse 50b, we read, "Have salt in yourselves, and be at peace with one another." Here the salt refers of course to a quality within the disciples which will make them beneficial to each other, perhaps as salt is beneficial to food in bringing out the flavor of the food. We can see here, rather amusingly, the danger of overpressing a metaphor. A little salt is a good thing for this purpose, but too much defeats its purpose. This would lead us to the ludicrous conclusion that Christians should be good enough to produce peace but not so good as to cause disturbance! The saying, for lack of a true context, remains obscure. The second use in verse 50a, "Salt is good; but if the salt has lost its saltness, how will you season it?" is the clearest in itself, but there is no hint as to its application. Since this saying of the three is parallel with the versions from Q, we shall consider it below.

In the Lucan version the Evangelist has also the saying, "Salt is good." We find the observation of the impossibility of restoring flavor to unsalted salt (v. 34) expanded in verse 35, where the deteriorated salt is cast out as "fit neither for the land nor for the dunghill." This obviously means that salt without its flavor is not fit for fertilizing the soil, nor for the manure pile—which is another way of saying the same thing. Something, apparently, has happened to the text, but scholars have found no acceptable way of correcting it. Evidently the meaning originally was: It is not fit for its original purpose (seasoning or preserving), nor will it help the land as a fertilizer. It can be only thrown away.

This is emphasized in Matthew's version: "It is no longer good for anything except to be thrown out and trodden under foot by men," the obvious meaning of which is that it cannot be put on the soil but, as Matthew is careful to emphasize, only on the road, where nothing is expected to grow. The saying in Luke follows the discourse on "counting the cost," with its similitudes of the Tower Builder and the King Preparing for War, a context in which it is difficult to see any meaning. Matthew has overcome this difficulty by introducing the saying, with the phrase addressed to the disciples (the multitude in the background, 5:1), "You are the salt of the earth." Here the salt is not, as in Mark, a quality within the disciples but the disciples themselves, or the people as a whole.

The three versions have a minimum saying in common, namely, *"If the salt has lost its taste, how can its saltness be restored?"* It is with this that we must work as the original similitude. Here a little observation of the Eastern scene is worth a good deal of dogmatism. Salt, as known to the laboratory, does not lose its taste. But apparently the Gospels visualize the possibility. We find that in the Near East salt is obtained by mining it from cliffs, such as those that existed near the Dead Sea, and by evaporation from the salt marshes or the sea. It is probably impure salt by our standards, either in origin or through storage. Salt is so essential to human life and animal husbandry that it has often provided a convenient form of reward and a certain source of revenue. As recently as this century, Gandhi led his followers on a march to the sea to obtain salt by evaporation rather than pay the salt tax. (I found in teaching at Serampore University that the Bengal students were unfamiliar with this incident in their history, having been born since Gandhi's death.) We would then assume the admixture of other chemicals deleterious to the salty flavor. W. M. Thompson reports an observed case of salt stored on earthen floors which spoiled and was thrown into the streets, and adds that the reason it is thrown into the streets is because it is actually harmful to the soil.[32] We recall that sites were "sown with salt" in Old Testament times in order to make them uninhabitable.

The meaning, then, becomes clear. Nothing was so useless as salt that had lost its saltness. The only reason for gathering it was to enjoy its flavor. Its saltness was the only reason for its use. When this had gone, only more salt could produce saltness; why dilute the new salt with the old? It thus appears as a strong metaphor, not yet become a simile until we find with what it is compared. For Matthew, it is the disciples; for Mark, a quality within. Taken by itself, however, it suggests something that exists for a simple and specific purpose and without that purpose its reason for existence is at an end. It is hard to see how this could mean anything other than Israel. Cadoux rightly argues that Jesus did not adopt this view of the individual, since the individual could be redeemed; he says, "It was simply true of the nation in view of their world-destiny."[33] The parables do envisage the possibility of Israel's being "thrown out" if it does not fulfill its purpose, and in a brief but striking figure the salt as a similitude would stand as a similar warning. With this Dodd also agrees: "It becomes a poignant comment on the whole situation at the moment."[34] We can again easily see that when the situation in which Jesus spoke had come to an end and the church had emerged, the original meaning would be lost and new applications found in the Christian life. We may, like the Evangelists, individualize the saying, but its primary reference is still valid for the church as an institution. Unless it is fulfilling its divinely appointed task of salt to the world (whether we choose to think of salt as a preservative, an antiseptic, or an enhancement), it is "no longer good for anything except to be thrown out." Ignatius combines both aspects of the function of salt in Magnesians X.2: "Be salted in him, that none of you may be corrupted, since by your savor you shall be tested."[35]

The similitude does not stand alone but in Matthew is associated with that of the Lamp, at once suggesting a similar meaning.

## THE LAMP

**Mark 4**
[21]*And he said to them,* "Is a lamp brought in to be put under a bushel, or under a bed, and not on a stand?"

**Luke 8**
[16]"No one after lighting a lamp covers it with a vessel, or puts it under a bed, but puts it on a stand, that those who enter may see the light."

**Matthew 5**

[14]"You are the light of the world. *A city set on a hill cannot be hid.* [15]Nor do men light a lamp and put it under a bushel, but on a stand, and it gives light to all in the house. [16]*Let your light so shine before men, that they may see your good works and give glory to your Father who is in heaven.*"

**Luke 11**

[33]"No one after lighting a lamp puts it in a cellar or under a bushel, but on a stand, that those who enter may see the light."

As in the foregoing case, here again is an apparently simple saying (or most likely two sayings) that is divorced from its original setting and hence used in different connections by the Evangelists. Probably they found it so used in their sources. It is first necessary to recover the original similitude and try to arrive at its meaning without literary context by setting it against the background of the time. It then becomes a parallel metaphor to the Salt.

The simplest form occurs in Mark in the form of a question: "Is a lamp brought in [i.e., lighted][36] to be put under a bushel, or under a bed, and not on a stand?" Here it is parabolic in form since it requires a judgment—the quite obvious one: "Certainly, to be put on the stand."[37] The application in the Marcan context is, as we have noted, as a similitude on teaching by parables. The verse which follows it, concerning that which is hid in order (later) to be manifested, does not really fit the similitude and represents another viewpoint about parabolic teaching than that naturally suggested by our figure. One does not hide a (lighted) lamp and then produce it. It is senseless to talk of the lamp as hidden before it is lighted, since the similitude obviously visualizes only a lamp that is burning. The parallel to this in Luke is in more extended form and has equally what we have come to recognize as the parable form. The purpose of exposing the light is expressed. It has the same context as Mark.

The situation depicted in the original is that of a single-roomed Palestinian house where the human occupants sleep on the floor on the raised level and the animals occupy the lower level near the door. It was the usual custom to leave a light burning all night, with the obvious purpose that anyone entering, or arising from sleep, during the night for some purpose (cf. the parable of the Friend at Midnight in Chapter Seven) might not stumble over the sleeping forms. We should not miss the humorous note which visualizes putting the lighted lamp (of clay, with a floating wick) under a grain measure or under a bed. Under a measure it could give no light and would soon go out. Under a bed, which in a peasant home was a rug or mattress without legs, it would obviously be smothered. It would normally be put on a "stand" or in a niche in the wall.

In the second pair of versions from Q we notice two differences between Luke and Matthew in the central part of the similitude. Luke introduces the phrase "in a cellar" (some manuscripts omit here his reference to "a bushel") and where Matthew has, "It gives light to all in the house," Luke has, "That those who enter may see the light." Luke's changes suggest that he is thinking of a more elaborate home, perhaps a non-Palestinian one, where there might be a cellar and more than one room and where a slave, let us say, lights the lamp to greet the returning family. The sense of the similitude is not, however, changed. With regard to the difference in the last phrases, to attempt to find that Matthew is speaking of the Jews (those already in the house), and Luke is speaking of the gentiles (those who enter), is to turn a simple similitude into a conscious allegory. It is sufficient explanation that the Evangelists use the figure in terms of the scenes they and their readers know. The meaning is the obvious and simple one concerning the purpose of a light, which purpose will determine its use, and the application should not go beyond this.[38]

The application is indicated in Matthew, at least as it was understood in the church, by the words, "You are the light of the world. . . . Let your light so shine before men." In its setting this is said to the disciples. Its meaning is emphasized by the intrusion of the other metaphor of the city on the hill. In that exposed position it *cannot* be hid; with the lamp the point is that it *ought not* to be hid. In this sense it applies to every Christian and has a continuing valid meaning. But did it originally have this individual reference? I have indicated earlier why I believe the primary reference of such sayings for Jews would have been corporate. To interpret Matthew 5:16 as addressed to individuals does not harmonize (as Dodd has pointed out) with Jesus' deprecation of individual ostentation in religion. It is free of this difficulty if it is taken to mean the corporate national witness to God, in response to which mankind will praise God for the blessing his people have brought to the world. This is in line with the earliest statement of Israel's call in Genesis 12:2-3 (J): "I will make of you a great nation, and I will bless you, and make your name great, so that you will be a blessing . . . and by you all the families of the earth will bless themselves." This interpretation of the parable would be again an attack on the constant attempt to hedge Israel in and, in the terms of the parable, to hide its light. Again, as in the parables considered earlier, such criticism is based on Israel's nature and God's purpose for it, without which it has no meaning—as a lamp has no meaning unless it be used to diffuse its light. This, likewise, is the only raison d'être for the church, God's new Israel.

To attempt to narrow the application to the hiding of the Law under the Tradition (Dodd, followed by B. T. D. Smith) tends to be too allegorical by seeking too closely to identify the lamp. The similitude must be treated as similitude: As a lighted lamp is meant to be exposed where it will cast its light, so Israel is intended to be on display before the world to give illumination to the nations and to draw men's attention to God. It is interesting that Matthew, who by general consent expresses the Hebrew Gospel, most nearly sets out what seems to have been the original application. His drawing together of the two similitudes of Salt and Lamp indicates their parallel meaning.

The historic situation of Israel, when the parable is taken as addressed *to the people*, is sufficient explanation of the warning, particularly since it turns upon the use of a simile which involves the idea of purpose. The choice of the simile has this primary reason and has a wide Old Testament precedent. The servant of Yahweh is designed to be given "as a light to the nations (Isa. 49:6)" and "a dimly burning wick he will not quench (42:3)." The righteousness of Israel is to shine out: "For Zion's sake I will not keep silent, . . . until her vindication goes forth as brightness, and her salvation as a burning torch. The nations shall see your vindication, and all the kings your glory (Isa. 62:1-2)." Judging by Matthew's version, it is here surely, rather than in references to the Word or to posterity as a lamp (Ps. 119:105; 132:17; 1 Kings 15:4), that the precedent is to be found. The simile needs no justification apart from itself, but when a traditional use is to be allowed as influencing the hearers, the passages quoted afford sufficient endorsement of the application. It later, very properly, came to be applied to the gospel of Christ and those who exemplified it:

> And even if our gospel is veiled, it is veiled only to those who are perishing. In their case the god of this world has blinded the minds of the unbelievers, to keep them from seeing the light of of the gospel of the glory of Christ, who is the likeness of God.... For it is the God who said, "Let light shine out of darkness," who has shone in our hearts to give the light of the knowledge of the glory of God in the face of Christ (2 Cor. 4:3-4, 6). "Among whom you shine as lights in the world (Phil. 2:15)."

When we consider earlier and later use of the simile, we see by contrast with what certainty and clarity Jesus used it, bringing out the essential feature that a lamp, like salt, is meaningless unless it can fulfill its one and only purpose. The same emphasis, as we have seen, appears elsewhere: the fig tree is designed to bear fruit, a vineyard owner properly expects fruit from his establishment, and a trust is intended to be used to advantage. The reiteration suggests that Jesus offered to his people and their leaders not only a series of warnings but a central determinative philosophy of national existence which he believed was God's intention. The positive element in his teaching here is the underlying faith that what God has planned he will carry out, and what he purposes will be accomplished. "Hitherto you have asked nothing in my name; ask, and you will receive (John 16:24)." But to stand aside is to be lost. To neglect the one thing that justifies national existence is to lose all meaning, to be shut out from God's purpose of a new age, to be lost indeed.

The repeated emphasis is put into parable form where it cannot be escaped, as if Jesus would say (as the Fourth Gospel makes him say), "If I have told you earthly things and you do not believe, how can you believe if I tell you heavenly things? (John 3:12)." And yet it was Jesus' *right* to speak in this way which seemed incredible to his hearers, and the responsible leaders must take note of his presumption unless he can substantiate his parables by something more than his own words. The parables that have bearing on this aspect of Jesus' struggle will conclude our study.

# SEVEN THE RESPONSE OF GOD'S PEOPLE

It is necessary in conclusion to examine only the parables in which Jesus deals with the response to his work. They consist of those that resist the demand for a supernatural sign and call for vigilance and caution. They present the joy and trust and final assurance that response to Jesus makes possible.

The parables to be dealt with are gathered from many parts of the Gospels, and the attempt to place them chronologically is hazardous. Their general relationship is that each in some respect deals with the acceptance or rejection of Jesus' appeal, an acceptance or rejection, in the last analysis, of Jesus himself. This is the theme with which any study of the Gospels must end.

It is evident from the parables previously considered that Jesus taught with authority, an authority which, together with his activity, constituted an implicit claim. This was the people's impression (e.g., Mark 12:7: "And they were all amazed, so that they questioned among themselves, saying, 'What is this? a new teaching! With authority he commands even the unclean spirits, and they obey him' "). In the later stages of his ministry Jesus forced himself on the attention of the Jerusalem authorities, and the parables were one means by which he did so. Questions must arise, not only concerning the "cleansing" of the temple but about the tone of Jesus' teaching. "By what authority are you doing these things, or who gave you this authority to do them?" (Mark 11:28; cf. Matt. 21:23; Luke 20:2).

We have seen, however, that apart from the inescapable viewpoint of the church which tended to make Jesus' claim explicit, that claim is only *implicit* in the parables. There was no need for Jesus to attract attention and present himself as an "offense" to the leaders, aside from his own inner compulsion and his understanding of God's will. He returned again and again to the attack as if insistent on precipitating a crisis. This is not the place to consider the activities of the Passion story. In the parables, as was observed at the outset, we find no open declaration of his own person or nature. Many signs of later interpretation arise which are suspect as the work of Christian apologetic. They are valuable for understanding the life situation of the early Christian community. We have seen, also, that some of these indications are perhaps original to the parables when treated simply as parables. They have been read as christological elements because centuries of christological interpretation make it difficult for us to detach them from this context and look at them in their original setting, the life and time of Jesus. The point is that there is no single parable dealing with Jesus' own person, and yet we may well assume that a parable with that theme would have been preserved had there been one. The very fact that other parables have been used for this purpose strongly suggests that no parable existed that dealt primarily with Jesus' personal claim.[1]

The Jerusalem authorities, however, did not need an explicit claim to messiahship to be forced to action, much as they might need it at the trial. Their refusal of Jesus' appeal and their resistance to his charges find sufficient ground in the teaching of the parables alone. They were confronted with a situation that demanded action. When we consider the messianic atmosphere of the times, manifest in the apocalyptic literature, we can see that one who so clearly taught and acted as in the midst of a crisis which portended the breaking in of a new age should be capable of justifying his attitude by a "sign," some evidence of an otherworldly character (cf. Mark 13:4; Matt. 24:3; Luke 11:16; 21:7). Jesus' response is clear evidence that the demand was made. He refused to provide the proof which his enemies required. The demand for it was, to him, but another sign of the wickedness of that generation (Mark 8:11-12; Matt. 16:1, 4; Luke 11:16, 29; Matt. 12:38-39). The signs expected might, indeed, lead men farther astray (cf. Mark 13:5, 24; Matt. 24:4, 24). And yet, for Jesus, the warnings were clear and were to be found elsewhere. It is in this context that the first parables to be considered find their application.

## THE RICH MAN AND LAZARUS
### Luke 16

[19]"There was a rich man, who was clothed in purple and fine linen and who feasted sumptuously every day. [20]And at his gate lay a poor man named Lazarus, full of sores, [21]who desired to be fed with what fell from the rich man's table; moreover the dogs came and licked his sores. [22]The poor man died and was carried by the angels to

Abraham's bosom. The rich man also died and was buried; <sup>23</sup>and in Hades, being in torment, he lifted up his eyes, and saw Abraham far off and Lazarus in his bosom. <sup>24</sup>And he called out, 'Father Abraham, have mercy upon me, and send Lazarus to dip the end of his finger in water and cool my tongue; for I am in anguish in this flame.' <sup>25</sup>But Abraham said, 'Son, remember that you in your lifetime received your good things, and Lazarus in like manner evil things; but now he is comforted here, and you are in anguish. <sup>26</sup>And besides all this, between us and you a great chasm has been fixed, in order that those who would pass from here to you may not be able, and none may cross from there to us.' <sup>27</sup>And he said, 'Then I beg you, father, to send him to my father's house, <sup>28</sup>for I have five brothers, so that he may warn them, lest they also come into this place of torment.' <sup>29</sup>But Abraham said, 'They have Moses and the prophets; let them hear them.' <sup>30</sup>And he said, 'No, father Abraham; but if some one goes to them from the dead, they will repent.' <sup>31</sup>He said to him, 'If they do not hear Moses and the prophets, neither will they be convinced if some one should rise from the dead.' "

Probably there is no parable that tempts the preacher to extravagances more than this, when it is taken literally as Jesus' description of the situation beyond the grave. When it is so taken, it bristles with difficulties involved in reconciling its meaning with the rest of Jesus' teaching. Its uniqueness in the body of his sayings seems to call for explanation. It is another example of the difficulty that arose when the parables were transmitted apart from their original context.

There appear to be two distinct parts to the story, namely, verses 19-26 and 27-31, and the latter half has been under suspicion as a later addition. In that case the first section would be a simple story concerning the reversal of human lots in the afterlife and the finality of that reversal; the second section would be explained as commentary on the failure of the Jews to be converted by the resurrection of Jesus and their blindness to the true teaching of their own scriptures ("Moses and the prophets"). In neither instance could we call the material a parable as we have understood parable.

The key is to be found in the treatment B. T. D. Smith and other commentators have offered.[2] These reveal verses 19-26 to be parallel to a popular tale current not only in Palestine but in Egypt and the Near East generally. The reversal of fortunes after death has always been a common theme and still constitutes an element in the popular mythology of heaven and hell. There is no reason why Jesus should not have been aware of such stories, nor why he was not at liberty to use them. The most striking parallel (because it reveals so clearly the teaching that a careful examination of the first part of the Gospel passage makes clear) is that adduced by Smith from rabbinic literature, which goes back to an Egyptian tale.[3] In Askelon a dream was vouchsafed to a certain man concerning the contrast between the funeral of his pious friend and that of a publican. The godly man had had a meager funeral, ignored by all, in spite of his exemplary life. The tax collector's funeral, on the other hand, had been magnificent. The reason for this, made clear by the dream, was that the godly man had once made the error of putting on his phylacteries in the wrong order and the poor funeral was his punishment; the publican had once admitted the poor to a banquet when his original guests did not appear, and the magnificence of his funeral was his reward. The point is that the reward of an isolated good deed and the punishment of an isolated fault are duly meted out *in this world.* There is no chance that there should be the slightest detraction from the fit reward and punishment *in the world to come.* The good or evil that predominates is *there* rewarded or punished. Occasional deviations are rewarded or punished *here.* This is shown by the vision of the state of the two characters in their future life.

This emphasis on the complete disseverance of the life of this world and the life to come involving thorough-going reward or punishment is present in the Gospel story. In all probability Jesus is using a current tale. Without the concluding verses (vs. 27-31) there would be nothing about it characteristic of Jesus.

The picture of the rich man (who later acquired the name "Dives" to match the naming of Lazarus) is clearly intended to make the same point. He is rich, he wears expensive clothing, and his festivity is not occasional but constant ("feasted sumptuously every day," v. 19). When he dies, he is buried; to the very end all that a man could wish for is his. If he is a sinner no retribution has overtaken him, and he does not even suffer indignity in his dead body. On the other hand, nothing good befalls Lazarus in his lifetime. He is a beggar, dependent on others even for his place outside the rich man's house (he is "laid" or dropped down at the gate, *ebebleto*). His hope is to maintain himself on what the rich man and his guests throw away—the pieces of bread used in lieu of table napkins[4]—and the implication is that he is disappointed. He is so helpless that he cannot even protect himself from the dogs.

After death the reversal is complete. It is the rich man who is now in need and becomes the suppliant. The poor man is reclining with Abraham[5] in a state of bliss, enjoying the consummation of all Jewish hopes and able to observe the woes of the damned. The rich man, with an apparently corporeal body, is suffering the torments of fire and thirst, tantalized by the sight of those in bliss. He claims his standing as a Jew by addressing Abraham as "Father," and Abraham acknowledges him as such by replying "Son" (or "Child"). He modestly asks only minor relief, and perhaps it is a compliment to Lazarus rather than persistent presumption (as some have supposed) that he asks for Lazarus to be the messenger. But even minor alleviation is impossible; there is a gulf that cannot be crossed even though each side is in sight and sound of the other. But the real reason is not geographical or geological. The gulf, so to speak, is in the nature of things (v. 25). "Son, remember that you *in your lifetime* received your good things, and Lazarus in like manner evil things." There is no need to debate whether one was good and the other evil in the world. The point is the enjoyment or lack of all outward signs of comfort and good fortune—which, to the Jew, were in themselves evidence of God's approval or disapproval (cf. the assumption of the rich young ruler, Mark 10:20). The reversal is final.

If we assume this to be a popular tale adopted by Jesus for his own purposes, we need not go into detail about the viewpoint expressed in the scene and dialogue. We are on very uncertain ground if we assume it to involve Jesus' view of the life of the world to come. We probably cannot press it as the conclusive Jewish viewpoint of the time. Dr. Abrahams says, "The question as to the exact physical conditions of life after death has often divided Jewish opinion."[6] There was no settled doctrine that repentance after death was impossible. The Sadducees did not admit belief in the resurrection as the Pharisees did, and there is something to be said for the view that this parable is directed against the Sadducees rather than, as Luke 16:14 would imply, against the Pharisees.

So far, then, we may say that Jesus is using well-known and popular material. The story is complete, in this sense, with verse 26 and its affirmation of finality. But in verse 27 the conversation continues and takes another turn. The rich man, unable to mitigate his own misfortune, would like to warn his brothers. Lazarus, in his request, would "warn them." Just what that warning would be is not made clear. If the Sadducees with their doubts of the resurrection are in view, the testimony would initially be a proof that there was an afterlife to be taken into account. This the rich man himself had apparently not done. "Lest they also come into this place of torment," however, suggests that the testimony would include a warning of the state of affairs to be expected. The rich man expresses in verse 30 what he has in mind: "If some one goes to them from the dead, they will repent"; that is, the apparition of one of the departed would be a sign sufficient to warn them and recover them even though they had ignored the scriptures. The phrase, "Moses and the prophets," again suggests the Sadducees, since this was their sole reliance. But Abraham denies the effectiveness of the sign: "If they do not hear Moses and the prophets, neither will they be convinced if some one should rise from the dead." In other words, they have sufficient warning, and if that is ineffective nothing else will do. A supernatural sign will be of no avail.

Before we can proceed to the meaning of the passage as parable, we must consider two points. It has been held that verse 31, "If some one should rise from the dead," is a clear reference to the resurrection of Jesus. But the natural meaning of the story as it stands is, of course, that the one who is to "rise" is Lazarus ("send him to my father's house"). Some manuscripts read (v. 31), "If one go (*apelthē*) from the dead" in place of "rise (*anastē*) from the dead." Though Creed ascribes this to the influence of "go" *(poreuthē),* in verse 30, it does suggest that the verse has not always been taken to refer to the resurrection. Indeed, there seems no *necessity* so to read it, apart from the predominating power of that event to cause us to view everything in its light. The parable may mean no more than appears on the surface—a supernatural event, an apparition, a messenger from the other world.[7]

The second point is the naming of the poor man. Since Lazarus is also the name of the brother of Mary and Martha of Bethany, whom Jesus, according to John 11, raised from the dead four days after his decease, it has been supposed that the name here is dependent on that story. Another possibility may be suggested, however: not that the *name* Lazarus was applied to the brother in the Fourth Gospel in dependence on this parable, but that the *story* about the raising of Lazarus of Bethany is dependent on this parable in somewhat the same way that the story about the withered fig tree depends on the parable of the Barren Fig Tree. In each case an incident becomes a later reflection on the earlier teaching. In each case the incident confirms the teaching. The fig tree withers as Jesus' parable indicated it must. According to the Fourth Gospel the appearance of Lazarus of Bethany from the dead does perhaps convince a few of the Jews (John 11:45), but its major result is to arouse opposition to Jesus (vs. 46-53). So, far from proving an effective sign, it makes it necessary for Jesus to hide himself (vs. 54-57).

The name Lazarus is a brief form of Eleazar which means, "God is my help." In the story it probably emphasizes the pathetic fact that the poor man has no help but God. The dialogue is more easily carried on with the help of the name. Though it is the only case where a character in a parable is named, we need look no further than the freedom of Jesus to name the character or the freedom of the Evangelist to add the name, and in either case for its value as a name with a meaning and as a literary aid. It is not beside the point, however, to observe that the one who is to go as messenger from the dead is identified by name, and it strains the story as it stands to suppose that a supernatural being is contemplated. If the name is attributed to Luke, it still precludes the thought that the risen Christ was intended.

If we should explain the parable down to verse 26 as a popular tale used by Jesus with, at verse 27, a surprise ending, we then have to answer the objection that Jesus is endorsing the views of the folk tale. This does not appear a serious difficulty if we try to imagine the situation and remember that parables were used in part to "get through the guard." The hearers would find themselves approving the first phase of the story and be quite unprepared for the second phase.[8] In effect Jesus is saying, Your own story tells of the conclusiveness of death and the futility of expecting any result beyond that earned here; all the more reason, therefore, to heed Moses and the prophets, since not even a ghostly apparition or a miraculous revivification would touch those who are indifferent to the revelation of God already given. It says again that no sign will be given because no sign would avail. The story serves its purpose, not only because it holds attention and meets with popular approval but because it makes the point that what happens here and now is conclusive. The time comes when it is too late to repent. Every warning is given in the scriptures of the need not only for repentance but also for rendering to God the service for which he prepares us. If the burden of Moses and the prophets—the whole genius of Israel—has no influence, then those who remain unmoved will not be changed even by a supernatural sign.

Interpreted in this way, the difficulties diminish and the parable takes its place in Jesus' campaign. It is a parable because it argues that as the situation depicted in the story told is true, so with the situation that Jesus confronts. The demand for a sign is adroitly refused and the reason given. Not only would a sign of supernatural origin be unavailing; men are expected to respond to the revelation they have and not to postpone response on the ground that they have not been sufficiently assured of its eternal truth or supernatural origin. If they cannot recognize and respond to the truth when they meet it, there is little likelihood that their response to a more unusual (and amoral) manifestation will be worth having even if it could be secured. It would be a response arising out of fear rather than conviction.

We can hardly read the passage in this sense and fail to be reminded of Jesus' refusal of the temptation to cast himself down from a pinnacle of the temple in the wilderness story. We should not forget that right to the end, according to the Passion story, even on the cross, he was still challenged to offer a sign, with the promise that it would be met by instant belief. "So also the chief priests mocked him . . . saying, 'He saved others; he cannot save himself. Let the Christ, the King of Israel, come down now from the cross, that we may see and believe' (Mark 15:31-32)." It is also significant that among the first results of Jesus' resurrection was a new interest on the part of his followers in "Moses and all the prophets" (Luke 24:25-27). No doubt this new interest itself led to interpretation and use of this present parable as apologetic against the Jews who failed to respond to Jesus or to find in the scriptures the prophecy of his coming as the Christ. But this fact does not force us to the conclusion that the latter part was an afterthought of the church. Its genius is that of Jesus and of Jesus alone. In any case the New Testament record itself is very clear that there were no resurrection appearances to any but Jesus' own followers, so that his appearance to the Jews to persuade them is an argument that does not arise.[9] It was the testimony of the Christians to the (death and) resurrection of Jesus that failed to move the majority, not the rising of "some one from the dead." The crucifixion rather than the resurrection was the stumbling block that prevented the Jews from accepting Jesus as Messiah. But the crucifixion was the result of his work and teaching. The demand for a sign of his authority was part of the opposition that he faced. He diagnosed it as a refusal based not simply on lack of convincing authority but on something more fundamental—refusal to believe and to repent.

Once again, though the historic setting throws light on the parable, we cannot isolate it in its original setting and leave it there. Every parable was occasioned by the situation and must first be understood by its help. The genius of Jesus, however, is not limited to his polemical skill but is revealed by the endurance of the truths he first enunciated in the heat of action. This truth of the valueless sign is as pertinent now as it was then. We are still disturbed about authority and authorities. An authority enthroned as supreme *by that act* becomes invalid and ineffective and raises doubts about its ultimate nature—as attempts to enthrone the church and the Bible as absolute should have taught us. Still more, the refusal to believe and to act pending a testimony beyond our human experience is likely to be a symptom of refusal for some ulterior reason rather than an exhibition of detached rationality. Jesus is here, in resisting a move of the opposition to discredit him, putting his unerring finger also upon a perennial weakness of the human will.

Jesus elsewhere characterizes the inability or unwillingness to accept the sufficient signs which already exist and makes a further and more positive claim concerning what was happening unperceived—if we may so phrase it—"right under their noses." The demand for a sign is an implicit claim on the part of those who make it that they are ready to respond to a new age if only they can be assured by a sufficient testimony that it is about to happen. Jesus questions this.

## THE FIG TREE IN BUD

### Matthew 24
[32]"From the fig tree learn its lesson: as soon as its branch becomes tender and puts forth its leaves, you know that summer is near. [33]*So also, when you see all these things, you know that he is near, at the very gates."*

### Mark 13
[28]"From the fig tree learn its lesson: as soon as its branch becomes tender and puts forth its leaves, you know that summer is near. [29]*So also, when you see these things taking place, you know that he is near, at the very gates."*

### Luke 21
[29]*And he told them a parable:* "Look at the fig tree, and all the trees; [30]as soon as they come out in leaf, you see for yourselves and know that the summer is already near. [31]*So also, when you see these things taking place, you know that the kingdom of God is near."*

The opening of this similitude is rather unusual, "From the fig tree learn its lesson," and for it Luke substitutes a more usual formula. Luke also adds, "And all the trees," which is explained perhaps by his unfamiliarity with Judea or the question likely to arise for his readers as to why the fig tree was chosen. The fig tree belongs to the local scene, and the similitude itself causes no difficulty. When the tree began to awaken and its leaves to appear, men felt that summer had really started to come. In my childhood in England there was a saying current that seems to me an exact analogy: "Never cast a clout till the may's out!" The "may" was the blossom of the hawthorn. When it appeared, summer was no longer tentative but certain; then, and not before, it was safe to change one's winter clothing. The leafing out of the fig tree was likewise a certain sign which could be accepted with assurance. It guaranteed that summer was about to begin.

The difficulty arises over the setting and the application given in verse 29 of Mark: "So also, when you see these things taking place, you know that he [or it?] is near, at the very gates." Something is a certain sign of something, as certain as the fig tree in bud is a sign of summer. But what? It is likely that this verse takes its form from the necessity to fit the similitude to the discourse that precedes it. The earlier part of Mark 13 contains "the Little Apocalypse" with its apocalyptic signs, the description of tribulation and of the consummation. It ends (vs. 26-27) with the coming of the Son of man. It has been observed that this coming itself can hardly be what is referred to in "these things taking place," but the signs of that coming. The verses that follow are a collection of sayings somewhat separate in themselves but linked together by the Evangelist. We have already referred (see the parable of the Farmer and the Growing Seed in Chapter Three) to verse 32, in which knowledge of the day and hour is denied. The remaining verses emphasize the unexpectedness of the coming. With this the similitude seems on the surface to disagree.

Apart from its rather artificial context, we should probably interpret the similitude as one designed to illustrate in what sense Jesus used the words, "The time is fulfilled, and the kingdom of God is at hand (Mark 1:15)." It is in this sense that the kingdom is "at hand," the sense of something already on the way, the first sure evidences of which may be observed. Like the leaves of the fig tree, which testify that summer is so near that it has already started to show signs of its presence, so there are evidences that the kingdom of God is beginning to make its presence known. We can only compare Jesus' words, from Q, "If it is by the Spirit [or "finger"—Luke] of God that I cast out demons, then the kingdom of God has come upon you" (Matt. 12:28; Luke 11:20). The impact of Jesus' own presence was a sign, and he pointed to his own "works" to reinforce his teaching (cf. John 10:38; 14:11). The attempt of his enemies to ascribe powers, the actuality of which they could not deny, to a compact with evil spirits may be taken as another sign of that unwillingness to believe of which we spoke above, and which merited Jesus' scornful analysis (Mark 3:23-26). The similitude may be understood as a parallel to Jesus' complaint, "You hypocrites! You know how to interpret the appearance of earth and sky; but why do you not know how to interpret the present time? (Luke 12:56)." It indicates the presence of something which could not be missed except by those who wanted to overlook it. "The kingdom of God is in the midst of you (Luke 17:21)." Perhaps "in your midst" is the best interpretation of the sense in which these much-debated words are used, for that sense seems to be in keeping with many of the parables.[10] If the certain signs of the kingdom were present as clearly as Jesus seems to suggest, then they could not always be ignored. To refuse to see them sooner or later would mean to reject not merely the signs but that to which they pointed—the kingdom of God itself. The parables that speak of its being taken away from the nation now appear to speak of no arbitrary act of God but of something that is inevitable because it is the removal of what is not really wanted— like the talent taken from the man who had revealed that he did not care for the trust it involved. And since Jesus is speaking of signs which in the last analysis are occasioned by his presence, this refusal must become the refusal of himself. It begins to appear, indeed, that Jesus is intending to force the issue, to leave his opponents finally no alternative.

The sense in which Jesus used the terms, "If it is by the finger of God . . . then the kingdom of God has come upon you," is made more clear by another brief parable.

## THE STRONG MAN

### Matthew 12
[29]"Or how can one enter a strong man's house and plunder his goods, unless he first binds the strong man? Then indeed he may plunder his house."

### Mark 3
[27]"But no one can enter a strong man's house and plunder his goods, unless he first binds the strong man; then indeed he may plunder his house."

### Luke 11
[21]"When a strong man, fully armed, guards his own palace, his goods are in peace; [22]but when one stronger than he assails him and overcomes him, he takes away his armor in which he trusted, and divides his spoil."

The saying would appear to have been found in both Mark and Q. The form in Matthew is quite similar to that in Mark except that it is cast in the form of a question. That in Luke is quite distinct. The variation is of little moment. Luke's picture is a more elaborated one and presupposes a situation more developed and military than the domestic setting of the Marcan version. The question form in

Matthew is more akin to a similitude, and the form in Luke more nearly approaches a narrative. In either case the point conveyed is clear. The man who is strong can protect his house and its contents so long as no superior force is brought to bear. The enemy who would plunder his camp or the thief who would rob his house must first overcome the strong man and fetter him so that he can no longer interfere.[11]

The Evangelists provide what would otherwise be either an obscure saying or trite observation with a setting that makes it important. It occurs in the debate on exorcism occasioned, in Mark, by the accusation of "the scribes who came down from Jerusalem" (3:22) that Jesus casts out demons by the power of the "prince of demons." In Mark, Jesus replies "in parables," but the phrase there means cryptic or proverbial sayings: "If a kingdom is divided against itself, that kingdom cannot stand," etc. Jesus points out that there can be only two explanations of the power to cast out demons.[12] In each case the result is the same, namely, Satan's kingdom is doomed. If one in league with the adversary undoes the adversary's work, the kingdom of evil is doomed. If, on the other hand, the power is of God, then even more certainly the result is the same.

The saying we are considering shows that Jesus claims the second of the two alternatives. The fact that Satan's work is undone shows that a stronger than Satan has taken control and Satan's power is at an end. It was a tenet of Jewish thought that the end of the adversary's power meant the coming of God's kingdom. Jesus here expresses this belief in picturesque form, not as a general truth but as an experience to be experienced. Its importance comes from the association with his own work, and it is to this he points. His work has attracted attention, but his opponents refuse to read its obvious meaning—that the kingdom of God has broken into history, that it is "at hand," that its effect is already being felt in their midst.

There is always a tendency to turn to this passage, taken apart from its context, as a support for arguments that favor a strong military and naval establishment.[13] Taken as a similitude, with its meaning found in its settings, it is obviously useless for this purpose. When Jesus in the parables uses an observed fact of human life, he does not necessarily endorse human life as he finds it—any more than he endorses the shrewdness of the characters in his parables or the views expressed in the story on which the Rich Man and Lazarus is based. He appeals to the human situation and asks if it is not so on that plane. This is clearest in the question form of the saying in Matthew. As soon as we ask *how much more* true it is in the spiritual realm, we come face to face with the end of all human devices. To the Jew the things of this world were under the control of the enemy, and Jesus proclaims the end of that situation and the beginning of a new age. So that the end of all reliance on human might is implied here rather than its endorsement.

Once again Jesus asks his contemporaries to look about them. The signs are there, but even when they see them they attribute them to evil and refuse to see their true significance. This is not only an "eternal sin" (Mark 3:28-30) and an obstruction to God's work (Matt. 12:30) but an attitude that no further signs could alter. With Jesus' presence and work the kingdom of God is known to be operative. It is useless to ask whether Jesus brings the kingdom or the kingdom brings Jesus. The two are concomitants. Jesus is both Agent and Manifestation. Neither does the activity of the kingdom as a present reality preclude the fact that it is yet to come in its fullness and the consummation of history to be brought to pass.

An analogy can be found in what has often happened in military campaigns, when a hitherto uncontrollable invader in conquered territory has been defeated and thus proved already to have lost his hold, although much campaigning remains yet to be suffered before the war can be ended in victory. Much arduous work remains, many lives will yet be sacrificed, long crises endured and dark days met, but the enemy is no longer invincible.[14] In some such sense we may understand this parable. In the sphere to which our Lord belonged, the victory has been achieved. In our sphere, we "see not all things put under him," but we know the enemy has been vanquished.

There are those who do see and interpret the signs of God's kingdom, who, in Jesus' phrases, "seek" and "enter" the kingdom, and of them certain attitudes are expected. The parables to which we now turn deal with these attitudes. Earlier we have seen that Jesus warned against interference and against aloofness, commending wholehearted commitment. The joy that such commitment brings is suggested in a short similitude.

## THE WEDDING GUESTS

### Matthew 9
[14]*Then the disciples of John came to him, saying, "Why do we and the Pharisees fast, but your disciples do not fast?"* [15]*And Jesus said to them, "Can the wedding guests mourn as long as the bridegroom is with them? The days will come, when the bridegroom is taken away from them, and then they will fast."*

### Mark 2
[18]*Now John's disciples and the Pharisees were fasting; and the*

*people came and said to him, "Why do John's disciples and the disciples of the Pharisees fast, but your disciples do not fast?"* [19]*And Jesus said to them, "Can the wedding guests fast while the bridegroom is with them? As long as they have the bridegroom with them they cannot fast.* [20]*The days will come, when the bridegroom is taken away from them, and then they will fast in that day."*

## Luke 5
[33]*And they said to him, "The disciples of John fast often and offer prayers, and so do the disciples of the Pharisees, but yours eat and drink."* [34]*And Jesus said to them, "Can you make wedding guests fast while the bridegroom is with them?* [35]*The days will come, when the bridegroom is taken away from them, and then they will fast in those days."*

It is well known that Mark 2:1 to 3:6 form a collection of stories dealing with the causes of opposition to Jesus. We have seen their relation in Mark's scheme to the introduction of the passage on teaching by parables which uses the Sower as its first major example. They have no necessary chronological connection and provide an uncertain basis for conclusions based on their position in Mark.

In its present form (most clearly in Luke) the similitude appears as a discussion of fasting and has been attacked as a construction of the early church to justify its practice. Some would eliminate, on this basis, all but the words (Mark 2:19a), "Can the wedding guests fast while the bridegroom is with them?" It might then be a general observation of the inappropriateness of fasting when the messianic banquet had already begun, when the kingdom of God had already made its appearance. The rest of the passage, including the occasion (v. 18), would be later elaboration and an attempt to justify the revival of fasting by the Christians. In this sense "the bridegroom" would be the heavenly Bridegroom, the Christ. However, in Christian thought the Bridegroom is yet to come to claim his bride, the church.

It has been suggested that the combination of the disciples of John with the Pharisees indicates the passage was originally connected with a fast in mourning for the Baptist rather than a regular Jewish fast ("mourn" in Matt. 9:15) which has been adapted to deal with the broader question by references in each Gospel to the Pharisees in order that it may fit into the series of stories. Be that as it may, we can see how the basic point has been developed to fit the later purpose of the church. The basic similitude consists in the question of Mark, verse 19a and parallels, "Can the wedding guests fast while the bridegroom is with them?" It may even be a proverbial saying of which Jesus was making use. The rest of verse 19, peculiar to Mark, is a pretty obvious gloss providing an answer where none is needed. Verse 20 is equally obvious but has been introduced to justify the practice of fasting by Christians in solemn recognition of the cross. The simple question of Mark (v. 19a) as scarcely permitting anything but one answer and consistent with experience is typical of what we have seen to be Jesus' method. The emphasis is on the presence of the bridegroom which occasions a feast. Taken apart from its context, the saying deals with a joy akin to that of guests in the presence of the person who occasions the festivity (in the East the bridegroom was the center of interest rather than the bride). Such a joyful occasion obviously precludes fasting. The fact that it is a short-term occasion is not really part of the figure but as clearly provides the point onto which a developed application could be attached.

The saying would obviously be preserved for its value in Christian discussion of fasting. The association with Christ as bridegroom would be almost inevitable. We may read it in the first instance, however, as Jesus' emphasis on the joy that the kingdom produces. Fasting has its place, but not in the presence of him who reveals the kingdom to be in their midst.

Self-identification on the part of Jesus as the bridegroom is impossible to conceive. His audience would take the saying to refer to the ordinary case and extend no further than the plain meaning of the words. Otherwise "the bridegroom" would have to suggest to them, in Old Testament terms, Yahweh as the bridegroom of Israel, and it is altogether unlikely that they would suppose Jesus to be referring to himself as God or even as God's Messiah. The attitude of joyful response which precludes fasting is the immediate point of significance, and that it is associated with the presence of him who is the cause for the occasion.[15] In short, Jesus here implicitly claims to determine times and seasons.

To respond to the signs which exist, to be aware of the reality with which the presence of Christ confronts one, and to enter into its joy—this requires constant alertness and instant service. Jesus brings this home in four similitudes, which we may consider as a group (pages 175-80).

## THE THIEF
### Matthew 24
[43]"But know this, that if the householder had known in what part of the night the thief was coming, he would have watched and would not have let his house be broken into. *"There you also must be ready; for the Son of man is coming at an hour you do not expect."*

**Luke 12**
[39]"But know this, that if the householder had known at what hour the thief was coming, he would have been awake and would not have left his house to be broken into. [40]*You also must be ready; for the Son of man is coming at an hour you do not expect.*"

Here Jesus characteristically appeals for a judgment from everyday experience. The opening words could be read, as the NEB aptly renders them, "Remember." There is no need to think that an actual event is in view, as some commentators do. The image is used also at 1 Thessalonians 5:2ff., 2 Peter 3:10, Revelation 3:3 and 16:5.

The saying presents no difficulty except that of its context in Matthew 24.[16] Treated as a similitude in its own right, it suggests that the success of the thief depends upon the lack of warning. If he were expected, he would be unsuccessful. The unexpectedness of his design and descent upon the sleeping household makes constant vigilance necessary. The unexpected nature of the kingdom's impact likewise demands constant preparedness. This is not a clear case of teaching by contraries, for it applies alike to friends and foes of the kingdom, since both, though for different reasons, would like to know in advance when God is to draw near in power. Here in a more unusual form is the theme so often illustrated by the absent and returning proprietor.

## THE DOORKEEPER
**Mark 13**
[34]"It is like a man going on a journey, when he leaves home and puts his servants in charge, each with his work, and commands the doorkeeper to be on the watch. [35]*Watch therefore—for you do not know when the master of house will come, in the evening, or at midnight, or at cockcrow, or in the morning—*[36]*lest he come suddenly and find you asleep.* [37]*And what I say to you I say to all: Watch.*"

The central character of this little similitude is the doorkeeper, upon whom the chief responsibility for watchfulness rests. The other servants are mentioned as having been given authority and each his special work in order to emphasize the particular duty of the man at the gate. The others have their tasks; he has his. He may exhibit other virtues, but none of them is important if he be not vigilant.

It is possible that the similitude extends no farther. The case visualized is again the case of the owner absent on a journey, which need reflect no more than (as has been said before) a favorite theme of Jesus drawn from commonly existing situations. The watchfulness would be necessary to preclude the successful activity of thieves as above, but verse 35 extends it to introduce the warning that the master himself may also come at night, due to the vicissitudes of travel, and he will expect to find the doorkeeper watchful. The exhortation of verse 37 reads like a phrase from a Christian sermon.

The emphasis on the special function of the doorkeeper, in the light of other parables of Jesus, may well have been originally interpreted to apply to the people of God, as having above all others the responsibility to be alert for the coming of God's kingdom or of God's agent that they might prepare others (cf. Ezek. 33:1-7). Certainly we should not be in error to interpret it so of the church, and we can see that it has been legitimately used of the ministry in Christian tradition.

## THE WATCHFUL SERVANTS
### Luke 12

[35]*"Let your loins be girded and your lamps burning,* [36]*and be like men who are waiting for their master to come home from the marriage feast, so that they may open to him at once when he comes and knocks.* [37]*Blessed are those servants whom the master finds awake when he comes; truly, I say to you, he will gird himself and have them sit at table, and he will come and serve them.* [38]*If he comes in the second watch, or in the third, and finds them so, blessed are those servants!"*

The opening verse with its phraseology, more especially used in the sense just referred to of the ministry of the church, would seem to belong more appropriately with the Doorkeeper verses and perhaps has "wandered" in transmission. The whole passage suggests that it embodies a simile, used by Jesus many times, which has become confused in constant reuse. The last part of verse 36, with its knocking on the gate, again suggests the Doorkeeper. In general, however, in this passage a master has gone from the house for only a short time, leaving uncertainty about the precise hour of his return. All is clear except the last part of verse 37, "he will gird himself and . . . come and serve them," which seems to owe something to later reflection on the humility of Christ and suggests the foot-washing scene in John 13:1-16 (one of many instances where John seems an expansion of Luke). Those who are found girded ready for service will *receive* that which they were prepared *to offer.* In John 13, Peter had to suffer the humiliation of receiving *from* Jesus what he should have offered *to* Jesus. Verse 37b reads as a later expansion, in the fuller understanding of Jesus, and as a similitude is the opposite of the Slave in Field and House. The original element is the emphasis on preparation for the unexpected call to service. The stress on service, whether under the master's supervision or not, is more clearly brought out in the next passage.

## THE SERVANT PROMOTED
### Matthew 24

[45]"Who then is the faithful and wise servant, whom his master has set over his household, to give them their food at the proper time? [46]Blessed is that servant whom his master when he comes will find so doing. [47]Truly, I say to you, he will set him over all his possessions. [48]But if that wicked servant says to himself, 'My master is delayed,' [49]and begins to beat his fellow servants, and eats and drinks with the drunken, [50]the master of that servant will come on a day when he does not expect him and at an hour he does not know, [51]and will punish him, and put him with the hypocrites; *there men will weep and gnash their teeth.*"

### Luke 12

[42]*And the Lord said,* "Who then is the faithful and wise steward, whom his master will set over his household, to give them their portion of food at the proper time? [43]Blessed is that servant whom his master when he comes will find so doing. [44]Truly I tell you, he will set him over all his possessions. [45]But if that servant says to himself, 'My master is delayed in coming,' and begins to beat the menservants and the maidservants, and to eat and drink and get drunk, [46]the master of that servant will come on a day when he does not expect him and at an hour he does not know, and will punish him, and put him with the unfaithful."

Another variation is found here, and a further refinement of the point. One of the servants is to be promoted as overseer and caretaker of the rest. Jesus asks (in true parabolic fashion) which slave will be entrusted with this honor and responsibility (Luke 12:42, "will set," *katastēsei*, rather than "has set," *katestēsen*, in Matt. 24:45). Will it be the one who, on his return, he finds already assuming this responsibility (Luke 12:43) or the one who takes advantage of his master's absence to ill-treat his fellow servants and indulge himself (v. 45)? The issue will be decided by the situation that the returning master finds to prevail on his unheralded return. As in the parables of the Talents and the Pounds, reward and punishment are fitted to the behavior. The servant who has taken upon himself, because of the absence of the master, the ordered care of the others will be rewarded by a post in which just that will be his function. The other, to whom the absence afforded not a chance for service but an opportunity for domination and self-gratification, will be surprised in the act and receive severe treatment. Objection has been taken to the closing phrase, "put him with the unfaithful" (v. 46; "hypocrites" in Matt. 24:51), as foretelling hell. It may, however, belong to the similitude, since if the evil servant had expected his master he would have been found, no doubt, acting commendably. His master classifies him where he belongs. One additional phrase in Matthew, "men will weep and gnash their teeth," is a typical addition of that Evangelist.

This theme might have been treated in the previous section, with which it has much in common, but its emphasis on the unexpected return—which is the crux of the story—suggests its treatment here. It does, however, point to an original application to the Jewish church. Jesus' people had always looked for a position of dominance, and their kings and hierarchy in turn, failing to secure it outside, had exercised it within on their fellow countrymen. Whether applied in the first instance to the nation in relation to the world, or to the leaders in relation to the people, the point is the same. God's calling is to responsibility and care, and the critical judgment which determines future function and standing is made without warning. It therefore argues constant employment "so doing." There is every indication throughout the Gospels that Jesus did not find that evidence of qualification for the place in God's economy that is implied here. The discourse commonly known as "the parable of the Sheep and the Goats" (Matt. 25:31-46) indicates that the sin that will bring about rejection is failure to see the opportunity presented for service and surprise to learn that it had existed (Matt. 25:44). That passage and this series of similitudes (which even in their confusion testify to a frequent theme) reveal alike that Jesus found his people guilty of blindness. We can scarcely resist the implication that the interest in a sign was that there might be an advance warning so that reform might be geared to the occasion—which is at least the implication of "An evil and adulterous generation seeks for a sign (Matt. 12:39)," as if to continue in its evil and adultery as long as it could be certain that there was no chance of being surprised in the act!

In the present instance, the introduction in Luke (12:41)—"Peter said, 'Lord, are you telling this parable [the parable of the Thief which precedes] for us or for all?' "—indicates that when the initial situation no longer obtained, the church found this similitude an effective code for the ministry. The story, which provides the answer to the question with which it begins, challenges the hearer to judge for himself. What decision the master in the parable would make is clear. Peter is likewise encouraged to see that the ministry and its authority belong to those who exercise its proper function, or provide orderly, watchful care over the "household."

Thus, in this little series in which the emphasis is always on the unexpected demand of a sudden confrontation, Jesus sets forth the response expected of those who "see," to whom the kingdom is not something that comes "with observation" but is already in their midst. It is an instant response, revealing constant vigilance and the continual preparedness of being engaged in the master's interest. These sayings came to be connected more especially with the "Second Coming" and the Christian ministry, but that does not diminish their initial impact on the situation of Jesus' time and hence on the church as he knew it—and as we know it. Instant concern for the God-given task, expressed in service as diligent as if its Lord knocked at the gate, is the prime presupposition of its life. When Jesus found no such response, there was but one possibility for himself—to take Israel's place—and but one for Israel—to be called to account.

The final suddenness of the demand is set forth in Luke 12:16-20, the "parable of the Rich Fool." It is not strictly a parable, for there is no comparison and the Evangelist's opening and closing verses into which the story is set (vs. 15, 21) indicate what is evident, that the incident is an example, a case in point. It deals with complete absorption in material things.[17] The man has more than he can use, more than he can store, so much that his security seems assured and no further effort is needed on his part. The soliloquy he engages in reveals all this, and the story might be called "The Man Who Talked with Himself." What he has forgotten is cleverly introduced by the words of God. But God breaks into the private conversation; this was what the man said, but *God* said . . . ("your soul" in v. 20 should be taken in the Hebrew sense, "life"). The "many years" on which the man counts are contrasted with God's mention of "this night." His preparation and concern have been for an uninterrupted future, but a crisis breaks in. Its meaning is clear, and its relevance to the situation of Jesus' time. It is not a parable, but the element of absorption that leaves one unprepared for the unexpected action of God further indicates the place this theme had in Jesus' teaching. The wisdom of this world is foolishness in God's world.

When our Lord warns of the danger of ignoring the signs of the kingdom and refusing its call, and speaks of the need for vigilance, he also utters a note of warning to those who would undertake its work and seek to enter the new age. This warning is found in two brief parables of caution.

## THE TOWER BUILDER
Luke 14

[28]"For which of you, desiring to build a tower, does not first sit down and count the cost, whether he has enough to complete it? [29]Otherwise, when he has laid a foundation, and is not able to finish, all who see it begin to mock him, [30]saying, 'This man began to build, and was not able to finish.' "

## THE KING PREPARING FOR WAR
Luke 14

[31]"Or what king, going to encounter another king in war, will not sit down first and take counsel whether he is able with ten thousand to meet him who comes against him with twenty thousand? [32]And if not, while the other is yet a great way off, he sends an embassy and asks terms of peace."

The parables are treated as a pair because the Evangelist has added the moral of Luke 14:33 to both: "So therefore, whoever of you does not renounce all that he has cannot be my disciple." It will be seen that this meaning can be obtained only by forcing the parables, and that the probable explanation is the desire to unite the parables with the preceding discourse on renouncing all to follow Christ (vs. 25-27). There are no parallels in the other Gospels by means of which to discover the meaning. The setting implies a period of popular following, since Jesus addresses his words (v. 25) to the great multitudes who "accompanied him." It suggests something of the spontaneous and unthinking enthusiasm exhibited by three would-be disciples in Luke 9:57-62, two of whom had afterthoughts that disqualified them. "Yes, and even his own life" (v. 26) indicates that the saying teaches the complete renunciation which is taken up again in verse 33.

The parables themselves have a different emphasis. They adopt the characteristic form of questions: "Which of you?" and "What king?" They are again an appeal to the average intelligence, operating on the normal worldly level. In the first case the man, for fear of the mockery that suggests a lost reputation for foresight, quite deliberately makes a preliminary calculation as to whether he can complete the structure. He first sits down, which depicts something different from an occasional hesitation and reflection while the work is in progress. This is a realistic view. It suggests that to be carried away by enthusiasm is not sufficient. Jesus' call involved a great deal; some of what it involved we have seen in other parables. All that could be foreseen in the changed relationships of life, a new sense of values, the doubtfulness of a hard future, and more must be taken into account. The follower must weigh his chances of persistence. But Jesus is not, certainly, referring only to a man's innate abilities but surely also to his faith, his ability to trust God, to put himself entirely in God's hands. Other parables (see below) suggest that this is a factor to which Jesus gave an important place and one which, at Gethsemane, he himself supremely demonstrated. This must be weighed because to withdraw after beginning is more dangerous than to draw back at the start. "No one who puts his hand to the plow and looks back is fit for the kingdom of God (Luke 9:62)." The reasoning is that if this is true of a mundane undertaking, how much more necessary is it for him who would serve the kingdom of God.

The same reasoning is followed in the second parable, though a somewhat different outcome is involved. The question here is not whether to embark on the task of meeting the opposing king. The rival ruler is coming "against him" in any case. The question here is one of method. Shall he take arms and fight it out? Or shall he pay homage and submit to the other's demands (the meaning of the phrase "asks terms of peace")? The question is to be resolved, however, in the same manner. By calculating his own resources and those of his opponent, the king will know whether to engage in war or to capitulate without fighting. It is perhaps implied that some decision relative to the kingdom is involved for all, but the nature of one's commitment must be decided by deliberation.[18]

In each parable some loss is envisaged if one does not feel able to commit himself—in the first case, being without the proposed building; in the second, the restricted life lived under the terms of surrender. We inevitably think of the parables of the Treasure in the Field and the Pearl Merchant. If the parables apply to Israel in the first instance, they will deal with the future to which Israel has been called, the fullness of which cannot be realized without deliberate and full commitment. If they apply (as they always must in the Christian life) to the individual disciple, they will deal with Christian vocation and suggest that the full joy and blessedness of the Christian life can be experienced only by complete commitment in faith. It was for this complete trust that Jesus appealed, rather than establish two levels of Christian discipleship. This is suggested by the two parables next to be examined. In passing we may note the high compliment Jesus paid two of his apostles in spite of their immediate misunderstanding of his purpose. "Are you able to drink the cup that I drink, or to be baptized with the baptism with which I am baptized? . . . The cup that I drink you will drink; and with the baptism with which

I am baptized, you will be baptized (Mark 10:38-39)." Mark and Matthew do not contain the parables, nor does Luke contain the incident of James and John, but the same question is posed in different ways: "Are you able?" It is not complete renunciation so much as complete commitment that is asked, but, in times of crisis like those in which Jesus spoke, complete commitment is likely to involve complete renunciation. Complete abandonment to the cause would not be possible without the assurance that God and all his resources are committed to the undertaking. That is the assurance offered in two whimsical pictures.

## THE FRIEND AT MIDNIGHT
### Luke 11
*5And he said to them,* "Which of you who has a friend will go to him at midnight and say to him, 'Friend, lend me three loaves; *6for a friend of mine has arrived on a journey, and I have nothing to set before him'; 7and he will answer from within, 'Do not bother me; the door is now shut, and my children are with me in bed; I cannot get up and give you anything'? *8I tell you, though he will not get up and give him anything because he is his friend, yet because of his importunity he will rise and give him whatever he needs."*

## THE WIDOW AND THE JUDGE
### Luke 18
*1And he told them a parable, to the effect that they ought always to pray and not lose heart. 2He said,* "In a certain city there was a judge who neither feared God nor regarded man; *3and there was a widow in that city who kept coming to him and saying, 'Vindicate me against my adversary.' 4For a while he refused; but afterward he said to himself, 'Though I neither fear God nor regard man, 5yet because this widow bothers me, I will vindicate her, or she will wear me out by her continual coming.' " 6And the Lord said, "Hear what the unrighteous judge says. 7And will not God vindicate his elect, who cry to him day and night? Will he delay long over them? 8I tell you, he will vindicate them speedily."*

It is editorially indicated that each of these parables is understood as a parable concerning prayer. The first comes between Luke's version of the Lord's Prayer (Luke 11:1-4) and further sayings about petition, and the second is introduced by the words, "He told them a parable, to the effect that they ought always to pray and not lose heart" (18:1). Each parable, taken by itself apart from its context, is based on common experience of the small Oriental village and is full of playful humor. This seems thoroughly characteristic of Jesus in his parables, and it is difficult to ascribe them to anyone but himself. They have also, along with a certain playfulness, a certain daring. To allegorize either would, of course, be fatal, for God would then be depicted as willing to answer persistent prayer because to do so is the lesser of two evils! It is significant that it is in the little similitude in the passage that follows (Luke 11:11-13) that the clue is found to the interpretation of many parables by use of the principle "from the lesser to the greater" or "how much more."[19]

The nature of other parables provide the clue to the first parable, namely, that the whole, to the end of verse 7, is a single question, "Which of you . . . give you anything?" It expects the answer "No one" or "None of us would behave like that" (which the RSV makes clear as previous versions did not). The problem arises in two ways. First there is the manner in which the actors are presented, which probably did not confuse the original audience. The suppliant is the "which of you" who is addressed, in which Jesus appeals to the experience and judgment of his hearers. Second, the problem arises from the understanding of the term used in the application (v. 8) where *anaideian* is commonly translated "importunity" (e.g., RSV) and *understood* to mean "persistence." This misapprehension is influenced by the second parable where, as we shall see, the situation is quite different.

In the first parable we are introduced to a midnight scene in a peasant setting. The villagers have retired and are asleep in their one-room homes, surrounded by their families lying together on the floor. To one comes a hungry traveler and surprises his host without the means of hospitality. Let us call the host "A" and his sleepy neighbor "B." Neighbor A finds himself in an unexpected and grave emergency, the arrival of a guest for whom he can provide no food. A therefore goes to B's door to seek help, in spite of the fact that B has been long abed. He has no hesitation in doing so, for everyone in the East would recognize his predicament as a serious one. The question is not whether A should have disturbed B, but what B will do when A comes. Will B answer that he cannot comply with A's request because of the disturbance it would cause? The obvious answer (to the times) was that, under the circumstances, B would not so reply. Understanding it was a real emergency A faced, he would immediately do what he could to help.

This is understood in verse 8, which is interpretation ("I tell you") rather than part of the parable. It correctly grasps the point of *anaideian* as, literally, "lack of shame," hence, without hesitation. It is because A knows B will respond that he does not hesitate to arouse B, knowing that B will immediately sense his neighbor's straits and come to his aid at any cost of confusion to himself or his family. Not because A is his friend, but because B knows that only a serious matter would enable A to overcome his reluctance and bring him to his door at midnight. There is neither in the parable nor in the interpretation any suggestion that neighbor A has to keep on knocking until, in despair, B is forced to get up and provide the bread. The misinterpretation comes from the persistent belief that prayer has to be *persistent* rather than constantly faithful, a view which finds no support from what follows in Luke (vs. 9-13). It probably comes in part from a transfer to this parable of the content and meaning of the parable about the Widow and the Judge (Luke 18:1-8). In the present case the person applied to is a friend, not one "who neither feared God nor regarded man," as is the case with the judge. Thus there is no question here other than instant response or instant refusal. When the question is put, the answer can be counted on, "He would not so reply; he would not refuse." His night might be disturbed, but that is little to be weighed against the loss of face his neighbor would suffer by being unable to offer even the simplest hospitality.

Properly understood, the parable is an excellent example of the open-ended question which can expect an assured answer and makes possible the application, "How much more . . . ?" As noted above, this principle appears in the context at verse 13, parallel to Matthew 7:11. The parable says, If this is the case among neighbors over a simple matter of lending bread, how much more may we expect God to respond when we ask in need? And this, of course, in Luke, is preceded by his version of the Lord's Prayer (vs. 1-4) and is followed by an explicit statement of the truth drawn out by the parable. "Ask, and it will be given you; seek, and you will find; knock, and it will be opened to you" (v. 9) is precisely illustrated by the parable when its method is understood, as by the further analogy of the father who responds to his son's request. If a neighbor can be counted on in real need, if a father can be counted on to deal kindly with a child, how much more will God respond with equal immediacy, with equal understanding, when our sense of need removes our hesitation or our childlikeness gives confidence that we shall not be deceived or frustrated? Whether we pray to meet need (ask), or pray to understand (seek), or pray to find an open way ahead (knock), it is the same. There is no idea here of a reluctant God who has to be persuaded by constant reiteration (see Matt. 6:7f., the introduction to the Lord's Prayer). There is much more, of course, to be said about prayer, about its content and aim, but of it all this teaching is the groundwork.

The other parable (Luke 18:1-8) is dealt with here, not because it has the same teaching nor, perhaps, even the same subject but because both are related to prayer by Luke's redaction and because they have therefore been treated as a pair or, at least, interpreted together—to the detriment of a true understanding of the first. This tendency is increased by the fact that verses 1-8 are followed by another parable dealing with an aspect of prayer, the Pharisee and the Tax Collector (vs. 9-14).

The editorial introduction (ch. 18:1) applies the parable to the teaching that one ought to keep on praying and not give up (to paraphrase the words). We can well imagine that in the early church, when the Parousia seemed long-delayed, this counsel was necessary. That the Evangelist has something of this in mind, heightened by the suggestion of intense persecution, is shown by the verses that follow the parable proper and fasten upon what is probably a mistaken though possible interpretation of the widow's plea. In verse 3 she begs, "Vindicate me against my adversary" (*ekdikēsov me*). The Greek, judging from contemporary evidence, might well be read, however, "*Do me justice* with regard to my opponent." The idea of vindication is taken up again in verse 7 with reference to the "elect." This is another indication that verses 7-8a are an interpretation applicable to the persecutions suffered by Christians.[20] What is suggested is the provenance of Revelation 6:9-11, where the souls of the martyrs cry from beneath the altar, "How long before thou wilt *judge and avenge* our blood . . . ?" The latter part of Luke 18:8 is a further addition, linking the whole discussion to a preceding section (Luke 17:22ff.). Both at the beginning and at the end it is indicated that the Evangelist felt the parable needed a context. Luke is reproducing here the use to which it had been put in the church. The parable needs a context that indicates the *object* of the prayers, and this is precisely what is provided in Luke 18:7.

The parable, taken alone and ending with verse 5, is strangely free of intensity and has the same peasant-life playfulness of the other parable. An unworthy judge who respects neither God nor man, and therefore is concerned only for his own interests, is pestered for an indefinite time by a widow, in what we may properly assume to be a minor suit (to the judge, not to the widow). Widows were traditionally figures of misfortune in the Bible and were the victims of unscrupulous dealings and of exactly this type of judge (Deut. 24:17; 27:19; Job 24:3, 21; Isa. 10:2, etc.). He ignored the biblical injunction to be no respecter of persons (Deut. 16:18-19; Prov. 24:23). The suppliant, being a widow, was not worth his trouble, since she may be presumed to have been incapable of rewarding him, and we may assume further that it would probably be to his advantage to let her oppressor have his way. In the end, however, her persistent pestering turned the scale. It was more trouble to ignore her than to grant her request and do her justice. He had no interest in her cause except that, after a time, to settle it was less trouble than to endure her dogged application. The scene is adroitly and artistically allowed to speak for itself, in the words that close the parable, by drawing attention to the judge's soliloquy—which is unnecessarily elaborated unless it is the real point: "Hear what the unrighteous judge says."

The scene is different, though from the same village life. The same danger from the use of allegory arises and the same difficulty of interpretation. A context is needed that will indicate that the point of its application is to be found in the *object* of prayer rather than in the *mode* of prayer. Here the judge does not immediately respond because his concern and interest are not involved. His self-interest is much more to the point. He finally acts, not because he has come to see the justice or importance of the widow's case but because it is less trouble, the lesser of two evils.

Only by interpreting the parable by the contrary can it be brought into harmony with what we have deduced to be the general trend of Jesus' teaching. In the case of prayer for the kingdom of God and all that concerns it, both the one who prays and the prayer he offers are of the utmost interest and concern to God. Where the one who prays submits himself thereby to God's will, and where that for which he prays furthers God's kingdom, the whole matter is of instant importance and will receive immediate response. Repetitious prayer represents an unworthy view of God, since it implies that God will yield to pressure, and it becomes a further item in Jesus' criticism that current religious practice was based on an inadequate understanding of God's nature. The Father knows what we need before we ask, and it is the Spirit who teaches us what to ask (Rom. 8:26-27). Jesus is represented in John 15:16 as saying, "You did not choose me, but I chose you and appointed you that you should go and bear fruit and that your fruit should abide; so that whatever you ask the Father in my name, he may give it to you" (cf. John 14:12-14; 16:23-24). The whole meaning here is that what is asked in harmony with Christ's perfect obedience to the Father's will shall be granted (cf. John 15:7).

We may then read these parables in connection with those concerning commitment and, as was said above, we must allow in interpreting the latter for the efficacy Jesus ascribed to the prayer for the kingdom and the kingdom's resources. The act of deliberation which is to precede commitment should make allowance for the fact that the concern for the kingdom is primarily God's, who, if we may say so, is more deeply involved and more heavily committed than we. It is always his gift and dependent on his will, and while persistence may seem to us the most necessary element in our prayers when they concern our own interests, it is a very different matter when our prayers reflect a concern that we share with him and when their aim is the doing of his will. Then the response is instant and certain. For the one and through the one who so prays the answer can be immediate. In his humanity our Lord himself had to learn in Gethsemane what this meant, and learn it to the last syllable.

We conclude our examination of the parables with one which, when interpreted, endorses all that has been said. The note of authority and assurance which is always apparent in the parables here sounds most clearly and with finality.

## THE TWO BUILDERS

### Matthew 7

[24]"Every one then who hears these words of mine and does them will be like a wise man who built his house upon the rock; [25]and the rain fell, and the floods came, and the winds blew and beat upon that house, but it did not fall, because it had been founded on the rock. [26]And everyone who hears these words of mine and does not do them will be like a foolish man who built his house upon the sand; [27]and the rain fell, and the floods came, and the winds blew and beat against that house, and it fell; and great was the fall of it."

### Luke 6

[47]"Every one who comes to me and hears my words and does them, I will show you what he is like: [48]he is like a man building a house, who dug deep, and laid the foundation upon rock; and when a flood arose, the stream broke against that house, and could not shake it, because it had been well built. [49]But he who hears and does not do them is like a man who built a house on the ground without a foundation; against which the stream broke, and immediately it fell, and the ruin of that house was great."

Each Evangelist closes his major collection of Jesus' teaching, the great "sermon," with this parable. It forms the climactic warning that hearing alone is insufficient and must be followed and implemented by action, or what we are accustomed from New Testament usage to call "good works." An examination of the two versions leads to the conclusion that Matthew has preserved the more original form. His is more Hebraic in that it maintains the parallelisms, while Luke's is more influenced by the Greek. Matthew's is the more indigenous, while Luke's generalizes and changes the point from one of choice of a site to digging deep to lay a foundation. Luke has added (v. 47) "comes to me, and" to "hears my words." In verse 48 he has put the emphasis on construction rather than site by introducing the words "because it had been well built," and this is made clear in verse 49 by the words "who built a house on the ground without a foundation," where the site does not matter provided a secure foundation is laid. Matthew's point is that the house is built on rock (v. 24), i.e., the choice of a place to build is what matters. The foolish builder (v. 26) took no care to choose a secure site but built on sand. For Matthew the danger lies in the storm with all its features (v. 25 and its parallel in v. 27), characteristic of the steep hills and wadis of Palestine, which undermines the site unless it is well chosen. It is assumed that the building is equally good in each case.

It has sometimes been felt that the parable concerns the houses, and the introduction, "Every one . . . will be like a wise *man* who," has then caused difficulty. But this assumes that the emphasis of the Lucan version is authentic, or is influenced by rabbinic parallels where the nature of the construction is the main point. The most frequently quoted parallel is as follows:

> A man who does good works and who learns much Torah, with whom is he to be compared? To a man who builds [a house] with stones for its foundation [lit., underneath], and bricks of clay [above]. Though the floods [lit., much water] come and beat upon the side thereof, they cannot wash it away from its place. And a man who does not do good works and [yet] learns the Torah, with whom is he to be compared? To a man who builds with bricks of clay first, and thereafter with stones. Even if but little water flows, it falls at once.[21]

There are other forms of essentially the same parable, and it is clear that the emphasis is on the building of a foundation and not on the choice of a site on which to build. It is possible that Luke was influenced by the parallels and modified the original form. Much of the preaching one hears on the parable takes the Lucan theme. But in the Matthaean form it is a parable of the Two Builders, one of whom chooses well the place on which to build and one of whom makes a poor choice.

If this be granted, we have then to find the application that this requires. The comparison is with those who hear the words of Jesus —and all who are addressed are included. Out of the one group of hearers two types emerge—those who follow hearing with works and those who do nothing as a result of hearing. The usual illustration of the two types was by means of parables like the one quoted above. But Jesus here takes another line. The good works are not the stones or bricks of the building which rests on a foundation of mutual hearing, for both build alike. Neither is the doing of works the foundation laid, for nothing is said of foundation as it is in the rabbinic parable.

The point is that activity that is a result and interpretation of Jesus' words represents a decision that his teaching is the ground on which to build. The hearer has, in this case, made a decision and chosen Jesus' words as a basis upon which to act or, in the metaphor of the parable, upon which to build his life. The other hearer, likewise, has made a decision, but it is a different one. He has decided that Jesus' teaching is not the basis on which he will build, is not to be the ground of his action. He will base his action on other teaching. He has heard what Jesus said but rejected it as a basis for life. To return to the discussion of the purpose of parables, he is one of those who hearing hears not. The parable then says that the first, who has chosen to act on Jesus' teaching, has chosen a basis that will give his structure enduring security against all storms; the second, who has decided not to act on Jesus' teaching, has chosen to build on a basis (whatever other basis it be) that will not hold up the structure he builds upon it when the time of testing comes. In brief, the parable says that Jesus' teaching is the only secure basis for life.

The daring and the finality of this teaching then become clear. It is no wonder that Matthew adds (vs. 28-29), "And when Jesus finished these sayings, the crowds were astonished at his teaching, for he taught them as one who had authority, and not as their scribes." The parable is another way of saying what is elsewhere attributed to Jesus, "Heaven and earth will pass away, but my words will not pass away" (Mark 13:31; Matt. 24:35; Luke 21:33). The difference between this and the teaching of the rabbis must be apparent. Their counsel concerned the knowledge of the Law and the doing of its commandments. Without "the works of the law" the knowledge of the Torah was unprofitable and the life devoted to it insecure. Jesus, in the parable before us, says that action that carries out his teaching is the only secure structure of life because the choice of his teaching as a basis for action is the choice of that which can support a way of life secure against all shocks. Jesus here does not equate his words with the Law but puts them in a more fundamental place than the Law. To do so is to claim that he himself is the fulfillment of the Law.

It is the Gospel of Matthew that sets forward the Sermon on the Mount as the new law and Jesus as the lawgiver of the new age.[22] He does not so much set aside the law of Moses as reveal its deep demands, its inwardness, its judgment which is a call for perfection. It may be said, therefore, that this parable is the work of the church, seeking to establish Jesus as a new and greater Moses. Yet the parable seems to have been found in the earliest tradition (Q) and its Hebraic style, its departure from the conventional parallels, and its daring stamp it as his. Its note of authority is missing among the rabbis, and with Jesus is not found alone in this case. If Jesus made the claim implied here as well as, in less obvious forms, elsewhere in the parables, it was inevitable that he be dealt with by the authorities. It is a claim that, unless substantiated, must be designated blasphemous. It is a staggering claim. Yet it is in a form not likely to have been invented by the church. There seems to have been a confused echo of something of this kind in the attempt at the trial to find evidence that he had said something about destroying the temple and rebuilding it (Mark 14:57-59; Matt. 26:61). It is not those who merely call Jesus "Lord" who enter the kingdom, but those whose actions are an effort to fulfill the will of God (Matt. 7:21), which according to Luke's Gospel is to be known in Jesus' teaching (Luke 6:46). Both versions of this saying are followed by the parable that, originally, distinguished the fate of the work of the two builders by the choice of foundation that each made. Here Jesus' claim upon us as individuals is clear. For the church, after the resurrection, not the teaching alone but the Teacher in his person and office, together with his teaching, became the foundation for Christian life. "For no other foundation can any one lay than that which is laid, which is Jesus Christ (1 Cor. 3:11)."

# EIGHT THE JESUS OF THE PARABLES

Jesus makes a claim to be heard, and when his claim is opposed he points to the situation in which he and his people stand. "Look about you," he says, with the assurance that eyes that can foretell a change in the weather can also read the signs of the times. But in demanding attention to the times, he inevitably draws attention to himself. He intends to be seen. For this reason he plunges into the precariously poised situation in the Holy City and will not let the authorities ignore him. From the beginning in Galilee to the end in Jerusalem, his parables are addressed to the situation at hand. By this fact their form is determined, each demands an occasion, and the point of emphasis is dictated.[1] They are inseparable from the time and from his own presence in it. The history owes its peculiar meaning to the activity of a person. The parables do not form an abstract speculative system, reasoned at every point, addressed to the ages. They are distinct from the cool, dispassionate production of the porch or the classroom, to be accepted or rejected in calm and friendly debate. The issues of life and death are in the balance—his own life and his own death. This, in itself, is of small moment, least of all for himself, when the issue of the destiny of God's people, upon which the divine purpose centers, is to come to decision. Unlike the precepts of a philosopher, his teaching depends upon his person. Christianity is something other than a school of thought like the wisdom of Socrates or the idealism of Plato. It may be difficult to say where Socrates ends and Plato begins, and it probably matters little to the schools. But Christianity depends upon Christ, and it is not Christianity without him, no matter how well systematized his teaching or how widely it be rendered lip service.

This, again, explains why the understanding of the parables involves a close scrutiny of the Gospel texts in which they occur. As William Manson stated it:

> It is worthy of notice that, wherever the intuitional method is favoured, the tendency has been to take the origins of Christianity

back to an *idea* in the mind of Jesus, and therefore to assume that an ideal unity and simplicity will have characterized the original terms of his message and of the earliest Christian kerygma. From such a standpoint the complications and involvedness of the Synoptic tradition cannot but be suspected and deplored. But if the actual starting-point of the Christian confession and of the Christian conception of the revelation of God in Christ was not an idea but a life, a spiritual history, a drama of divinely inspired and guided personality, the case is different. The probability is that the testimony borne to Jesus from the start will have exhibited elements as various and as heterogeneous as those which within a generation are found entering into the composition of the Q source and of the Gospel of Mark.

It needs to be remembered in this connection that Christianity did not originate in a vacuum but at the heart of the most highly developed and self-conscious religious system which the world had known.[2]

The parables reveal this clearly. Because Jesus, a Jew, lived and worked among Jews, the question of his relation to his people's calling must always occupy us. The parables were not simply vehicles of teaching. They were instruments forged for warfare and the means by which his strategy was vindicated—until no further words could serve, but only an act.[3] The parables are aspects of a campaign, the final step of which was his surrender to the cross. The crucifixion cannot be ignored in the study of his similitudes, nor the similitudes in the study of the crucifixion. They explain in large part how it happened and why it happened. Jesus' death cannot be omitted in the attempt to understand the Gospels any more than his resurrection. When we understand the parables as the sharp spearhead of his teaching and a major contribution to the tragedy, we approach a comprehension of his sacrifice and begin to sense the impact his words made upon his time.

## THE NATURE OF THE GOSPELS
The literary form known to us from the first four books of the New Testament as Gospels is an utterly distinct phenomenon, a new literary genre. As far as we know, we owe the form to Mark. A Gospel is not a history, not a biography, not a theological treatise, but contains elements of all these. It takes its rise from interest in a particular historical person who is treated as a Person, ultimately in the highest and most profound sense possible.

The distinct genre "Gospel," so baffling to describe in simple unmodified categories, has, however, one element of which modern scholarship has begun to take more careful account. The main thing which makes the works of the Evangelists into Gospels, while other works which appear to be of the same order are not Gospels in the same sense, is that each reaches a climax with the crucifixion and death of Jesus, followed by accounts of the appearances of the risen Christ, demonstrably identified with the "same Jesus." This is not true, for example, of the so-called Gospel of Thomas or of the hypothetical document Q. Each of these is a catena of the sayings of Jesus without a climactic "passion story." Within the Gospels themselves it is clear that other genres are embodied whose existence as units or collections antedated the Gospels. These were forms of expression known to the Jewish and Hellenistic world of religious literature or oral tradition. They included stories of great deeds accomplished by notable persons and enhancing their stature (aretalogies), miracle stories, wonder tales, epiphanies, healings, exorcisms, and the like, and of course maxims, fables, allegories—and parables. The important thing about collections of such genres within the Gospels is not so much the patterning of their forms as the influence the Gospel genre itself has had upon them by their incorporation in the Gospel. They have undergone modification as they have become part of the drama which leads up to the cross. They are, therefore, properly assessed only when seen as sharing the overall thrust and theme which leads to the destination which makes of the whole this distinct genre, the Gospel of the death and resurrection of Jesus Christ the Lord.[4]

The previous pages have set out to show in cumulative fashion that this influence of the end on the forms was true of the parables incorporated in the first three Gospels (there are none in the Fourth Gospel). Because, as Kähler noted,[5] the Gospels are passion stories with extended introductions, the emphasis on the relation of the teaching by parables to Jesus' passion is a clear example of how all the genres in the Gospel have been influenced, as studied in "genre criticism." It is this that makes us cautious about treating the similitudes and parables as solely aesthetic structures or allegories of theological dogma, or as exclusively related to purely personal religious experience, in any way detachable from the person of the Crucified. It is significant, for example, that Luke has embodied all his distinctive parables (other than those paralleled in Mark or the source he shares with Matthew) in the section of his Gospel which is held together by the editorial framework of Jesus' journey to Jerusalem. The literary and aesthetic inheritance of the parables as they have come down to us has aspects which can be most fruitfully studied and the result appropriated in most helpful ways, but such interpretation must always return to the Jesus who first illuminated the Christian understanding of God and man by using this genre and about whom, by his very use of parable, we learn something of significance for the Gospel itself.

The ability to detect the distinctive Christian voice of the scriptures depends in the end on the reality of our conception of Jesus. It is indeed the risen Christ who speaks through his Word, but he does not speak with any words whatsoever that the Christian community cares to supply. There is an authentic note; we come to realize that it is the voice of Christ incarnate, the Jesus who was actually encountered in history. There is a visage, not simply the reflection of our own faces. We see that it is the profile of a man who was himself and not just anyone: not an idealized being, not a dehumanized demigod, but a man.

It would be difficult to overestimate the effect the parables have had in forming this impression, in teaching us to distinguish this voice. The parables and similitudes by themselves occupy a relatively large proportion of the Gospels.[6] Apart from extended discourses which are, like the Sermon on the Mount, patently constructions, the two most original forms which convey the teaching are parables and "pronouncement stories" (or "situation sayings"). In Mark, where little of the teaching is divorced from narrative, the pronouncement stories occupy twice as much space as parables. In Matthew and Luke the case is reversed, and the parables take up just about twice the space.[7] The parables represent, therefore, apart from the passion story, a large proportion of the account of the public activity of Jesus. It would seem proper to give to them a foremost and determinative role in forming our impression of him.

## THE "SECULARITY" OF THE PARABLES

It is part of the paradox of Jesus to find that hardly any of the parables are "religious" in the direct sense of the word. Boris Pasternak in his novel *Doctor Zhivago* remarks on this. His hero says:

> It has always been assumed that the most important things in the Gospels are the ethical maxims and commandments. But for me the most important thing is that Christ speaks in parables taken from life, that He explains the truth in terms of everyday reality. . . . For into this tasteless heap of gold and marble, He came, light and clothed in an aura, emphatically human, deliberately provincial, Galilean, and at that moment little gods and nations ceased to be and man came into being—man the carpenter, man the plowman, man the shepherd with his flock of sheep at sunset, man who does not sound in the least proud.[8]

It is apparent that in approaching the common people Jesus was able to talk of the concerns of God in everyday terms.

The popularity given by Dietrich Bonhoeffer to the terms "religion-less Christianity" and "secular religion" finds here an echo in the heart of the Gospel.[9] The only parable that deals specifically with religion as a distinctive activity is the parable of the Pharisee and the Tax Collector at prayer in the temple (Luke 18:9-14). This is unique, and that it should be so is important. In the parable of the Good Samaritan two religious figures appear, only to be rejected in favor of a layman (Luke 10:29-37). This "secular" aspect of Jesus' teaching is sometimes obscured, but it cannot be overthrown by the observation that some of the parables start with an introduction which identifies the subject as a likeness of "the kingdom of God." On examination this proves to be a peculiarly Matthaean contri-bution.[10]

Jesus' ability to draw analogies between the things of God and the homely affairs of daily secular living is itself the clue to the theology of the Gospels at an early stage of its development. It was not apparently necessary for Jesus to exploit or even to invent a particular vocabulary to elucidate his view of the ways of God with men, nor was it necessary to erect a great divide between human life and the divine impact on it. At the least it is possible to say that we see from the parables that the religious issue could be encount-ered in the daily experiences and decisions of life, work, and rela-tionships. It follows also that the religious issue could not, therefore, be evaded either by staying apart from formal religious activities or, for that matter, by engaging in them as a thing apart from the rest of life in the hope that the issue might be limited to a controllable area.

The significance of this element in the parables is stressed by Amos Wilder, who says, "One can even speak of their secularity" and adds that to insist that every figure is an Old Testament allusion is "to pull the stories out of shape and to weaken their thrust." Both about Jesus and about the people, the naturalness of the parables tells us something. Of Jesus, Wilder says, "In the realism and actuality of the parables we recognize Jesus the layman. . . . We insist that these sharply-focused snapshots of life do reveal something very important about the story-teller himself." Of people, he writes, "Jesus without saying so, by his very way of presenting man, shows that for him man's destiny is at stake in his ordinary creaturely existence, domes-tic, economic and social. . . . It is implicit that man can be saved where he is."[11] Funk, with a critical appraisal of Dodd's and Wilder's views, observes that "more is involved than a pleasant or amusing anecdote, even one which relieves the coarseness of life by jesting. . . . The parabolic imagery lays bare the structure of human exis-tence that is masked by convention, custom, consensus. . . . It is the element of ultimate seriousness that is implicit in the patent every-dayness of the parable." Further, "The parable does not direct attention by its earthy imagery *away* from mundane existence, but *toward* it. The realism of the parables is not merely a device."[12] That the transfer is not literal or immediate (as we have seen, they are not allegories, and there is the "how much more") is stressed when Via says, "No figure or action in the parable tells us literally what God is like, but the parables do tell us that God meets us and we are put in touch with him in the everyday and that when we respond to him our existence is structured like that of the prodigal and not like that of the unforgiving servant."[13] Even when Jesus seems to have had a polemical purpose aimed at specific situations, he does not cheat; the people in the stories are people, intended to be real, and the situations are possible in everyday life even if, as we shall see, at sometimes critical moments or under unusual circumstances.

The attempt to control the many detailed decisions and circumstances of life by bringing them within a casuistry under Torah was the point at which Jesus came into dispute with the religious leaders and had to vindicate his association with people whose way of life put them outside the area of control. As Eta Linnemann has more than once expressed it, "Jesus stands before his listeners as one who disturbs God's order. He ignores the difference which the law erects between the righteous and the sinner."[14] This applies not only to the content and thrust of the parables but also to the method Jesus used, which in itself was, in spite of Mark's theory, an act of compassion for the alienated. Father Kahlefeld not unjustly describes it as an act of friendliness: "speaking in parables is explained, therefore, as a sign of the friendliness with which Jesus preached to the people." In discussing Mark's theory, he says, "There is apparently an older way of thinking that is closer to the words of Jesus, and therefore takes precedence, which in principle sees in the parable a means of understanding, spoken out of the desire to unlock the truth for the hearers, to provide them an access to the meaning, to convince and win them."[15] This friendliness to the common people, to "sinners," was in itself a basic cause of conflict, and the parables were also a means of judgment on those who would not be convinced.

## JESUS' METHOD IN THE PARABLES
The religious aspect of the parables is sometimes held to be in their allegorical nature; until the work of Jülicher, this was the prevailing method of interpretation. Evidences of allegorical use and modification are, as we have seen, present in the New Testament itself. Those who wish to preserve at least a partial allegorical character for the

parables can point to an element in them which would better be described as their "allusive" character. Certain analogies or types or allegorical figures had become customary through the Old Testament and its interpretation and carried a power of suggestion. This meant that a reference to such seemingly everyday things as vines, sheep and shepherds, kings and their servants, or banquets and bridegrooms might readily suggest a previous religious symbolism for those to whom it was familiar. Allusive features of this kind are not, however, absolutely dependent on previous use; they still describe what goes on. Crops were still grown, sheep still herded, houses still run, and business affairs still managed in the same way, so that the words could be taken to mean simply what they pointed to and the necessary application be found at that level.[16] That in some instances this did not exhaust the possibilities is true, and for those with eyes to see and ears to hear there were further enriching reflections possible.

There is a sense, however, in which the teaching of Jesus was, as it were, thrown out with a divine "carelessness,"[17] permitting the hearers to make of it what they would—except, as we shall see below, that there was an "engagement" involved which demanded of them something in the nature of a decision. Many of the specific applications of the parables in the Gospels, as we have seen, must be attributed to the Evangelists or to the church. Jesus' use of traditional themes may be elucidated by reference to the Old Testament, but even there, it is fair to observe, they first appeared because they referred to familiar experiences. Jesus' use of them is in the first instance natural, and the incidents and stories are in the main openended, so that the hearer is allowed to form a judgment for himself, to come to a conclusion, to apply the material; Jesus not only intends him to do so but trusts him to do so.[18]

There is here a marked contrast with all gnostic or esoteric types of religion. For Jesus, the familiar is full of clues to the Divine, and it is not esoteric in the sense that the secular hides the spiritual until the enlightened can elucidate it. There is no gulf of meaning between God's way with man and ordinary life involved with people and things of the world, though there is between man in his sin and God in his heaven, and the similes point to a "how much more."

We are thus enabled often to distinguish between Jesus' teaching and the applications and amplifications of the church, to detect the reasons for the changes in the parables when they appear in the gnostic Gospel of Thomas, and to try to maintain some of the lack of concern for enforced meaning which Jesus seems to have been willing to risk in contrast with the rigidities of later interpreters. It is when the parables are allegorized and each item in them pinned down to a specific meaning other than its natural one, so that the whole must be interpreted *en bloc,* that rigidity takes the place of the carelessness or open-endedness of Jesus' method.

In this respect another function of the parables appears. The verisimilitude which inheres in them, and the capacity of the hearer therefore to recognize and accept the situation portrayed, is an essential part of their capacity to do more than merely *illustrate* timeless truths. The recognition involved on the part of the hearer—whether it be of the familiar, or the expected, or the unexpected but feasible, or an already well-known tale with a new twist, or an allusion which brought echoes of traditional meaning, or even aspects of humor—this recognition took hold of the hearer and made it possible for a sudden change of insight to take place or stimulated an opposing reaction which, however, must know itself to be a choice. The hearer's interest is engaged by the integrity of the material presented with his own experience or observation, and this enables Jesus to expect an involvement which must issue—as did some of his acts in the pronouncement stories—in decision for or against, or in the sullen, silent effort at disengagement. This in large part explains their perennial power, for the characters, especially, still engage our "existential" understanding, a fact which has been effectively developed by interpreters such as G. V. Jones, Funk, and Via.

## THE NATURE OF THE PARABLE MATERIAL
It would be misleading to create the impression that all the parables deal with simply everyday incidents. Bultmann's distinction between similitude and parable is useful here. We can observe that the point of similitudes such as those about the salt or the lamp, about the sower or the farmer and the growing seed, the leaven in the meal, the dragnet, or the mustard seed, is dependent on their being instances of the normal or typical. Salt is always in demand for its saltiness, and a lamp is lighted only that its burning should give light. There is process and a result always to be expected about the growing of seeds and the making of bread dough. There is, in a sense, an inevitability about it. Here the engagement of the hearer was not so much demanded as already involved. Examination shows that parables proper assume more the form of an occasional occurrence, sometimes with an element of the unexpected or the unusual, often the critical. Caring for sheep is a typical everyday undertaking, as is sweeping a floor. It is only rarely that a sheep strays so far that it has to be sought to the exclusion of all else, or a floor swept exhaustively to find a lost coin. Likewise, sons who stay at home and others

who leave in search of freedom are not unusual, but the reception accorded the returning good-for-nothing is not to be expected to happen every day or in every family. Travelers all too frequently were attacked and robbed between Jerusalem and Jericho, but our attention is directed to a special instance of one who was ignored by the ecclesiastics and aided by a layman or a foreigner. Pearl merchants and purchasers of fields are not uncommon, but those who dispossess themselves of all they own to secure one surpassing pearl or a treasure trove in the field are special cases. There is nothing unusual about vineyard practice or about hiring laborers for the vintage, or about absentee landlords, but an employer who paid the last-hired the same as the first in their presence may be considered eccentric. Tenants who rejected all overtures for rent may not have been entirely unknown, especially in a time of revolt, but an aggravated case is presented by the parable. Nothing beyond good practice is proposed by the cutting out of a barren fig tree, but the year of grace granted it is intended to be a special concession. For guests to find they preferred their own pursuits to attending a banquet would not be unheard of, but the decision to exclude them by bringing in everyone who could be found was a significant reaction, even if anticipated in Jewish lore. There have been dishonest stewards, but they were not always shrewd enough to cut their own commission as a means of countering the inevitable loss of office.

So we could go on. The narratives of what amount to special cases, or at least typical ones with a critical turn, suggest that, however isolated the case, it must be within the bounds of possibility, conceivable if not usual, a crisis breaking into the habitual, the whimsical arising out of the normal. Otherwise its power to engage the hearer in Jesus' dynamic method would not exist. Some parables expressly set out to make the engagement by extended and rhetorical questions, even if they do not all begin with "What do you think?" or "What man of you?" or end with some such query as "Which of these?" or "What will he do?" The response intended can be expected only because the situation, if unusual, is possible; if surprising, conceivable; if eccentric, yet commendable.

Along with the recognition that the critical moment or the unexpected emergency has a frequent place in Jesus' parables, the essential element of realism or verisimilitude is lost only when there has been adaptation or development at work or a change has taken place because the clue to the situation was mislaid. The modification or mystification leads us to suspect a deliberate intent to shift the emphasis or provide the means for a different application. In all probability this explains the versions found in the Gospel of Thomas when the parables have become bare statements of fact, or have introduced an exaggeration like the statement that the lost sheep was the biggest of the flock, or have adapted the details with what appears to be an urbanized and commercial intent. The authenticity of the images used in the Synoptic parables defies many attempts at distortion because this realism is a reflection of the life of the times, not in and of itself of value to the adapter. It can either be recovered from a study of the background of the period or still observed in primitive localities to this day.

## DISTINCTION FROM RELIGIOUS MOTIFS

The setting forth of much concerning the ways of God with man in symbols of ordinary life is quite distinct from the use of religious motifs or cultic symbolism. Cultic symbols are historical in origin but, apart from the recital of historical happenings, they tend to be arbitrary. One does not necessarily become involved in them or with them. One could live his whole life without ever being in Jerusalem or taking a sheep to be slaughtered at the temple or knowing the detailed regulations of Torah. One might be aware of these things because they were part of the culture or of a society which, by its pressure, gave one a sense of obligation about them or a wistful desire to be able to participate if one's work or conditions ever permitted. But one could be ignorant of them, uncertain of the refinements of their use, very possibly of their meaning. It is therefore part of Jesus' attack on the situation of his day, which one might call his "revolution," that his parables did not deal with religious matters in that sense.

The areas of life to which he pointed did not *demand* involvement; the involvement *already existed*. The engagement was not recommended; it was pointed to as an already compelling fact. Fatherhood and family relationships are already part of our existence, seldom experienced without some reflection or discussion with neighbors and friends. So with business, agriculture, and the like, matters in which some were directly involved and which indirectly but unavoidably affected the lives of others and about which they knew. If they did not happen to operate a vineyard, fish with a net, tend sheep, or grow figs, they, by analogy, did comparable things, and the principles which arose were the same, within their capacity to appreciate and judge. Questions are steadily posed by the parables, and a demand for a judgment arises from them, because people's existence and the practice of living are tied up with just such discussion. They are not *optional* activities in the same way as religious undertakings (or there would not have been so many *'am ha'aretz*), not to the same extent matters which one could take or leave, enter into or avoid. They had already a "thereness."

These experiences and encounters were not self-explanatory. But they needed only the Word which pointed to them. The Word declared the secular (in this sense) to the religious (in this sense). It did not have to fence off a whole new area of life to provide a religious arena, nor did it have to produce a special audience trained in a sacred dialectic. Religion here, to use today's jargon, was not an additive; it was life itself, life as the housewife, the shepherd, the parent or child, or subject of a king knew it. What made the secular religious without ceasing to be secular, or the religious secular without ceasing to be religious, was the "how much more," the bringing to a new focus, the intensification, the heightened seriousness of the very same things seen from a new angle. Funk aptly refers to it as "a whole new vista—i.e., the penumbral field."[19] The Word creates the new angle of vision. In the same way, the basic sacraments of the historic church do not create entirely new means but inform by the Word and "lift up" the age-old and customary means of washing, the elements of feasting, the earthy instruments of water, wine, and bread.

## THE MORAL ASPECT OF THE PARABLES

Some of the parabolic tales in the Gospels have been classified as example-stories. It may at the moment be left as an open question whether such a classification does not need reconsideration. What would be a serious misconception would be to extend this designation to all the parables, making them thereby moral tales.[20] To treat the parables uniformly as good examples would yield ludicrous results. It may be, for instance, good business to invest all one's stock of pearls in the purchase of one superlative pearl, especially if there is a sure market for it; it would be prudential to liquidate one's few assets to secure the right to dig up a long-forgotten treasure. But Jesus was not concerned to teach business methods or prudential action; his hearers hardly needed such instruction. Because they did not, they could get the point or even share in the humor or tragedy involved. The level of example would often leave matters on a purely moralistic—indeed, on a merely mundane—level: domestic, economic, or agricultural. The hearers of Jesus were familiar enough with the a fortiori or lesser to greater, *a minore ad majus,* principle of interpretation, not to be so misled. One might emulate the diligence or the shrewdness or even the compassion of the characters depicted, but to be content to do so would be to ignore the "how much more" (*posō mallon*: Matt. 7:11 and Luke 11:13; cf. Matt. 10:25; Luke 12:24, 28) which assimilated the image to the things of God.

The inadequacy of the exemplary point of view is even more grotesquely apparent when we consider the distortion which would arise if we imitated all the ways of the parabolic characters. It would be a curious way of life which would be depicted, at variance with even commonsense morality. We are not expected, for example, to take our cues from the parables and justify sleeping when there is work in the fields to be done or a meeting to be honored; to be careless in sowing seed or unwatchful enough to allow a sheep to stray; to be "hard men" expecting to reap where we have not sown; to be content to have nothing to offer but our sins; to pay workers with no regard for the work done; or to stay away and leave the dangerous business of collecting the rent to others![21]

From following this line it can be seen that the parables are from life, not from an ideal realm. The people in them are good, bad, and indifferent because they are natural, doing what they do in the way they usually do it, not dressed up to strut before us as sketches of good behavior. Neither is judgment brought to bear on them for being what they naturally are. As Bornkamm wrote, "The only presumption which is made in Jesus' parables is man, the hearer himself, man indeed in the plain, unadorned reality of his world, which is neither put to rights according to high moral standards, nor deplored with righteous indignation."[22] The purpose of Jesus' parables is more incisive, and their ability to penetrate defenses testifies to the reality of the situation which Jesus faced.

This has been the basis for the modern understanding of the parables and of the genius of their creator. By it we gain a better grasp of the fact that Jesus was done away with for reasons which seemed good to those who were officially responsible. Jesus' uniqueness, unique in his time, unique in his person, and a unique problem for our understanding, is revealed not in claims he made for himself but in the way in which his parabolic teaching penetrates the surface impressions of life to uncover unsuspected issues and put inescapable decisions before his hearers. This is not an invention of the tradition, not contrived by the compilers of the Gospels. It is when the deposit of tradition and the work of later hands are removed that we catch these unmistakable glimpses of a person quite distinct and, once recognized, not to be forgotten until we have come to terms with him—on his terms.

## CRITICAL TIME IN THE PARABLES
The problems faced by the primitive church can at many points be distinguished from those faced by Jesus, though this does not mean, as some critics seem to believe, that every problem found in the

church is thereby excluded from Jesus' time. The situation in which Jesus was caught was essentially Jewish and fin de siècle. To bring in problems from another area or a later stage (what Jeremias termed the "change of audience") and force the Gospels to provide a solution is to distort the teaching of Jesus, especially in its parabolic form. Where the material needs no forcing but can be shown to apply to a later situation only, we can detect that later interests have already been at work.

Jesus spoke and acted as a Jew, though paradoxically he spoke and acted as no ordinary Jew of the time would do. Only so can we understand his death and why it was that this crucified one, among so many others crucified in those days, became the Lord of the church. His people were in a state of crisis, even if some of the people refused to see that the situation was critical. Jesus commented on their view of providence when in Luke 13:5 he said, "Unless you repent you will all likewise [that is, just as suddenly] perish." To be unaware of the crisis, or deliberately to close their eyes to it, meant that they must be to that extent the less aware of God's call to them to be his witnessing people. Jesus' call was to believe that God was still at work, in the actuality of the harvest which presents itself *when* it presents itself (Mark 4:29). We see it is so in the parables of the Sower, of the Farmer and the Growing Seed, of the Dragnet, in spite of redactional elements due to their collection in the work of the Evangelists. It is still clear when we consider the allegorical work based on them in Matthew's creation of the allegory of the Tares Among the Wheat (Matt. 13:24-30, 36-43). No less a critical element is found in the parables of the Pearl Merchant and the Treasure in the Field, in the Tower Builder and the King Preparing for War. It appears as well in the many which deal with preparedness to respond to a situation, as with the bridesmaids when the bridegroom comes, or the father when the son comes home, or the servants when the king returns to ask a reckoning. In so many cases immediate action is required. The fig tree in Luke 13:6-9 is granted a period of grace, but only as preliminary to a final drastic decision. It is this to which Mark points in the incident of the barren fig tree, so closely related to the temple at a point where it has lost its proper function (Mark 11:12-14).

## JESUS AS THE CRITICAL FACTOR
The conclusion can hardly be escaped that Jesus spoke as if his own presence itself constituted or precipitated the crisis. It is in just those passages where it seems Jesus is most clearly distinguished from the Son of man who is to come that the critical moment *now*

determines the outcome *then* (Mark 8:38 and Luke 9:26; Luke 12:8f.). Bultmann is surely correct when he insists on the radical nature of Jesus' demand, though this alone does not constitute the whole of Jesus' appeal. The call for radical obedience is existential even now to the extent that Christ is realized as present in our own time, the same One making the same call for decision. The Christ who confronts this secular age is recognizable as the same Jesus who confronted his religious countrymen then.

It becomes clear from the parables that the crisis of decision is a call to complete commitment. It will not do to risk being hailed into court, to haggle for the field, or to postpone deciding whether to meet the price asked for the pearl, even though what is asked is all that one has. Neither will it do to give up sowing because some seed is bound to be lost, or even to be niggardly in its use.

Closely involved with this frequent element in the parables falls another which is not always given an adequate place in Christian teaching, yet it has a curiously modern ring to it. That is the constant emphasis made by Jesus, and carried over into the work of the Evangelists, that the value, test, and continued existence of anything is determined by its purpose, its inherent and God-given function. This can be seen clearly in the parable of the Barren Fig Tree, and it applies to the duties of tenants, to the use of entrusted wealth, to a house furnished and decorated to be lived in, to salt, to a lighted lamp, and to those who are to carry lighted lamps in a given procession. It is nonetheless true, in a derived sense, that it is the function of a neighbor-by-proximity to be a neighbor-in-action (Luke 11:5-8) and, even when out of his place, to *be* a neighbor still rather than to ask *to whom* he should be a neighbor (Luke 10:29-37). Invited guests are tested by whether they act upon the invitation, employers have a concern to provide a living wage for their employees, and it is the high function of a father to be ready to receive his son and of a shepherd to seek his sheep. There is inherent in the situation, as God has ordained it, a built-in demand and therefore a built-in judgment. Both demand and judgment are inexorable in character, and no casuistry will serve to make the situation other than it is.

The element of time is critical, as a little reflection will show. The time comes when the son has arrived and found no father watching, when the sheep has already perished, when the starving villager can wait no longer for work or wage, when the seats at the banquet are already filled, when the bridegroom has come and the door is shut, when the days of grace for the fig tree have expired. The metaphor in Jeremiah 8:20, "The harvest is past, the summer is ended, and we are not saved," receives in Jesus' parables, for all their charm, a trenchant and terrifying meaning within which and beyond which lies true redemption.

## THE PARABLES AND JESUS' WORD AND ACTS

The most significant point of all is that the parables are not mere illustrations of Jesus' teaching. They are less peripheral and more essential than those of the rabbis. In the parables is found the core of the teaching itself; they convey it. They are the dynamic means of its impact on the times, piercing through defenses and laying bare hypocrisies. The sayings of Jesus are much more open to modification than the parables, so that the original Logia are more difficult to recover by form-analysis. It could be said that the sayings are very often illustrations of the parabolic teaching. The tendency of the preaching tradition was, in fact, to append such sayings as hortatory addenda to the stories themselves.[23] The sayings do not so clearly authenticate the parables, since in many instances the sayings can be judged to be original because there are parables which drive home the point.[24]

The same thing may in a sense be said about Jesus' action. The recovery of the parables as a means of understanding Jesus and the continuity between him and the kerygma of the church is exemplified in the work of Ernst Fuchs. He quite regularly turns to the parables to elucidate the nature of Jesus' own proclamation and stresses its basis in Jesus' life. Maybe he tends to stress the relation between teaching and action in too absolute a manner. In his essay, "The Quest of the Historical Jesus," he points to the parable of the Prodigal Son(s). He says, quite correctly, "The usual interpretation tends to argue *somewhat too hastily* from the father's conduct to God's. Closer examination shows that Jesus is defending his own conduct." He adds, "Hence it is not the prime purpose of the parable to explain the conduct of Jesus, although Jesus does vindicate himself in it; on the contrary, Jesus' conduct explains the will of God, by means of a parable drawn from that very conduct."[25] From this Fuchs deduces that to understand Jesus' proclamation we have to understand Jesus' conduct. One might ask whether he does not go too far or too quickly when he asserts that this is because "he himself stood in God's place."[26] That there is an implicit claim conveyed by the convergence of Jesus' teaching and action, notably in connection with his relations with sinners and outcasts, is of the essence of the paradox involved in the Gospels.

The impression we get, that the parables very largely carried Jesus' defense of his practice in drawing close to the outsiders, may have served the *Sitz im Leben* of the church but can hardly have been created by it.[27] As Kahlefeld suggested, the resort to parabolic teaching was itself part of that approach to the despised and neglected. The close relation of word and act is to be found chiefly here. It is not, as Fuchs could be taken to imply, that Jesus did certain things in order that he might base teaching on the action. Rather, the actions (as the pronouncement stories show) made clear an attitude which could be attacked and was. Jesus did not hesitate to demand from his opponents, as well as from his friends, a judgment, based on their own experience, as to whether his activity was not the better response to the demand of God. The final act of all, the surrender to the cross, is the end result and issue of this conflict in which word and work go together and in which the parables play a decisive part.

## THEOLOGY IN THE PARABLES

As suggested in Chapter Two, parables which found their original context in the critical questions of the time for Jesus' own people came to be applied in the early Christian community more universally to the individual—often by being addressed specifically to the disciples. Yet their secular character and lack of what we might consider theological concepts complicates the question of the continuity between the teaching of Jesus and the proclamation of the church. The adaptation, as we have seen, was largely accomplished by resort to allegorization. There is nothing that without some such reapplication can easily be taken to express the doctrines, for example, of Incarnation, Atonement, or Christology. Their secularity, their largely Jewish nature in method and content, the sense they make when set in the situation of the times—this still tempts interpreters to seek a measure of allegorical intention, if not content, in the parables and encourages existential and personal treatment in sermons. The latter is in itself valid as an extension of the original points, provided the basic community relevance is kept in mind.

We see the process beginning in the Gospels where the pericopes containing the parables have already been adapted to the life situation of the early church. In what way, therefore, are the parables of use theologically for the proclamation of the Gospel of Christ by the church, and to what extent were they in Jesus' use "religious"? How could one who proclaimed the kingdom of God or a new era in God's dealings with men, so sharply that it constituted a crisis, put so much of his teaching into this form? The question is urgent for a modern age in which the church must take the radical secularization of the world with absolute seriousness.

## THE JEWISHNESS OF THE PARABLES

Our answer has already been suggested. The parables (and all of Jesus' teaching and activity) were within the context of Israel: its institutions, its worship, its way of life, its critical position at the time. This context, even for its political concerns, *was* religious. It is in a sense consistently Jewish that religious teaching should be expressed in mundane terms and that the everyday concerns of life be the stuff of religion. Only an age correctly described as "post-Christendom" can again adequately bring this into focus. It is at the end of his discussion of the parables that Bultmann lays down his basic criteria: "We can only count on possessing a genuine similitude of Jesus where, on the one hand, expression is given to the contrast between Jewish morality and piety and the distinctive eschatological temper which characterized the preaching of Jesus; and where on the other hand we find no specifically Christian features."[28] This provides a solid safeguard and preliminary test but is limited as a final delimitation and reflects some prior understanding of Jesus. As we have seen, Jesus may well have used for his own purposes already existing Jewish proverbs and tales. His hearers would hear all his teaching with Jewish ears, conditioned by time and place and circumstance. This at once makes some proposed theological interpretations impossible as descriptions of Jesus' meaning. A certain Jewishness in the teaching would therefore be necessary for authenticity, even though a measure of divergence, transcendence, or eschatological awareness would characterize it as belonging only to Jesus. On the other hand, we should have to allow that some of the church's teaching and its characteristic way of life, including its primitive worship, was the product of what had been observed and learned of Jesus if there is any continuity at all between Jesus and the Christian church. All this would, of course, be transmuted and refracted by the experience of the resurrection and by movement into even more hellenized circles.

## CHRISTOLOGY AND THE PARABLES

In saying this, we should exclude anything that reflects Jesus as an object of worship and the christological affirmations involved. Attempts have been made to show a measure of self-identification or self-designation, an at least incipient Christology, in the parables, attempts which seem, on the basis of considerations derived not from the parables alone, to be misleading.[29] We have seen this in parables or similitudes which involve a bridegroom, since both Matthew 25:1-18 and Mark 2:19a are capable in the first instance of understanding on the ordinary level and do not involve self-identification by Jesus.

The extension of Mark 2:19a by verses 19b and 20 involves the later situation of the church and clearly belongs to another layer.

It was natural for the church to make such identifications and so attempt to use the parables as allegories of the Parousia. Attempts to identify Jesus as the shepherd in Matthew 18:10-14 and Luke 15:3-7, or as the returning lord in Matthew 25:14-30 and Luke 19:12-27 (or in any of the sayings about attendant servants), or as the vineyard owner in Matthew 20:1-16 or in Luke 13:6-9, or as the sower in Mark 4:1ff., and so forth, even by implication, are precarious when treated as embodying claims of Jesus, though not as interpretations by the church. Where such identification seems to be made, as with "the son" in Mark 12:1-12, Matthew 21:33-46, and Luke 20:9-19, or with the "Son of man" in Matthew 13:36-43, the instances can be judged *on other grounds* also to be inauthentic.

Two aspects of the parables, however, provide christological possibilities as a basis for later development. We have the right to speak of the impression of spontaneous, independent authority embodied as recollection in the tradition behind the Gospels.[30] This comes out especially in the parables. They are the work of no authorized rabbi and yet are superb examples of the method, in a class by themselves. They convey a tone of self-authenticating demand which raises in itself the question of authority, for that is what is implicit in them. It is, as far as Jesus is concerned, left as a question for the hearers to decide; he nowhere offers any explanation for this attitude of weighty finality.

While the peculiar situation of Jesus' people at the time was critical and heading for an eventual catastrophe, the impression retained is that the parables imply the crisis is in some ways heightened, made more immediate—and response or failure to respond to it more irrevocable—by the presence of Jesus himself. Again this is implicit and not explicit—as, for instance, in Mark 3:27 where a general truth about a stronger man, better equipped, being able to put another at his mercy, clearly speaks to the situation and, for those who are prepared, suggests that Jesus' presence is the overpowering factor. And yet we know how easy it was (and is) to interpret this in terms of a wrong kind of power or a wrong manifestation of the right power. In the Q passage (Matt. 12:28; Luke 11:20) Jesus is presented as having pointed to what was taking place, but the deduction he makes, "if it is by the Spirit (finger) of God that I . . . then the kingdom of God . . ." is not, however, identity between himself and a messianic figure. There is, in other words, that which is implicit in the parables (quite apart from amplifications by the church) which might result in some form of christological *response,* but it is not explicit and is not a form of self-designation. The response of the Christian community as it develops after the resurrection has provided the identification. The implicit pointers in the parables do not stand alone. They are part of a wider set of circumstances involving Jesus' other modes of teaching, his exorcisms and healings, and his approach to the institutions and sources of power of his time. In none of these are explicit signs given; they are, rather, refused.

## THE KINGDOM OF GOD AND THE PARABLES

An overall theological embrace of the parables is found—sometimes too readily—in the proclamation by Jesus of the kingdom of God. The parables which are introduced by a reference to the kingdom are not the only ones which must be considered under this head, nor is the introduction always an essential guide to the interpretation but is, as shown above, largely the creation of the Matthaean school. Basically, the declaration that the kingdom is at hand proclaimed an imminent change which would mean not the "end of the world" in some cataclysmic sense but the end of an "age," the effective end of men's institutions as known and possessed, which would involve at the very least a radical reorientation (or "repentance"). We tend to interpret the parables by some concept of the kingdom we have already in mind (as was illustrated by a period which titled some parables as those of "Growth" in the sense of a progression by stages), rather than interpreting the concept of the kingdom by an independent exegesis of the parables.

The radical factor of God's essential difference from men and of his intention, or "will," is not to be seen in a disparity between the life of men and the kingdom of God. It is to be found in the transmutation of the ordinary affairs of life into the nexus of divine-human confrontation and decision. In other words, the secularity of the parables must be taken with utter seriousness. It is there that the kingdom is defined, paradoxically, and not in the religious-institutional-regulative affairs of some kind of theocracy. This is seen particularly in the one parable which deals with a religious topic, the Pharisee and the Tax Collector (Luke 18:9-14). Here both men are engaged in a religious activity, the approach to God through prayer. Yet the point is precisely that the one who is by definition, because of his employ, excluded from the possibility of any formal religious life at all is "justified," or accepted, rather than the one whose obedience to the rules is scrupulous, whose religious qualifications are impeccable. In fact, in no parable does the secular impact make itself so felt as in this exceptional religious scene.

Watchfulness for the new "action of God," response to the proclamation (which is essential to any understanding of the Sermon on the Mount), means an openness which the life of regulated minutiae does not permit—which may explain why many of the parables themselves are open-ended. At the same time response, adequate response, could mean only thoroughgoing commitment without any clear definition or limitation as to what one was committing oneself. This is how we must read Jesus' "Follow me." God is to that extent unpredictable or, better, is not by any human measure predictable. If Mark's insistence on "repentance" is to be read as part of the original proclamation of Jesus, it can be accepted if read in this sense. We are not to read the parables (again, as with the kingdom) in the light of some prior understanding of repentance or prescription of what "faith" is. Rather, we must understand the turn to faith and its consequences in the light of the parables, so many of which involve a moment of decision and trust.

## THE CHURCH, THE INDIVIDUAL, AND THE PARABLES
The "theological possibilities" of the parables do not come essentially from their acute analysis of man's situation as man (or man under God), though this is part of their genius. They come primarily from their challenge to Jewish man in his religious situation as a member of the Jewish people, self-conceived as the people of God to whom a particular destiny has been revealed. The germ is found here of so much more than mere ecclesiology. In a very real sense (as well as by self-description) the Christian church takes the place in the world—or part of the place—of Israel as biblically conceived. But if it claims to take over the *function* of Israel, as, for instance, the vehicle of God's ongoing revelation, the community of spiritual power, the missionary instrument of God to the world, the expectant community, it also becomes subject to the warnings and promises we find applied to Israel in the parables.

It is not to man as individual man, initially, that the parables apply, but to man in his religious context as part of a community, yet they do so in nonreligious terms, at once identifying his religious life with life itself and the community of the religious with the human community. For the basic modern question in human relationships, interpersonal or international, is whether other people or peoples are to be treated as human beings. The importance of the modern critical study of the parables is not to limit their interpretation to what may be recovered of their impact in Jesus' time, nor even their meaning in the *Sitz im Leben,* the life situation of the church in the Evangelists' times. The importance of the analytical survey of the original import is that they be not treated as offering generalized universal "truths" but as proclamations concerning the situation of man under *this* God in a situation which, since Jesus and because of Christ, has been and always will be critical. Quite obviously this has its application to the individual, but if God's purpose be not needlessly and invalidly confined to the church, it applies mutatis mutandis to the succeeding generations of men and to the social structures which, since the decline of Christendom, carry the burden of fulfilling God's work in the world—or fail to do so. For example, the Empty House and the Barren Fig Tree are but two examples of many parables which, as has been suggested, depend upon the fulfillment of an inherent or appointed function. This applied originally to Jesus' own people in the presence of a crisis they were not prepared to identify or acknowledge as God's doing.

The same judgment or promise applies always to the church, which, properly aware of Christ's presence spiritually now as physically then, stands always under his judgment—the judgment of function fulfilled or unfulfilled. Does it not apply, therefore, to any institution of man, from the state itself through courts of justice, schools, economic systems, banks, social organizations, and the family? What Jesus is reported to have said of the sabbath, and must, to the Jews, apply to any lesser institution also, is spelled out in parable after parable: "The sabbath was made for man, not man for the sabbath." The assurance of their original bearing on Jesus' own situation, on his people's institutions and calling, only reinforces the point; it does not deprive us of it.

## RELATIONSHIP AND THE PARABLES

As suggested, the secularity of the parables *is* their religious power, and this is diminished when allegorical identifications are made which, when they become dogmatic or official, restrict the meaning. On the other hand, the recovery of their original existential meaning sets them free to be interpreted as sui generis in all times and places; not in spite of their "Jewishness" or "first-century-ness" but because of it. The teaching which they contain in nonreligious form this age is perhaps prepared to recover as no other, for it suggests the truly God-given and God-judged and God-promised nature of the human, social, and historical situation.

In many of the parables, for instance, the essential point revolves about relationships—their loss and restoration, their demanding nature, their opportunity for acceptance or rejection. The best-known parables, the Prodigal Son and the Good Samaritan, are cases in point. They have been distorted, as so many others, by having acquired non-Gospel titles. The overall problem in the Prodigal Son is the problem of two opposed responses to a relationship broken and suddenly available for restoration and advancement, depicted by the contrasted reactions of the father and the brother to the returned younger son. The point really depends upon *not* identifying the father with God but leaving open the opportunity of identifying ourselves (or our social systems) with either father or brother. *Then* we can ask which is the more like God. The Good Samaritan (in its Lucan context, the only one we have) changes the question asked, which postpones decision and action, "Who is my neighbor?" to one which permits of no evasion, "Which of these *was* neighbor?"; from object to subject. In the issue, the parables of the Two Sons, of the Slave in Field and House, the Rich Man and Lazarus, the Laborers in the Vineyard, the Unmerciful Servant, the Tenants of the Vineyard, the Approach to Court, the Friend at Midnight, and the Banquet (especially in the Lucan version) all essentially involve relationships of one kind or another. So does Christianity at its very core. The purpose of the particular relationship—the proper response within it, its reflection of the relationship to God within and through and over it—comes into question. The Gospels, indeed, the whole New Testament, do not deal with "relationship" as an abstraction but with relationships— this relation and that relation and the other. This very particularity of the parables keeps them from being general rules, since they remain analogues of crucial decisions confronting all men in similar conditions under God. For though the form may derive from first-century Palestine, relationships in family life, business, government, and social activities have their analogies currently and always will. In fact, the highest name of faith for the understanding of Jesus and of our destiny in Christ is the relationship term "son." There is here, indeed, an element far beyond the abstraction "sonship."

## THE PARABLES AS "SITUATIONAL"

The secularity of the parables is the heart of the impact of Jesus in the Gospels because it is not a feature confined to the Gospels alone. Jesus was not an academician or an ecclesiastical lawgiver. It is obvious that his conflict with the Pharisees, with whom his teaching had more in common than with any other group, centered upon the rigidity of even their case rules by which they applied Torah. Jesus, in the parables, lays down no maxims or universal laws. The particularity of relationships suggested above, and of critical confrontations inherent in the times, reveals that his teaching was "situational"—as were the Epistles of Paul and his treatment of the problems which arose for Christians in his churches. Religion for the Jew was solidly based on Torah, "sound instruction." To the Gentile world of hellenic culture (many Jews had been influenced by hellenization) religion basically meant an esoteric or gnostic salvation, deliverance of an inner man from the estrangement and defilement of a world involved in decay and death. Law, which could easily lead to making a claim on God and to the exclusion of lesser men, and "knowledge," which implied a private salvation, find no support in the parables until they are allegorized out of their situational Jewish setting.

The Christian religion, as Paul so clearly saw, is different from both—a scandal to Jews and confusion to Greeks—as the parables should be allowed to make clear. Jesus, the prophet and teacher who was to become celebrated as the Wisdom of God and the Savior of man, spoke in terms of the situation in secular language and everyday images, a paradox which has given Christianity self-renewing power, the power to reform itself when it becomes institutionalized, legalized, exclusive, or esoteric.

Yet the Gospels are not simply the record of the teaching of an uncongenial Jew. They have much to do with what happened *to* him and, therefore, what happened *because* of him. Thus the situational character of Jesus' teaching reflects the immediate situation in which he was placed and in which he himself was the catalyst, and which resolved itself in the situation of the cross. The study of the Gospels as a distinct genre affecting all the parts which go to make up a Gospel has made this even more clear. The suffering and death of Jesus are not separate items but the precipitate of his whole ministry, in which, as we have seen, the parabolic teaching could lead only to making the issues clear and making the confrontation in Jerusalem inevitable.

It was not with joy that Jesus entered upon the final task. In any case the part did not permit it. It may be thought from our treatment of the parables of warning that there is an element of—should one say "glee" or "vindictiveness"?—in Jesus' self-vindication. This would be completely to misinterpret the record. It is reported that on the way to Calvary he said to women who wept for him (Luke 23:27-31), "Daughters of Jerusalem, do not weep for me, but weep for yourselves and for your children." His own weeping and doubt were over, and all that remained was the final carrying out of the decision made. As he looked down on Jerusalem he had been reduced to tears—again for the city and not for himself (Luke 19:41-44). In another account he cried, "O Jerusalem, Jerusalem . . . how often would I have gathered your children together" (Matt. 23:37-39; Luke 13:34-35). The "agony" in Gethsemane is unexplained except on this basis. It is impossible to believe that it was prompted by physical apprehension, human though Jesus was, for there is nothing elsewhere to indicate it. Human nature requires, psychologically and physically, enough fear to stimulate heroic action, but it is surely not fear that explains why he "began to be greatly distressed and troubled (Mark 14:33)" or why, according to Luke, "his sweat became like great drops of blood falling down upon the ground (22:44)." Fear scarcely explains his prayer, "If it be possible, let this cup pass from me; nevertheless, not as I will, but as thou wilt (Matt. 26:39)." We may reject also the explanation that the agony was produced by the burden of "the sin of the world" as being clearly too theological. We are left then with the actual situation. While Jesus might not be in agony over himself, he might well be in agony over his people, over the Holy City, over "God's chosen." He was, as we insisted at the beginning, a Jew. We cannot ignore the passionate devotion of the Jew to his people and to Jerusalem. It is, in plain fact, still news. If our interpretation of the parables is correct, Jesus foresaw the rejection by Israel of his call to the nation, a call which he saw as final. To reject him meant to reject its place in God's purposes. Jesus himself must ask whether there is no further hope. Would not one more prayer avail? Could there be no other way but the disaster that must follow his own rejection? We can never imagine that a Jew would visualize the final answer and all it involved with composure. And yet if there be no other way, then the will of God be done! It was a bitter cup, for it meant the failure of his immediate mission, even while he committed the ultimate outcome to the inscrutable wisdom of God.[31]

It was, then, only in agony of spirit, that Jesus preached his message and pursued the strategy in which the parables are tactical elements. His strategy was completed by his own self-offering in place of his people. But before he went, he sealed in the upper room the covenant of the new fellowship that was to find its life in his death. Whatever else we may see in the Last Supper, it was this without doubt—a new consecration of the Twelve and a new binding of the ties that had so doubtfully held them to his real purpose. It was an act that could not have meaning as yet and, indeed, must always be bereft of its full meaning until "he . . . come again," for it was and is an eschatological meal.

In the interim we who claim to be of his following are faced with the fact that the parables as well as the cross—or, more strictly, the parables as part of the drama of the cross—present us with the problem of the person of Christ. This can only be solved by the response people are inspired by the Holy Spirit to make to him, in the making of which and in fellowship with the church they will come to know who he is.

This presents us with the serious task of preaching. The preaching of the Jesus of the parables involves not only the parables as material but the study of the parables as used by Jesus to form our own method of presenting the Gospel. If at first the result of study seems to deprive the preacher of favorite themes, as is the case with many of the better-known parables, it is in the interest of bringing the preacher nearer to the source of inspiration. The allegorical method promises more scope only on the superficial level. The preacher is well advised to limit what he says on each occasion to one topic only, for sermons are difficult to listen to with profit and the bulk of the hearers have the capacity to assimilate only one point. Jesus' technique in the parables was precisely this: his stories and comparisons focused attention on one point, and scenery, character, psychology, and action all reinforced it. It is just here that allegory fails the speaker, for that form needs the leisurely attention of the reader rather than the active participation of the hearer. It was by its appeal for a judgment, expressed or unexpressed, that the parable called forth participation and provided that living relationship between speaker and audience which so much preaching fails to secure. In order to do this the similitude, by its very nature, called upon the ordinary experience and everyday observation of the people. This sense of identity between pulpit and pew can profitably be learned again from our study.

But the parable was also related to the situation and addressed itself to some positive response. Although the response was fatal to Jesus, there is no reason to say that he failed. His impact, notably in his parables, was inescapable; increased enmity as well as increased following was a sign of their effectiveness. It is sometimes impossible to discern what the modern preacher aims to achieve unless it be admiration or the performance of a task. To see Jesus at work with the parables leads us to seek again the power of a message that will "not return . . . void." The issues to which Jesus addressed himself were of burning importance at the time, and the timeliness of truth must always be a prime concern of the pulpit.

The particular moment and its issues have passed, but Jesus' words are not swallowed up by the moment. The surrender of allegorical spread in favor of pointed concentration in the interpretation of the parables forces us to deep consideration of the fundamental issue Jesus raised in each case. Here the preacher also must learn to discern the signs of the times. God and the nature of his kingdom, dependent on his will; the church with its very nature to which it dare not be untrue; the perpetual frailty and lovableness of the human spirit—these, finding their solution in the Christ who dealt with them, are perennial themes and take us to the heart of the Christian religion. With these the parables deal, and by doing so reveal their central concern with a theology that is always related to the real world rather than to a world we would create after our own desires. The preacher must become again, in H. H. Farmer's fine phrase, "the servant of the Word."

It is not simply that God speaks through Jesus and his parables but that through Christ God acts. "In the *words* of the Lord are his *works* (Ecclus. 42:15c)." The parables alone—so often neglected as no more than *illustrations* of Jesus' teaching—confront us with the will of God, the nature of his kingdom, the centrality of his mercy, the inevitability of his judgment, the inescapable function of his church, and the response expected of his people. And all find their focus in the crucified and risen Christ, whose concern in the parables was that none should misunderstand or escape God's claim, and least of all himself. To respond to him is to respond to his teaching as the sacrament of God's present confrontation of us, as surely a means of grace as Baptism or the Supper of the Lord. The parables viewed as organic to his person and ministry demand a personal commitment.

When we thus read them, as those who have within themselves and in the long life of the church the testimony of the resurrection, they become the divine Word and their teaching the law of life. If we be redeemed into his following, then we too cannot be deterred in the task God seeks to accomplish through us by any failure or opposition. The kingdom of God is discovered for us as present reality and the inescapable catalytic agent of history and society. To discover it is to count all else worth the sacrifice. Our concern must always be to prevent its manifestations from being used as a means instead of only as the end. For the kingdom is not ours to use to our own purpose, and God is not the servant of any civilization or institution, no matter how cherished. We cannot even profess to build the kingdom, for it is beyond our control, existing by the inherent right of its own laws which are not less than the will of God. We are permitted to make way for it, to level the hills and fill the valleys on the highway along which it is to march. Above all we may pray for it, if we can also pray for ourselves, "Thy will be done."

When Jesus' struggle becomes for us not simply that of a human champion but the impact of an invasion from heaven, we find the church faced with the solemn responsibility of Israel and subject to the judgments which fall in greater and not less measure on "the household of God." It is first of all a missionary obligation. Truth cherished is truth lost until it is shared. No exclusiveness can narrow the field, nor may any considerations, dogmatic, ecclesiastical, social, or personal, be allowed to keep us from whatever will implement the church's God-given purpose. We cannot allow ourselves to be governed by our flagging sensitivity to need, for back of the springs of sympathy lies the declared will of God in its uncaused and loving initiative.

With the God revealed by his Son in the parables and in his life, there can be no bookkeeping, nor pressing of claim, but only surrender to God's grace in childlike faith and trust. It is God himself who presents us with the alternative of freely chosen love or judgment. And it applies to churches as much as to individuals. The grace of God and the Christian institutions which are the instruments of its mediation are given for use, for his use, and when not so used are taken away and the misusers rejected. The Gospel is a trust. There is required therefore of Christians and churches faithfulness, watchfulness, and diligent service with confiding prayer. For we were "bought with a price." The Day of the Lord is still to come, and the hour no man knows. The church is an eschatological reality and the Christian life in its fellowship is but an "arrabon," a first installment of the life to come when "we shall see him even as he is."

For, much as we may learn from the parables when we know their accents to be His who is the "fulness of the Godhead," still more important is what we may learn from them of our Lord himself. The cure for sentimentality in the presentation of Jesus is to know the Jesus who appears in the parables no less than to consider the "mighty acts" which God accomplished for our redemption in him. For in the parables Jesus appears as no Eastern sage or objective moralist but as the Initiator of God's new age and the Agent of his purpose. He is not the kindly advocate of brotherly love but the revealer of the dreadful love of God and the awe of the divine mercy. He is no passive victim of circumstance or preordained plan but the active doer of God's perfect will in the face of scorn, opposition, and death, fearless in his consistency and consistent in his fearlessness. He is no Jewish prophet, not even the greatest, but the Servant of the Lord: Israel, the true Israel, incarnate. Not merely prophecy is fulfilled in him but the purposes of God which had come to but faltering fulfillment in the history of his people. And equally he is the church, for we are of the church only when we are "in him and he in us."

To us, then, as to those who first heard the parables, he says, even now, "Blessed are your eyes, for they see; and your ears, for they hear" because "unto you is given the mystery of the kingdom of God."

# ABBREVIATIONS USED

*ATR*   Anglican Theological Review
ET     English translation
*HTR*   Harvard Theological Review
*JBL*   Journal of Biblical Literature
KJV   King James Version
NT     The New Testament
*NTS*   New Testament Studies
OT     The Old Testament
RSV   Revised Standard Version
RV    Revised Version
*SBT*   Studies in Biblical Theology (1st and 2nd series)

# NOTES

**PRELIMINARY NOTE**

Since 1948 the following treatments of the parables have been published or revised in English. Dates in parentheses indicate the original edition. References in the Notes to the works listed here are by the name of the author. Only a few articles are referred to, but these works will lead the student to fuller resources. Periodical literature may be traced in *New Testament Abstracts* for the years since 1956. Linnemann gives a good bibliography down to 1964. (English editions are given where they were used, but in some cases there are also American editions, and frequently the page numbers will be the same.)

Dodd, Charles H. *The Parables of the Kingdom* (1935). London: Nisbet & Co., rev. ed., 1961.

Jeremias, Joachim. *The Parables of Jesus* (1947). ET of 6th German ed. New York: Charles Scribner's Sons, 1963. This revised edition takes account of and quotes the parables in the "Gospel of Thomas."

Linnemann, Eta. *Jesus of the Parables* (1961). ET of 3rd German ed. New York: Harper and Row, 1966. An exposition for teachers with extensive critical notes dealing with thirteen parables.

Jones, Geraint V. *The Art and Truth of the Parables.* London: Society for Promoting Christian Knowledge, 1964. Includes a good summary of developments leading up to the modern study. Gives an "existential interpretation" of the Prodigal Son.

Kahlefeld, Heinrich. *Parables and Instructions in the Gospels,* Part I (1963). ET. New York: Herder & Herder, 1966. A Catholic work using the modern method. Index and bibliography will appear in a second volume.

Via, Dan O., Jr. *The Parables: Their Literary and Existential Dimensions.* Philadelphia: Fortress Press, 1967. Deals with eight parables.

Bultmann, Rudolf. *The History of the Synoptic Tradition.* ET. Oxford: Blackwell, 1963.

Perrin, Norman. *Rediscovering the Teaching of Jesus.* London: S.C.M. Press, 1967.

Kingsbury, Jack D. *The Parables of Jesus in Matthew Thirteen: A Study in Redaction-Criticism.* Richmond: John Knox Press, 1969.

Reumann, John H. P. *Jesus in the Church's Gospels.* Philadelphia: Fortress Press, 1968. Uses the parables to illuminate the preaching.

Derrett, J. Duncan M. *Law in the New Testament*. London: Darton, Longman & Todd, 1970.

Black, Matthew. *An Aramaic Approach to the Gospels and Acts*. 3rd ed. New York: Oxford University Press, 1967.

Robinson, James M., and Helmut Koester. *Trajectories Through Early Christianity*. Philadelphia: Fortress Press, 1971.

Guillaumont, A., Puech, Henri-Charles, et al. *The Gospel According to Thomas*. New York: Harper & Brothers, 1959. Coptic text and translation.

Grant, Robert M., and D. M. Freedman. *The Secret Sayings of Jesus*. London: Fontana Books, 1960. Uses a different notation from Guillaumont for the Logia but gives plate and line numbers.

Metzger, Bruce M. Translation of the Gospel of Thomas in Appendix I to Kurt Aland, ed., *Synopsis Quattuor Evangeliorum*. Greek. (Uses same Logia notation as Guillaumont.)

Montefiore, Hugh. "A Comparison of the Parables of the Gospel According to Thomas and of the Synoptic Gospels" in Hugh Montefiore and H. E. W. Turner, *Thomas and the Evangelists*. SBT 35. Napierville, Ill.: Alec R. Allenson, 1962.

Kümmel, Werner G. *Promise and Fulfilment*. ET. *SBT* 23. Napierville, Ill.: Alec R. Allenson, 1957. A study of eschatology.

Fuchs, Ernst. *Studies of the Historical Jesus*. ET. *SBT* 42. London: S.C.M. Press, 1964.

Bornkamm, Gunther. *Jesus of Nazareth*. ET. London: Hodder & Stoughton, 1960.

Wilder, Amos N. *The Language of the Gospel: Early Christian Rhetoric*. New York: Harper & Row, 1964. Especially Chapter V.

Funk, Robert W. *Language, Hermeneutic and the Word of God,* Part Two. New York: Harper & Row, 1966.

These popular and homiletical books are among those suitable for lay use:

Barclay, William. *And Jesus Said*. Philadelphia: Westminster Press, 1970.

Hunter, Archibald M. *Interpreting the Parables*. Philadelphia: Westminster Press, 1961.

Jeremias, Joachim. *Rediscovering the Parables*. New York: Scribner, 1966.

Straton, Hillyer H. *A Guide to the Parables of Jesus*. Grand Rapids, Mich.: Eerdmans, 1959.

Thielicke, Helmut. *The Waiting Father* (sermons). New York: Harper & Brothers, 1959.

## CHAPTER ONE: THE PARABLES AND THE CRUCIFIXION

1. Leslie Weatherhead, *In Quest of a Kingdom* (Nashville: Abingdon Press, 1944), pp. 57f.; cf. Jeremias, p. 21. There has been, of course, literary refinement by the Evangelists. A new interest has arisen in the form and function of the parables as literary aesthetic forms, theologically as a function of the concept of "word-event" (various terms are used). The latter may be traced in Fuchs and his pupil Linnemann, Funk, Jones, and Via. Linnemann and Via

have noted that this approach does not necessarily exclude the line represented in this volume. See Via, p. 55, note 23, on anticipation of the "language-event" in essence by Dodd and Thomas W. Manson. Via remarks, "Jesus' parables . . . do have a translatable content, and they also bear in a peculiar way the stamp of Jesus' mind and relate to his historical situation. . . . We in turn try to interpret Jesus' ministry in the light of the parables and, secondarily and to a lesser extent, the parables in the light of his ministry" (p. 37). That is basically our theme.

2. For earlier discussion of the background and nature of parable, see B. T. D. Smith, *The Parables of the Synoptic Gospels* (London: Cambridge University Press, 1937); William O. Oesterley, *The Parables in the Light of Their Jewish Background* (New York: Macmillan, 1936); C. H. Dodd, *The Parables of the Kingdom* (London: Nisbet, 1936); and Arthur T. Cadoux, *The Parables of Jesus, Their Art and Use* (London: James Clarke & Co., 1930; New York: Macmillan, 1931).

The lecture basis of my book was given in 1946-47 at the College of Preachers in Washington. In 1948 when the book was in the press I read Jeremias' *Die Gleichnisse Jesu* with mounting excitement, since I found we had pursued essentially the same method and arrived at substantially the same results in general. As will be seen, there are points at which I still have reservations and others where his superior personal knowledge of the background has corrected or amplified my views. Jeremias' revised ET lists (p. 24) the parables of "The Gospel of Thomas" and quotes them (*in loc.*). Whether they represent "an independent tradition" is open to question (see below).

3. Here I am particularly indebted to the discussion in Cadoux. Jeremias made the same stress and, in later editions, quoted my book. Jesus' method of involving his audience is particularly developed by Linnemann. She uses the term *Verschränkung* (German ed., p. 35; ET, "phenomenon of interlocking," p. 27). See Via's comments on her presentation, pp. 53-56; cf. Bultmann, pp. 191ff.

4. This biblical term covers also: proverb (Ezek. 18:2; Matt. 5:14), taunt (Ps. 69:11; Isa. 14:4), prophetic utterance (Num. 23:7ff.), riddle (Prov. 1:6), allegory (Ezek. 17:2ff.; Matt. 13:36ff.), moral counsel (Prov. 1:1; Luke 14:7ff.), and discourse (Job 27:1). The judgment of the Son of man (Matt. 25:31ff.) falls into the last category, containing only the incidental simile of the sheep and the goats. Though popularly known as a parable, it is not treated here; cf. Jeremias, p. 20, p. 206, n. 77.

Bultmann, following Jülicher (see Note 6), distinguished, apart from metaphors, two divisions: (1) similitude (*Gleichnisse*) with more detail, often as a rhetorical question rather than a comparison (and, of course, without formal application), developed either out of figures (*Bildworten*) or a comparison (*Vergleich*); and (2) parable *(Parabel)*, which "transposes the acts which serve for a similitude into a narrative . . . gives as its picture not a *typical condition or a typical, recurrent event*, but some interesting particular situation [*Einzelfall*]" (ET, pp. 170, 174; italics added, as this describes more fully a similitude). But, Bultmann adds, "the boundaries fluctuate."

To these are added "exemplary stories," pp. 177-79. I would question whether, although these are not obvious comparisons, there is not a sense in which they are parables, certainly in function.

5. For a modern revival see, e.g., C. S. Lewis' stories of Narnia. On the literary technique of the similitudes and parables, see Bultmann, pp. 188-91, and B. T. D. Smith, op. cit., pp. 35f. Bultmann is quoted in full in Linnemann, pp. 12-16, and paraphrased in Kingsbury, pp. 7f.

6. Jülicher's *Die Gleichnisreden Jesu* was first published in 1888. More recently there has been renewed discussion, arguing that allegorical elements may be found in Jewish parables (e.g., Kingsbury, pp. 3-7) and may be admitted in the teaching of Jesus. For a careful Catholic discussion, see R. F. Brown, "Parable and Allegory Reconsidered," *Novum Testamentum*, 5 (1962). See Linnemann, pp. 5-8, who shares the nonallegorical view: "The parable is used to reconcile opposition, the allegory pre-supposes an understanding. For the uninitiated the allegory is a riddle" (p. 7). See also Via's chapter, "Parable and Allegory," pp. 2-25. He says, "I would conclude that those stories which do not *need* to be taken as allegories *ought* not to be so taken" (p. 16). See Chapter Eight below.

7. The "one-point" method of interpretation has recently been questioned; see, e.g., Via, pp. 13-17, who concludes that "while the meaning of Jesus' parables cannot be restricted to one central point of comparison, that does not mean that they are allegories" (p. 17). Good questions are raised, but the discovery of the overall thrust or central point on which judgment is to be made, or which is critical to the telling of the parable, still provides the important *starting point* for interpretation and is a safeguard against a still-persistent tendency of interpreters and preachers to fall back into allegory. On this see Via's comments on Fuchs, pp. 19-21. Via's own method is stated: "What is needed is a hermeneutical and literary methodology which can identify the permanently significant element *in* the parables and can elaborate a means of translating elements without distorting the original intention. It will then not be necessary to allegorize or to add anything" (pp. 23f.). See also Funk, chapter 5, "The Parables as Metaphor," and his criticism of Jeremias' "single point" approach (p. 147; cf. pp. 149f. and his note 75). See references below to Wilder.

8. See, e.g., Weatherhead, *In Quest of a Kingdom*, and George A. Buttrick, *The Parables of Jesus* (New York: Harper & Brothers, 1928) for older homiletical treatment. The emphasis in Dodd was largely on "realised eschatology." More recently there has developed a new interest in hermeneutics (see James M. Robinson, *The New Hermeneutic*, New Frontiers in Theology, vol. 2 [New York: Harper & Row, 1964], for an account, as well as more briefly in Funk). Treatment of the parables as "language event" has a clear justification in the aspect of involvement with the listener and demand for a judgment on his part, as in these chapters. The words of the parable bring things to pass, but they also make possible an understanding of Jesus' "style of life" which thereby comes to expression and is involved in his fate. See especially Funk's application, where he deals with the Great Supper and the Good Samaritan (pp. 124-222), and Via, pp. 26-29. "Jesus' parables were a language-event in that (1) they injected a new possibility into the situation of the hearers . . .

(2) because they called for a judgment from the hearers" (Via, p. 53). The self-involvement of the interpreter is crucial, but of initial importance is putting ourselves in the position of the original audience, trying to hear as they heard. Here such works as Derrett can contribute (see notes to chapters below). To that step, as an aid in preaching, my book was primarily directed, but it also made initial suggestions as to "translation" (Via's term).

9. This study does not attempt to deal with every saying in the general category (estimated between thirty and one hundred!) but with those which seem clearly related to the central understanding of Jesus and his mission.

"Redaction criticism," the study of the use of the tradition by the Evangelists, taken into some account here and in Jeremias, etc., has begun to be applied to the parables. An example is Kingsbury on Matthew 13. See also my article, "The Mixed State of the Church in Matthew's Gospel," in *JBL* 82 (1963), pp. 149-68 (hereafter referred to as "Mixed State"). See below on "the situation in the life of the church" (*Sitz im Leben*).

10. Further comments on the systematic or theological aspects will be found in Chapter Eight. Cf. the last chapter of my *The Paradox of Jesus in the Gospels* (Philadelphia: Westminster Press, 1969; hereafter cited as *Paradox*).

There is general agreement on topics for grouping the parables. See, e.g., Perrin's list, p. 83, which differs from our five in treating the "seed" group last. Jeremias' list is strongly eschatological. Via, treating eight as basically aesthetic literary entities from an "existential" point of view, essays to group them under the headings "tragic" and "comic" (see further below). See Kahlefeld's justification for thematic treatment: "The reader should be able to linger awhile with one theme and to see how one parable assists another" (p. 13).

11. There is not space here to discuss the "new quest of the historical Jesus" and the continuity of teaching from Jesus to the church. Jeremias showed that the process must be reversed—"The Return to Jesus from the Primitive Church." See Fuchs, Bornkamm, and Perrin and, for further review, James M. Robinson, "A New Quest of the Historical Jesus," *SBT* 25 (1959); Joachim Jeremias, *The Problem of the Historical Jesus* (Philadelphia: Fortress Press, 1964); Carl E. Braaten and Roy A. Harrisville, eds., *The Historical Jesus and the Kerygmatic Christ* (Nashville: Abingdon Press, 1964) and *Kerygma and History* (Nashville: Abingdon Press, 1962), especially N. A. Dahl, "The Problem of the Historical Jesus." Note Dahl's comment: "Accordingly, no one can maintain that historical research has access only to the preaching of Jesus and not to his life. Rather, we must state that an historical understanding of his preaching can be attained only when it is seen in connection with his life, namely with the life which ended on the cross" (p. 159).

Much more interest has been shown in the content and function of the parables in the last decades. Two among many examples may be given as indications: Perrin on Jeremias—"At this point he is able to argue that the tradition in this form must be ascribed to Jesus rather than to the early Church, because it now fits the situation of the ministry of the historical Jesus much better than that of the earliest Christian community" (p. 21)—and Helmut

Koester (see Robinson and Koester in Preliminary Note) on the Gospel of Thomas—"The second conspicuous element is the use of parables, the most genuine vessels of Jesus' own proclamation of the Kingdom" (p. 139).

In view of the foregoing discussion, the eighth chapter of the 1948 edition (which was largely a summary) has been replaced by my present Chapter Eight.

12. The discussion here may be reviewed in the light of much debate since, but the theory that it is Mark speaking, not Jesus, has in general been maintained by most writers on the parables, including Kahlefeld (pp. 36, 38). Bornkamm holds that the saying in its present form does not go back to Jesus and comments that "this interpretation of the parables, as designed to alienate, breaks down in every parable of Jesus, and conflicts with the evangelist's own words at the end of his chapter" (p. 71). An attempt by C. F. D. Moule to restore the saying to Jesus is feasible only if it is possible to read "those outside" to mean those who exclude themselves (see "Mark 4:1-20 Yet Once More" in Edward E. Ellis and Max Wilcox, eds., *Neotestimentica et Semitica* [Edinburgh: T. & T. Clark, 1969], pp. 95ff.). Dr. Moule rightly commends Eta Linnemann's fourth chapter, on communication, where she says, "The narrator with his parable . . . can compel his listener to a decision; but what the decision is rests with the listener" (p. 22). Note also George B. Caird's remark that "even an open secret remains a secret from those who do not wish to learn it" (*Gospel of St. Luke* [Baltimore: Penguin Books, 1963], p. 118).

## CHAPTER TWO: THE PARABLES AND THE RESURRECTION

1. Useful studies of this development are found in Martin Dibelius, *From Tradition to Gospel*, ET (New York: Charles Scribner's Sons, 1935); Vincent Taylor, *The Formation of the Gospel Tradition* (New York: Macmillan, 1933); Charles H. Dodd, *The Apostolic Preaching and Its Developments* (Chicago: Willett, Clark & Company, 1937), and in the many developments of the "history-of-the-tradition" method. Jeremias contributed a useful phrase to summarize what follows, viz., "the change of audience."

In the chapters that follow, the italics in the texts of the parables indicate form-critical considerations.

2. In *Paradox* I tried to explore ways in which such controls may have operated. See also C. K. Barrett, *Jesus and the Gospel Tradition* (Philadelphia: Fortress Press, 1968), pp. 14-17. The cohesive force of the resurrection narratives, for all their discrepancies, is to insist that the Jesus known in the flesh was now the risen Lord (*Paradox*, pp. 182-200).

3. With the possible exception of a structured series of sayings (possibly in rhythmic form) like the Beatitudes. Cf. Black, chapter 7, especially pp. 162ff.

4. For a cautious discussion of Jesus' failure, see Charles Guignebert, *Jesus* (New York: University Books, 1956), pp. 212ff., and cf. *Paradox*, pp. 123f.

5. On the "historical Jesus" see Note 11 to Chapter One.

6. For further discussion see Chapter Five, Note 1.

7. For further study of the parables in Matthew and their relation to the situation of the early church see my "Mixed State."

8. Dodd, p. 25: "The teaching of Jesus is not the leisurely and patient exposition of a system by a founder of a school."

9. Joseph Klausner, *Jesus of Nazareth* (New York: Macmillan, 1925), p. 368. The assumption that Jesus taught in Aramaic and that "Aramaisms" are present in the Gospel texts should be treated with caution. See frequent references in Jeremias, and cf. Black.

10. Cf. Klausner's judgment: "He is as expert in the Scriptures as the best of the Pharisees . . . he can employ them for his own spiritual needs, he can expound them and adapt them and supplement them" (op. cit., p. 409). This would need to be modified by more recent studies of the use of the OT in the Gospels in view of the Qumran scrolls. See, e.g., Krister Stendahl, *The School of St. Matthew*, rev. ed. (Philadelphia: Fortress Press, 1966), and Barnabas Lindars, *New Testament Apologetic* (Philadelphia: Westminster Press, 1961).

11. Of the rabbinic parallels, see Claude G. Montefiore's caution that whether they are characteristic rather than frequent or infrequent needs to be determined (*The Synoptic Gospels*, 2nd ed., vol. I [London: Macmillan & Co. Ltd.], pp. cxxxviii ff.).

12. Vladimir G. Simkhovitch, *Toward the Understanding of Jesus* (New York: Macmillan, 1923), p. 3. The reference does not endorse his thesis but refers to his acute analysis of the situation. Since Simkhovitch's essay (1921), growing attention has been paid to this factor. See Note 14.

13. Ibid., p. 13.

14. See Klausner, op. cit., pp. 154ff. Since the 1950s much attention has been drawn to the Zealot movement and speculations advanced about Jesus' relation to it. See, notably, S. G. F. Brandon, *The Fall of Jerusalem and the Christian Church* (New York: Macmillan, 1951) and *Jesus and the Zealots* (Manchester: Manchester University Press, 1967). More soundly, William R. Farmer, *Maccabees, Zealots, and Josephus* (New York: Columbia University Press, 1956); also Oscar Cullmann, *The State in the New Testament* (New York: Charles Scribner's Sons, 1956), and, partly in answer to Brandon, *Jesus and the Revolutionaries* (New York: Harper & Row, 1970). See my comments on the Barabbas theme, the (so-called) thieves on the crosses, and the Zealot debate in *Paradox*, pp. 169-71, 217-22.

15. John Knox, *Christ the Lord* (Chicago: Willett, Clark & Company, 1945), p. 47.

16. See John Knox, *The Death of Christ* (Nashville: Abingdon Press, 1958); also P. Winter, *On the Trial of Jesus* (Berlin: 1961), and the symposium in honor of C. F. D. Moule, *The Trial of Jesus* (*SBT*, 2nd series 13).

17. The difficulty and limitations of a study of the "titles" dubiously used by Jesus but clearly used of him may be seen in, e.g., Vincent Taylor, *The Names of Jesus* (New York: St. Martin's Press, 1953), and Oscar Cullmann, *The Christology of the New Testament*, rev. ed. (London: S.C.M. Press, 1963); cf. Reginald H. Fuller, *The Foundations of New Testament Christology* (New York: Charles Scribner's Sons, 1965).

18. On the constantly debated subject of the title "Son of man" see list of

references in *Paradox*, p. 131, note 12, to which should be added Ferdinand Hahn, *The Titles of Jesus in Christology*, ET, 1969.

19. Albert Schweitzer, *The Quest of the Historical Jesus*, ET (London: A. & C. Black, 1931), p. 401.

## CHAPTER THREE: THE CALL OF GOD'S KINGDOM

1. For the temptation narratives as postresurrection retrospects on Jesus' ministry, see my *Paradox*, pp. 200-205.

2. The aorist may indicate "inceptive" action. Bultmann is tempted to put the parable among the similitudes except for its strongly narrative form. Of similitudes, he says, "They recount what a smart [literally, "crafty"] plowman, or a merchant, who understands his advantage, will always do" (German 3rd ed., p. 188; cf. ET, p. 174). In this narrative the similitude aspect of a *typical* event is important. On this and related parables see the detailed form-critical study by John D. Crossan, "The Seed Parables of Jesus," in *JBL*, 92 (June 1973), pp. 44-66, with an extensive bibliography. Cf. also Jeremias, pp. 28, 149ff.; Linnemann, pp. 115ff.; Perrin, pp. 155ff. Linnemann holds that the sower himself is not central, as opposed to Jeremias and Fuchs (see her comment on my view, p. 184).

3. The construction, *ho men . . . kai allo . . . kai allo . . . kai alla* ("some . . . other . . . and other . . . and others") suggests a rapid movement to the climax where the emphasis finally falls. Cf. Crossan, op. cit., p. 246; Black, p. 63. On the abundant harvest see Joseph Klausner, *Jesus of Nazareth* (New York: Macmillan, 1925), p. 175.

4. According to Jeremias the plowing followed the sowing in Palestine (p. 11; cf. Linnemann, p. 180, n. 3), but see the more recent discussion in Crossan (p. 245, n. 3, and references there given), which suggests that the plowman would not in any case plow up the path, before or after.

5. The parable in the Gospel of Thomas (Logion 9) is, characteristically, condensed yet has embellishments of its own. It is doubtful whether the Thomas parables are more primitive in spite of their seeming simplicity. They diminish, sometimes change, the point and evidently leave it open for an esoteric (gnostic?) interpretation. As opposed to Perrin, who accepts the independence of the Thomas parables as a "working hypothesis" (p. 36), Grant and Freedman (especially pp. 100-102) feel that the editing of the Gospel tradition is a "warping of the lines laid down in our Gospels."

6. Jeremias, e.g., spells out the reasons which convinced him (pp. 77-79); cf. Bultmann, p. 187.

7. See John M. Creed, *The Gospel According to St. Luke* (New York: Macmillan, 1930), pp. 116ff.; cf. George B. Caird, *Gospel of St. Luke* (Baltimore: Penguin Books, 1963), p. 118. See Kingsbury's study of the Matthaean redaction, pp. 32ff.

8. Titles given to the parables in Bibles and commentaries depend on the interpretation presupposed and are in no wise part of the text. Titles, when used, should be as neutral a description of the content as possible, as has been attempted here and in most of the books cited in the Preliminary Note.

9. *The Apostolic Fathers*, vol. I, ET by Kirsopp Lake (Loeb Classical Li-

brary), pp. 206-7. I have pointed to a similar transition in the New Testament use of the term "fishers of men" in my article, "Fishers of Men: Footnotes on a Gospel Metaphor," in *HTR*, vol. LII, no. 3 (July 1959), pp. 187ff. (hereafter cited as "Fishers of Men"). Hermeneutics does not require that the same term must mean the same thing in each stratum of the tradition: cf. Bultmann, p. 172; Kingsbury, pp. 84ff. See also I. Abrahams, *Studies in Pharisaism and the Gospel*, 1st series, chap. 4 (New York: Cambridge University Press, 1970).

10. Jeremias lists this and the Mustard Seed under "The Great Assurance" (p. 146). In Thomas, Logion 96 is surely an adaptation (Perrin, p. 158, "transformed in the service of gnosticism"). It starts with "a little leaven" which makes "large loaves"; the all-pervasive aspect is lost. Thomas adds the familiar "who has ears" saying and a non-Gospel parable (Logion 97) of the woman who lost meal from her jar.

11. The quotation is from the commentary on Jonah in *Parker's People's Bible*, p. 260. The reference was very kindly sent me in 1953 by the late Archdeacon Herbert L. Johnson of Marshfield, Mass.

12. Cf. Crossan, op. cit., pp. 253-59. See also Bultmann, p. 172; Jeremias, pp. 146ff.; Kingsbury, pp. 76-84. Thomas, Logion 20, stresses tilled ground and shelter for the birds (in which Perrin, p. 157, sees gnosticizing elements).

13. William O. Oesterley, *The Parables in the Light of Their Jewish Background* (New York: Macmillan, 1936), pp. 253-59. Cf. Jeremias, p. 148. In parts of the United States, "picayune" is used to refer to something neglible, originally a tiny coin.

14. On the Old Testament allusions to the birds see Jeremias, p. 31; cf. Crossan, pp. 225 (Q) and 275 (Mark). Crossan finds a literal basis in Psalm 104:12 but no Old Testament allusion in the earliest version of the parable.

15. Crossan holds that the redactional insertions by Mark in the Sower, the Seed Growing Secretly, and here indicate a process of growth in time, inculcating patience and perseverance. Mark's added stress on contrast, however, would suggest that growth as a process was not the point, even in his redaction, but the contrast of beginning and end grasped as one paradoxical whole (cf. Jeremias, pp. 148ff.). Whatever confusion there may be, the point of final conspicuousness still holds. It probably deals not with the eschaton apocalyptically but as the climax of history. Jeremias' emphasis on the allusions as pointing to inclusion of the gentiles is valid for a later gentile-mission reading. Cf. Kingsbury, pp. 81f. (apologia vs. the Jews; paranesis for the church).

16. On the historical problem of church and culture, see H. Richard Niebuhr, *Christ and Culture* (New York: Harper & Row, 1956).

17. The "kingdom" introduction is most likely to be treated as Matthaean redaction (for its distribution in the Gospels see Chapter Eight). Cf. Kingsbury, pp. 19-21.

18. The place of the farmer in these parables has been challenged by Crossan (p. 252) on the ground that the term used in verse 28, *karpophorei* ("produces" or "bears fruit"), is to be taken metaphorically, as in Romans 7:4f. and Colossians 1:6, 10. *Karpophoreo* is as germane to the growing as *didonai karpon* is in verse 29 (lit.; "when the fruit offers itself"; cf. the same

phrase in Mark 4:8 and Matt. 13:8; see Black, pp. 163ff.). It would seem that *karpophoreō* is used successfully as a metaphor in the Epistles because it is used in agriculture, and the fact it is used "literally" here in the NT (as against the two cases in the Epistles) is proof of its power. There is not on this ground sufficient basis for excluding the farmer as central any more than there is for ignoring the human actor in Matthew's equivalent (see the Tares Among the Wheat) or in the Sower, or would be in the Barren Fig Tree. On the other hand, Kingsbury (p. 34) goes too far in seeing Jesus represented, which would be true only of the postresurrection interpretation. Logion 21 in Thomas contains the final metaphor of the immediate response to the harvest.

19. This reference was supplied by the late Miss Claudine Clements, distinguished teacher of scripture at the National Cathedral School for Girls.

20. A similar point is amusingly made by E. B. White in "Book Learning" in *One Man's Meat*, 5th ed. (New York: Harper & Brothers, 1944), p. 306. He had expounded his theory learned from government pamphlets about cutting hay when its vitamin content was at the highest to a Maine farmer, and adds, "When I had exhausted my little store of learning and paused for a moment, he ventured a reply. 'The time to cut hay,' he said firmly, 'is hayin' time.' "

21. See Note 14. The activity called for is not necessarily the point (as in Arthur T. Cadoux, *The Parables of Jesus, Their Art and Use* [London: James Clarke & Co., 1930; New York: Macmillan, 1931], pp. 162ff.). The extension of this parable by Matthew in the Tares Among the Wheat (13:24-30) emphasizes noninterference, while his interpretation (vs. 36-43) ignores the point in order to put the emphasis on an apocalyptic climax (see below).

22. Both parable and interpretation may be attributed to Matthew or his "school," and each helps explain the other. Bultmann, p. 177, holds it is a "pure parable," not an allegory, yet it is obviously designed to prepare for the allegorical application. The Thomas version, Logion 57, is abbreviated, losing the directness and dialogue, so as to weaken the point. There is no interpretation ("no doubt because he has his own"—Grant/Freedman, p. 156). Crossan, pp. 260-61, finds an element of outwitting the enemy in the parable.

23. I have expanded this and explored further the church situation in my article "Mixed State." See Perrin, p. 113. Cf. Kingsbury's discussion, pp. 64ff. I do not find his objections compelling but can agree that there has been substitution (p. 65). His thesis of the redactional purpose in Matthew finds its best support here.

24. See Jeremias' detailed and conclusive reasons for the Matthaean nature of verses 36-43, though he attributes the parable to Jesus, which is unlikely in view of its relation to Mark (pp. 82-85).

25. *Pirke Aboth* IV, 20 (Herbert Danby, ed., *The Mishnah* [New York: Oxford University Press, 1933], p. 455). This example of a rabbinic introduction should be noted to avoid confusion in all cases of "likeness." See above on the Leaven. Bultmann holds the similitude belongs to the ancient tradition, but not the application to Jesus and John (p. 172).

26. Giving the neuter in Luke 11:31f. the sense of "occasion" and omitting the reference in Matthew 12:40 to whale and resurrection as redaction.

The added comment on "wisdom" in Matthew 11:19 should be treated in the context of the influence of the wisdom tradition on the Gospels. See M. Jack Suggs, *Wisdom, Christology, and Law in Matthew's Gospel* (Cambridge, Mass.: Harvard University Press, 1970).

27. Derrett, pp. 1-15. The application he makes, pp. 15ff., which he describes as "topsy-turvy," that God so treasures his servants, does not seem to me primary but (if surprise may be attributed to God!) a legitimate consequence. Derrett's work is important as far as it makes us aware of assumptions that may well have been understood by the listeners, which might not occur to us but are an important means of interpretation and may save us from grotesque misapplications. Cf. Kingsbury, pp. 110ff. Thomas, Logion 109, is more like a folk tale than a Gospel parable (the original owner dies without knowing the treasure is there and a *purchaser* finds the treasure). It may be an attempt to avoid the problem but in any case shows the predominant commercialism of the Thomas parables.

28. Thomas, Logion 76, has a "prudent" merchant who, "finding" the pearl, sells all his merchandise. Following is an exhortation, based on Matthew 6:19f., to seek for the treasure which endures. While Thomas does not pair the two parables, this addition may mean that he knew of the pairing in Matthew.

29. Eta Linnemann puts the two parables under one head, "Unique Opportunity" (pp. 97ff.), and reviews modern exegesis (notes 11-16). Against my emphasis on commitment as related to Israel she argues that Jesus was neither Pharisee nor Zealot (p. 173, n. 16). I would agree. The commitment for which Jesus appealed would, in the hands of Pharisees or Zealots, be distorted or misdirected. I suggested the "existential" aspect above, pp. 64-65.

## CHAPTER FOUR: THE WIDENESS OF GOD'S MERCY

1. On the Zealots, etc., see Chapter Two, Note 14.

2. I. Abrahams, *Studies in Pharisaism and the Gospel*, 1st series (New York: Cambridge University Press, 1970), pp. 55f.

3. Claude G. Montefiore, *The Synoptic Gospels*, 1st ed., vol. I (London: Macmillan & Co. Ltd.), p. lxxxv. Used by permission of Macmillan, London and Basingstoke. The 2nd ed. reads, "by seeming to countenance them."

4. Arthur T. Cadoux, *The Parables of Jesus, Their Art and Use* (London: James Clarke & Co., 1930; New York: Macmillan, 1931), p. 28. See my articles, "Fishers of Men" and "Mixed State," and Jeremias, pp. 224ff. (not an exhortation to the disciples, "Throw out your nets, you fishers of men!"). See also Kümmel's comment on my treatment, p. 137. In Thomas, Logion 8, "man" is like a fisherman who finds a large good fish in a netful of small fishes and throws out the rest. A very different parable, possibly of gnostic superiority?

5. Rudolf Otto, *The Kingdom of God and the Son of Man* (Boston: Beacon, 1957), ET, p. 127. More would see verses 49f. as Matthaean and verse 48 part of the parable. Kümmel (p. 173) finds the interpretation relevant, though a Matthaean formulation. Bultmann, p. 137, asserts the application is original. But the change of the words "good" and "bad" in verse 48 into "evil" and "righteous" in verse 49, and the stock Matthew phrases of verse 50 clearly

indicate redaction (see my articles named in Note 4). Cf. Kingsbury, pp. 117ff. He holds gathering and sorting to refer to present and future respectively, but that is dependent on the application. In "Fishers of Men" I discussed the possibility that the image was not originally missionary (Christian) but eschatological, and that this parable represents a transitional stage. The universal appeal was the meaning that to be fishers *came to have*, as in the related stories of Luke 5:1-11 and John 21:1-14. Cf. Kümmel's comment, p. 137, and Note 9 in Chapter Three.

6. See the action picture in Basil Mathews, *A Life of Jesus* (New York: Oxford University Press, 1930), p. 154, plate XIV.

7. The setting in both Gospels is editorial ("I tell you" is often a sign of later application). The Matthaean *form* is more authentic than Luke's assimilated version, though the *application* is more secondary. Bultmann agrees (p. 171); also Linnemann (pp. 65-73) and Perrin (pp. 98-101). Cf. Jeremias, pp. 38-40, 132-36 (joy the sole point, and at the final judgment). Fuchs speaks of "the joy over the recovery of what was lost" (p. 57). Linnemann makes the joy the climax but as "anchored in the finding" (p. 149, n. 17). It seems that in both parables the emphasis falls on the search and issues in the joy of finding. Cf. Wilder on the joy of discovery in the parables, "aware of cost and ordeal but also of joy" (pp. 94ff.). Thomas, Logion 109, completely distorts by making the lost sheep the largest and has the shepherd address the sheep directly!

8. Verses 25-32 are accepted as original and essential to the parable also by, e.g., Bultmann, p. 196; Jeremias, p. 131; Linnemann, pp. 78, 152; and Via, p. 163.

9. Derrett, pp. 104-12.

10. Leslie Weatherhead, *In Quest of a Kingdom* (Nashville: Abingdon Press, 1944), p. 90, wrote, "It is so very undignified in Eastern eyes for an elderly man to run. Aristotle says, 'Great men never run in public.' " I know of no other documentation. Via refers to Linnemann and she to Jeremias, who included it in his first English edition (1964). It seemed in 1948 a likely observation and, as the repetitions of the reference show, still does for its element of surprise.

11. Some readings (see Kurt Aland, *Synopsis of the Four Gospels*, p. 306) add the rest of the son's speech in verse 19 to verse 21.

12. See Derrett, pp. 113-16.

13. Via (p. 166) is right in emphasizing that his return home was to a "contextual" freedom, not a release from law except in the sense that he was released by his father from the "law" of having to work to earn reinstatement. That came, as Via emphasizes, as an unanticipated gift, as grace.

14. Via makes an interesting point when he suggests that, in the "comedy" structure of the parable, the two images of eating focus the prodigal's extremities of despair and redemption (p. 166).

15. Jones (pp. 167ff.) uses this parable as his only example, and Via treats it as a "comedy" with a picaresque theme, and both are worth study as examples of the existential interpretation building on the exegetical. The Gospel of Thomas, interestingly enough, has no parallel.

16. Cf. Derrett's analysis of the "sins" of the prodigal, pp. 111f.

17. Montefiore, op. cit., vol. I, p. cxl. On the biblical background of the "prayer parables," see my article, "Prayer," in the *Interpreter's Dictionary of the Bible*, vol. 3 (Nashville: Abingdon Press, 1962), hereafter cited as "Prayer."

18. On verse 14, cf. Bultmann, pp. 178f.

19. Jeremias, p. 140, accepts the first alternative (meaning, "took up a prominent position") as more Semitic; cf. Linnemann, p. 143, note 2. Jeremias notes there are more Semitisms here than in any other parable of Luke, and also quotes prayers similar in tone from the Talmud and Qumran (p. 142). Of Jeremias' exposition (pp. 139-44), Perrin says that "his exegesis of the parable is beyond all praise" (pp. 122). Linnemann, pp. 58ff., designates the parable an "illustration."

20. Cf. Joseph Klausner, pp. 180ff., and Derrett, pp. 19, 33 (with the references to other literature on p. 296). The Aramaic word behind *doulos* may mean both "child" and "servant" as the Greek word *pais* in the NT may do (see especially Luke 7:2, 7; cf. Matt. 8:6, 8 and John 4:36-53, where "child" and "son" alternate). In the parable of the Talents the word means agent ("they cannot have been slaves," Derrett, p. 19; cf. p. 33), but in the Tenants of the Vineyard the primary meaning "slave" is preferred (Derrett, p. 296). It would seem that Luke here has the slave of the Hellenistic world in mind, one not under Hebrew regulations. The unpretentious household depicted in the parable will be found also in Luke's version of the Banquet. It may be a touch which goes back to Jesus and the elaborations into the household of a king are redactions.

21. Bultmann, p. 170, holds that verse 10 "precisely repeats the meaning of the similitude: a slave cannot boast of any merit." Jeremias, p. 193, translates, "We are just poor slaves, we have only done our duty." (On the omission of "only" in Semitic speech see his p. 39, n. 59.)

22. Montefiore, op. cit., vol. II, 1st ed., pp. 1008f. See Jesus' statement, found only in Luke 22:27.

23. This parable is Jeremias' first major example in which he lays down his method (pp. 33ff.; further, pp. 136ff.). Fuchs also uses it as a guide to method (pp. 32ff.). Via (pp. 148ff.) treats it as his first example of a parable with a "comic" structure; a tragic plot (cf. Fuchs on verse 14a as "stern pronouncement," p. 33) subordinated to a comedy theme, its tendency to allegory overcome by its internal structure (p. 152).

24. The title is based on Luke's version, 18:18 for "ruler," and Matthew 19:20 for "young"; Mark's "from my youth" (10:20) seems to indicate maturity.

25. It is difficult to see why Jeremias (pp. 35f.) feels the order of payment unimportant, but we would agree it is not about reversal of rank.

26. W. H. P. Hatch suggested precedents for translating *en tois emois*: "Is it not lawful for me to do what I wish *on my own premises*?" ("A Note on Matthew 20:15," *ATR*, XXVI [4 Oct. 1944], pp. 250ff.). Jeremias (2nd ET) added support for this (p. 138).

27. Montefiore, op. cit., 1st ed., vol. II, p. 702. Via (pp. 153ff.) properly

stresses the "dismissal" of the complainers as suggesting why some "exclude themselves from the source of grace" (p. 154).

28. E.g., B. T. D. Smith, *The Parables of the Synoptic Gospels* (London: Cambridge University Press, 1937), p. 138. Also in Perrin, p. 117. (The latter well describes the reaction to the parable often characteristic of American congregations but rightly argues that this "intolerable situation" is the point of the analogy and uses it to reinforce the meaning of the parable concerning mercy as opposed to merit.) Cf. also Derrett, p. 150, note 3.

29. See the two chapters, "God's Forgiveness" and "Man's Forgiveness," in Abrahams, op. cit., 1st series, pp. 139ff., 150ff.

30. On the standing of the servant see references to Derrett in Notes 20 and 32 to this chapter.

31. Cadoux, op. cit., pp. 214ff.

32. What is said here and by many commentators possibly needs some modification in view of Derrett's explanations of the legal relations possible between a king and his ministers under non-Jewish law which accord with the parable even where it seems unreasonable to us (pp. 33ff.). He notes that both men were in the same business, standing in line with others, and both needed to see how they came out before settling other claims. This also explains how the fellow ministers were able to be witnesses. Cf. Jeremias, pp. 210ff.

33. See (without fully endorsing) Anders Nygren's discussion of the parables in *Agape and Eros* (New York: Harper & Row, 1969), Part I, pp. 59ff. Derrett, pp. 44f., says to forgive first in order to be forgiven is "apparently illogical" but defends it as a prerequisite for *asking* mercy. See his note on Perrin and Archibald M. Hunter (p. 44). A discussion of the petition in the Lord's Prayer will be found in my "Prayer." Derrett summarizes a midrash of R. Akiba which he feels helps to understand the parable (pp. 45f.).

34. It is worthy of note that none of the parables in this chapter are represented in the Gospel of Thomas except the Lost Sheep and a form of the Dragnet, and in each of these, unlike the Gospels, the emphasis is on the largest sheep, the largest fish.

## CHAPTER FIVE: THE CRISIS OF GOD'S CHOSEN

1. "Nation, People, Religion—What Are We?" address published by Hebrew Union College, 1943, p. 20. On the mission see *Paradox*, chapter 4. Fuller discussion in Joachim Jeremias, *Jesus' Promise to the Nations*, SBT, 24 (1958); George B. Caird, *Jesus and the Jewish Nation* (London: Athlone Press, 1965); Ferdinand Hahn, *Mission in the New Testament*, SBT, 47 (1965).

2. See a rabbinic parallel quoted by Perrin, p. 119.

3. The point is reflected in modern debates about "prescription" as opposed to "situation" ethic.

4. The differences in Mark's and Luke's use of the debate may reflect a changed church situation but, as Linnemann observes, the point of the debate fits Palestinian Judaism (p. 138, n. 1).

5. In Matthew 5:43, etc., "You have heard that it was said" means so to have understood or interpreted it. The corollary is illustrated, e.g., by Deute-

ronomy 23:19f., that interest may be charged a stranger but not a fellow Hebrew.

6. Arthur T. Cadoux, *The Parables of Jesus, Their Art and Use* (London: James Clarke & Co., 1930; New York: Macmillan, 1931), pp. 214ff. On the parable cf., Bultmann, p. 178 (artificially blended into context); Jeremias, pp. 202ff.; Linnemann, pp. 51ff.; Perrin, pp. 122-24. The two finest recent discussions are Funk, pp. 199ff. (one of his two examples), and Derrett, pp. 208ff. (who shows how essential the context is to the parable as parable). Most scholars, following Jülicher, treat it as an "example story." See below.

7. Martin Dibelius said of the parables, "The poetic fullness of this style does not consist in equal and uniform detail, but in expanding what is essential and abbreviating what is secondary" (*From Tradition to Gospel* [New York: Charles Scribner's Sons, 1935], p. 251). However, Derrett, who assumes the victim is a Jew, comments, "Stripped and unconscious as he was, the Jew's race and community were not ascertainable at a glance" (p. 209).

8. B. T. D. Smith, *The Parables of the Synoptic Gospels* (London: Cambridge University Press, 1937), p. 180.

9. Interestingly, Funk observes that the hearer is drawn in and, following Bornkamm, must "initially at least" put himself in the place of the victim (p. 212; cf. Bornkamm, pp. 112f.).

10. Smith, op. cit., p. 180. Derrett thinks the suggestion that the third was an Israelite (layman) "superfluous." He thinks the Samaritan essential as an antithesis, one who rejects the Jerusalem worship and priesthood (p. 211). Funk sees him as necessary, providing a "secular figure" who is unanticipated by the hearers (pp. 212-14).

11. See Morton S. Enslin, "Luke and the Samaritans," *HTR*, 36 (Oct. 1943), pp. 277ff. The author kindly drew my attention to it when I read this section at the 1945 SBL meeting. To dispose of the Samaritan does not, to me, make it necessary to deny the story to Jesus.

12. Derrett reveals the variety of risks the Samaritan took (pp. 217-19). The question of whether the priest and the Levite would risk defilement if they had been going to Jericho, not to the temple, is answered by Derrett. Even at Jericho the priest would at least be ineligible to participate in the tithe by which his family was supported and concerning which he had obligations (pp. 214ff.). The Levite only had more latitude (p. 211). The important point is that both had to decide between conflicting regulations, and their decision, while justifiable, revealed their priorities. Note Funk's references to the reactions likely among the hearers, lay and ecclesiastical (pp. 212ff.).

13. See John M. Creed, *The Gospel According to St. Luke* (New York: Macmillan, 1930), pp. 151f., 153. Cf. Black, p. 69, on the style of the parables.

14. It can be argued that verse 37b is not necessary to the story. It could well end with 37a, the lawyer's answer (though it is unnecessary). It is verse 37b which prompts the designations "example story" and "moralism." Funk says, "It is strange that Jülicher's reading of the Good Samaritan as a *Beispielerzählung* has gone virtually unchallenged" (p. 211, n. 52). He points to the Samaritan as the element which "shatters the realism, the everydayness of the story. The 'logic' of everydayness is broken upon the 'logic' of the

parable. It is the juxtaposition of the two logics that turns the Samaritan, and hence the parable, into a metaphor" (i.e., which does not "come to rest in the literal meaning"; p. 213, see p. 221). Derrett also agrees in part: "and it *is* a parable, as well as an illustrative tale, or 'wonder story' " (p. 208).

15. Thomas W. Manson, *The Teaching of Jesus* (London: Cambridge University Press, 1935), p. 41. Also note that all the parables peculiar to Luke (plus three from Q) occur in his central section (9:51–18:14), which is held together editorially as a journey to Jerusalem, therefore to the passion.

16. On the parable see Jeremias, pp. 170f., who holds that Jesus is using a folk tale found in *The Story of Ahikar* with a new ending. For a similar technique see below on the parable of the Rich Man and Lazarus.

17. On the basis that three years must elapse before the fruit may be treated as "clean," the tree would have been there six years (see Derrett, p. 290, n. 3; cf. p. 300, n. 3).

18. On this see my article on Mark 11:1–12:12, "No Time for Figs," in *JBL*, 79 (1960), and the further study, "Tabernacles in the Fourth Gospel and Mark," in *NTS*, 9 (1963). Luke, at a later date, in a different setting, was not so concerned to deal with the problem of the fall of the temple.

19. Jeremias properly observes, "the allegorical representation of the Messiah as a bridegroom is completely foreign to the whole of the Old Testament and the literature of late Judaism," and "Jesus' audience could hardly have applied the figure of the bridegroom in Matthew 25:1ff. to the Messiah" (p. 52). See below on Mark 2:19f.

20. On this see below on the Banquet and my article, "Mixed State."

21. On the parable see Jeremias, pp. 51ff., and, for a discussion of the customs, pp. 172-74. Cf. Bultmann, p. 176 ("an allegory constructed from the application"); whether a similitude underlay it can no longer be discovered. With this Linnemann agrees ("certainly a creation of the early Church"), pp. 189ff. In spite of her comments on my proposals (p. 192), I would still, in view of my article, stand by them.

22. See Via, pp. 122ff., treated as "tragic," with its climax the closed door (as above). Via says, "Older than Matthew and genuine." He helpfully remarks that "the foolish maidens too superficially supposed the world would take care of them . . . we find their abrupt exclusion shocking. This shock suggests the impingement of the divine dimension upon the everyday, the shattering effect of a crisis which breaks into our easy optimism and finds us without resources" (p. 126). Precisely the point.

23. Cf. Burnett H. Streeter, *The Four Gospels* (New York: St. Martin's Press), p. 244. See also Funk, p. 163, note 1. I would agree that the effort to fix a particular time or place for Jesus' parables, or to designate too precisely the audience addressed (as Jeremias too readily does) is unprofitable. Cf. Funk, pp. 177f., 181, on diversity of audience, a point I have tried to cover by emphasis on the address to Israel as a whole.

24. On the parable, see Bultmann, pp. 175, 201f.; Jeremias, pp. 63-66; Linnemann, pp. 88ff., 158ff.; Perrin, pp. 110ff. Via deals only with the Wedding Garment. See also Derrett, pp. 126ff. His attempt to exegete it on the basis of the holy war and a victory dinner seems to me to expect too much mid-

rashic lore of an audience, though it would contribute to later literary study. It also intends to justify Matthew's version. Funk's splendid analysis (pp. 163-98) issues in "theses" which are relevant for the study of the parables as a whole.

25. This incident is dealt with more fully in my "Mixed State." See also Bultmann, pp. 195f., 201f.; Jeremias, pp. 65, 68f., 187ff.; Funk, pp. 169f. It is thought that verse 2 in Matthew was probably the original beginning of the garment incident as a separate parable, and verse 10 the connecting link. Certainly "the bad and good" is a Matthaean concern (see "Mixed State"), and the garment incident picks it up. The situation is best understood through a parable of Joḥanan ben Zakkai, in which the wise guests were ready in suitable clothes when the call came (b. Shab. 153a, quoted in my article, pp. 156f.; see also Isidor Singer, *Jewish Encyclopedia* (New York: Ktav Publishing House, 1964; reprint of 1904 ed.), vol. 9, p. 514a). No special garment is provided. Jeremias tends to become allegorical (pp. 188f.). Via treats it as a separate parable among his "tragic" examples and cogently emphasizes the man's speechlessness (pp. 130-32).

26. Funk, pp. 183-85, supports questioning whether the final invitation in Luke was originally allegorical, and I am still convinced that it was integral to the intent of the story and is only later read as allegorical. In this edition verse 24 has been put in italics above, since "I tell you" ("you" plural) is not addressed to the single servant and betokens, as often elsewhere, an application—in this case properly deduced as the point of the parable. Funk rightly contends that the parable has no application, no ending, since the ending "is incorporated into the parable from the beginning" (p. 191). It is a parable of judgment and of grace (pp. 191f.). He notes that Thomas is interested only in those left out, not in those to be included (p. 183).

27. Dr. Nelson Glueck often made this point. See, e.g., *The River Jordan* (London: Lutterworth Press, 1946), pp. 175f.: "We could under no circumstances have refused his hospitality or stoned him with disdain or pity for his slender provender." Cf. Jeremias, p. 177. Linnemann tries to show the guests intended only to be late (p. 161) and rejects my suggestion of a later change of heart. Jeremias (p. 178, n. 23) rejects her view but adopts the suggestion (p. 179) that the host is a tax collector, based on the story of Ma'jan (see Note 16).

28. The parable in the Gospel of Thomas (Logion 64) does not seem to me more original. Though it has the basic form in common (cf. Funk, p. 166) with the Synoptics, the excuses are expanded, are more rational and commercial, and provide for the conclusion, "buyers and merchants will not enter the place of my father," with which compare the cleansing of the temple, especially in the Johannine version, John 2:16b, "You shall not make my Father's house a house of trade." On the Talmudic parable referred to by some commentators, see Chapter Seven on the Rich Man and Lazarus.

## CHAPTER SIX: THE JUDGMENT OF GOD'S CALL

1. Cf. Bornkamm's development of this theme (pp. 60-63) and Fuchs's perhaps overly emphatic discussion of the relationship of Jesus' action to his

(parabolic) teaching where "Jesus' conduct explains the will of God, by means of a parable drawn from that very conduct" rather than merely a vindication of Jesus' way of life (pp. 20-22).

2. Bultmann, e.g. (pp. 177, 205), states it is an allegory, a community formulation in its present form. Kümmel held it cannot be attributed to Jesus, nor can an earlier form be reconstructed (pp. 82f.; cf. n. 214).

3. In spite of this, Isaiah 5:1-2 has the characteristics of a parable, and the identification is made only with verse 7. By contrast, Psalm 80:8ff. is heavy allegory, with some terms completely transposed.

4. Martin Dibelius says, "Certain metaphors were already customary in Jewish exhortation, and the hearer was therefore prone to understand the words concerned in the usual sense" (*From Tradition to Gospel* [New York: Charles Scribner's Sons, 1935], p. 255). He adds, "Half-allegorical forms might have arisen in this way, for in retelling the parables these metaphors might have been unwittingly employed." Might not Jesus, however, have used the metaphor for that very reason? Derrett explains the importance of the property having been a newly constructed vineyard quite apart from Isaiah 5, where, of course, the emphasis is upon its having been newly planted (pp. 289f.).

5. The word *agapētos* here used has often the sense of "only," i.e., the heir.

6. See Dodd, pp. 124ff.; Jeremias, pp. 74f. The verb *apedemēsen* means to take up residence at a distance, possibly out of the country (RSV, "another country"), but it need not imply he was a foreigner. Only Luke stresses the length of absence, an example of his interest in a "delayed parousia." For Derrett's whole discussion see his chapter 13, pp. 286-310 (excepting the midrashic interpretation with which it ends).

7. Kümmel (p. 83) and Jeremias (p. 73) are correct in saying that the audience would not have taken a reference to the son, even as heir, to be a messianic claim on the part of Jesus. Only the church could so "hear" it.

8. In Mark, verse 7, "the inheritance will be ours," *klēronomia* may be read as "property," not that the tenants expected to inherit. See references in Derrett, p. 305, and William F. Arndt and F. Wilbur Gingrich, *A Greek-English Lexicon of the New Testament* (Grand Rapids, Mich.: Zondervan, 1963), p. 436). It need not be assumed, as I did in 1948, that they would think the owner dead.

9. Proposals akin to those I made in 1948 and have amended here tend to suggest that first Luke and then Thomas come closer to the original form. It is perhaps the best case for Thomas' use of a primitive parable form if purely literary criteria are used. However, there is at work in Luke's version traces of his style (cf. Jeremias, p. 72, n. 84) and in Thomas the tendencies we have noted to reduction. All reference to the setting up of the vineyard is omitted. Two servants are followed by the son. Some attempt to explain the owner's motives or the servants' failure seems implied by the latter's remark, "Perhaps he did not know them," and "This is the heir" is expanded to "Since those husbandmen knew that he was the heir." The beginning describes the owner as a "good" man, and the ending is changed by eliminating

the question and adding the logion, "Whoever has ears let him hear." The proximity in Logion 66 of a form of the stone testimony (though characteristically not quoted from the OT), seems to indicate a knowledge of the Synoptic tradition. There seems here no exception to the general impression of dependence on the Gospels. Cf. Grant/Freedman, pp. 162f.

10. Via (pp. 134-37), in his "tragic" treatment of the parable, has suggested that the tenants rather than the owner are central, and it may, of course, be treated from that point of view. However, the question of verse 9 (if retained) centers on the owner as the sower is significant in the "seed" parables, the host in the Banquet, and the owner in the Barren Fig Tree. This does not make the sower, host, or owner an allegory of God but makes the parables analogies of God's rule and kingdom, whether so designated editorially or not.

11. See M. Jack Suggs, *Wisdom, Christology, and Law in Matthew's Gospel* (Cambridge, Mass.: Harvard University Press, 1970).

12. See my articles cited in Chapter Five, Note 18.

13. Arthur T. Cadoux, *The Parables of Jesus, Their Art and Use* (London: James Clarke & Co., 1930; New York: Macmillan, 1931), p. 42.

14. Dibelius, op. cit., p. 257.

15. Dodd, p. 128.

16. Cf. Jeremias, p. 63, and Via, p. 121, who comments that nevertheless the parable requires some passage of time.

17. On this see "Mixed State." On the Matthaean style of verse 30, cf. Jeremias, p. 60, note 44.

18. Although Luke's reference reflects his interest in a church dealing with a delayed parousia, the comment may still have a historical basis not only indicated by its place in Luke's "journey section" but as reflecting what is documented elsewhere in the expectation that Jesus' purpose in going to Jerusalem was "to restore the kingdom to Israel" (cf. Mark 10:35ff. and Acts 1:6).

19. Cf. Bultmann, p. 176; Jeremias, p. 59. Derrett (p. 17) favors the Matthaean version. His note (p. 17, n. 1) that the parable has nothing to do with Archelaus does apply to the basic narrative, but it would be hard to see the Lucan verses quoted above as part of it even on Derrett's explanation.

20. Jeremias (p. 62) finds Matthew verse 28 and Luke verse 24 a subsidiary theme explained by primitive Christian teaching, but Via agrees they are essential (on aesthetic grounds in a "tragic" story) to give the parable completeness. Derrett says he cannot believe the third man expected commendation, as some have held.

21. Claude G. Montefiore says, e.g., "It is part of the dramatic environment of the parable, which must not be pressed in its moral" (*The Synoptic Gospels*, 2nd ed., vol. II [London: Macmillan & Co. Ltd.], p. 320. Used by permission of Macmillan, London and Basingstoke.). Derrett argues that the man's description of his lord may mean the latter was one who expected "an inequitably high proportion from his investments" which would leave the small trader with little if any profit (p. 25).

22. Derrett's discussion in general (pp. 18-29) substantiates what is said

here. He emphasized the element of "test" in the allotments, as indicated in the parable by the awarding or refusing of further opportunity, and observes that "even a small investment can detect unfaithfulness" (p. 28).

23. Jeremias' narrowing of the target to the scribes (pp. 61f.) seems unnecessary. Via (p. 115), as here, emphasizes that it is directed against those who held a limited view of Israel's obligation. He sees it as a "tragic" parable, centered on the third servant, and his excellent "existential" interpretation recalls the parable of the Children in the Market Place and its meaning for the individual within his relationships (p. 122).

24. Dodd, p. 128.

25. So, e.g., Perrin, p. 115.

26. See Derrett, pp. 48-77. The whole study should be read for its exposition of usury and the laws of agency, and for the literature cited. See also the Rich Man and Lazarus, in Chapter Seven.

27. Via, pp. 158, 161.

28. Ibid., pp. 159-61.

29. Perrin, p. 115.

30. Cadoux, op. cit., p. 135.

31. Jeremias (p. 198) argues that Matthew verse 44b reflects a conditional clause in Aramaic, "if he finds it empty," and links it with the parables which treat of persistence (see Chapter Seven).

32. W. M. Thompson, *The Land and the Book*, vol. II, pp. 43f. (New York: (Harper & Brothers, 1859). See further references in article by J. F. Ross, "Salt," in *Interpreter's Dictionary of the Bible*, vol. 4.

33. Cadoux, op. cit., p. 81. Similarly Jeremias, p. 168.

34. Dodd, p. 142.

35. *The Apostolic Fathers*, vol. I, ET by Kirsopp Lake (Loeb Classical Library), pp. 206-7.

36. Greek: "Is the lamp brought?" Western text: "Is the lamp lighted?"

37. There may be in Greek two questions: the form of the first ("under the bed?") implies a negative answer; the form of the second ("on a stand?"), an affirmative answer. Taken as one question, an affirmative answer is expected.

38. A third pair of sayings about the lamp (Matt. 6:22; Luke 11:34-36) deals with a different subject and are not treated in the text. See the standard commentaries.

## CHAPTER SEVEN: THE RESPONSE OF GOD'S PEOPLE

1. Discussing Matthew 11:27, Charles Guignebert said, "It is open to suspicion because, in those portions of the tradition which appear to be most historical, Jesus does not preach about himself as he does here" (*Jesus* [New York: University Books, 1956], p. 264). See Chapter Eight.

2. See B. T. D. Smith, *The Parables of the Synoptic Gospels* (London: Cambridge University Press, 1937), pp. 134ff. Bultmann, p. 178, feels there are two parts at variance with each other and that the purpose of verses 9-15 could not originally be to prepare for verses 16-18, except by Luke's editorial work in verses 14-18, but that both sections are "wholly Jewish" (pre-Lucan).

He thinks the "polemical" point destroys an original unity (pp. 196f.). See Jeremias, pp. 182ff.

3. Smith, op. cit., pp. 64ff. Also Jeremias, pp. 178, 183. Cf. Bultmann's reference, p. 196 and note 1, though I am not persuaded by his reasoning; I fail to see why purely Jewish material cannot be attributed to Jesus, especially as developed here.

4. Claude G. Montefiore, *The Synoptic Gospels*, 1st ed., vol II (London: Macmillan & Co. Ltd.), p. 1003; Jeremias, p. 184.

5. This suggests sharing in the messianic banquet. Attempts to find precedents for the phrase are unenlightening; cf. Abrahams, *Studies in Pharisaism and the Gospel*, 2nd series (New York: Cambridge University Press), pp. 202f., and Jeremias, p. 184.

6. Abrahams, op. cit., 1st series, pp. 168ff.; cf. Jeremias, p. 185.

7. Cf. Jeremias, p. 185.

8. See the method in the speech in Amos 1:3-8, 13–2:3, reminiscent of Marc Antony's speech over Caesar's body in Shakespeare's *Julius Caesar*.

9. Verses 28-31 in Matthew 14, an addition to Mark 6:45-52 (Peter's walking on the water) may well have been a resurrection story dealing with the demand for a sign that the appearances of the risen Christ are really appearances of Jesus. In that case the risen Christ rebukes this demand for a sign ("if it *is* you") as Jesus had done. See *Paradox*, p. 198.

10. Cf. Kümmel, pp. 33f. (who agreed with my interpretation [p. 21, n. 4; cf. p. 35, n. 54]). For the parable, see Jeremias, pp. 119f.

11. Thomas, Logion 35, is nearer Mark's version than Luke's except for the phrase "take it by force." (Jeremias does not list the Logion on p. 24 but refers to it on p. 122.) A somewhat related parable of the Assassin is found in Logion 98 (see Note 18).

12. The Q passage (Matt. vs. 27-28; Luke vs. 19-20) has the double argument based on the success of both Jewish exorcists and Jesus, and the assertion of verse 28 (Luke v. 20) applies in each case. Jeremias' suggestion (pp. 122f.) that the parable refers to Jesus' contest with Satan in the wilderness is not acceptable since, in my view, the temptation narratives are retrospect commentary by the church (see *Paradox*, pp. 200ff.), which, of course, then applies the similitude to the narrative.

13. This reference was originally prompted by a Congressman's question when I preached on this parable at Washington Cathedral during World War II.

14. In the 1948 edition I used the example of the victories in north Africa in World War II which were the prelude to the deliverance of Europe from Hitler; Oscar Cullmann used a similar analogy in *Christ and Time* (Philadelphia: Westminster Press, 1950). Another example from history would be Wellington's victories over the French in the Spanish peninsula in the Napoleonic wars.

15. See my use of the passage as an example in "Levels of Interpretation in the Gospels" in *Religion in Life*, vol. XXX, 2 (1961).

16. The image is found as a similitude in Thomas, Logion 21, and as a beatitude in Logion 103. See Jeremias, pp. 87f., 95; cf. pp. 48f.

17. The parallel Logion 63 in Thomas reveals the usual commercial inter-

est—the man has much money which he will use to produce more crops. There is no intervention of God; he merely dies. The frequently added, "Whoever has ears . . ." occurs here. For both, cf. Jeremias, pp. 164ff. His theory that the soliloquy is not original because absent from Thomas depends on his view of the primitive source of Thomas.

18. A similar type of parable is found in Thomas, Logion 98, in which "the kingdom of the Father" is likened to an assassin who first tests his strength by thrusting his sword into the wall of his house and then kills the powerful man. Cf. Jeremias, pp. 196ff.; Grant/Freedman, p. 177; Perrin, pp. 126ff. ("these parables challenge men to sober judgment").

19. The following paragraphs are a revision of the 1948 edition in which I was unable to escape from the traditional interpretation based on "persistence." Correction was first made in my article, "Prayer," pp. 863b-864a. Cf. Jeremias, pp. 157ff.

20. With which Linnemann agrees (pp. 121, 187ff., n. 14). She asserts (p. 121) that "we are certainly not dealing with a parable of 'the historical Jesus,' but with a word of the ascended Lord. . . . It is directed to a Church that is suffering under oppression and persecution." Jeremias (pp. 153ff.) appears to have changed his mind and attributes both parable and application to Jesus (not, of course, v. 1).

21. By, e.g., B. T. D. Smith, Creed, Oesterley. The literal translation given is from Oesterley, *The Parables in the Light of Their Jewish Background* (New York: Macmillan, 1936), p. 217. The author is R. Elisha ben Abuyah, c. A.D. 120.

22. A discussion of B. W. Bacon's theory of the five books of Matthew (each concluding with the formula beginning as in v. 28), and the mount of the "Sermon" as a new Torah and Sinai may be found in W. D. Davies, *The Setting of the Sermon on the Mount* (London: Cambridge University Press, 1964).

## CHAPTER EIGHT: THE JESUS OF THE PARABLES

1. This is still true although we can no longer recover the exact situation in detail. It is not necessary, however, to abandon the attempt to relate the parables to the conditions of the time and the issues which were already coming to a head as known from other sources, the general background, and some still reliable and undesigned) indications in the Gospels.

2. William Manson, *Jesus the Messiah* (1946), pp. 202f. Used by permission of Hodder and Stoughton Ltd.

3. We may have deep sympathy with Funk's demand that we consider Jesus as having put himself also on the side of the hearers and to this extent question the view that the parables were directed primarily to adversaries (pp. 180f.). That there was an element of counterattack in Jesus' teaching (and action) may be understood while Jesus still "moves to the side of the sinners and 'hears' the parables with them as a word of grace." See remarks below on Jesus in Gethsemane. We can agree to a wider understanding of the terms without neglecting the impact of Jesus' parables as a factor in his encounters. Funk says (p. 181), "What is being urged, to put it simply, is the

metaphorical range of the terms 'opponent,' 'critic,' 'Pharisee,' etc., I.e., the literal and non-literal meanings grasped concomitantly, and the expansive horizon of the parable as a mode of language, as opposed to an understanding of parable as a technique of debate."

4. On this whole subject see especially Robinson/Koester, particularly pp. 126-29.

5. The designation is found as a footnote in Martin Kähler, *The So-Called Historical Jesus and the Historical Biblical Christ*, ET (Philadelphia: Fortress Press, 1964), p. 80, note 11.

6. Apart from the birth narratives and the passion story, the parables account for 36 out of 534 verses in Mark, or 6.7 percent. Mark has a smaller proportion of teaching, so the proportion of parables to other material rises in Matthew and Luke: in Matthew, 17.6 percent (152 verses out of 862); in Luke 26.7 percent (190 verses out of 739). If added interpretation were included, the proportion would be somewhat higher.

7. The pronouncement stories or apothegms or paradigms (those listed by Dibelius and Bultmann as more or less pure examples of their kind) occur in the following proportions: Mark, 17 percent; Matthew, 9 percent; Luke, 13.4 percent.

8. Pasternak, *Doctor Zhivago,* Signet edition (New York: New American Library, 1972), p. 40. The passage was called to mind by a sermon and the reference supplied by the Rev. Theodore A. McConnell. Cf. a similar comment in Bornkamm, quoted on page 204.

9. For the point of view see D. Bonhoeffer, *Prisoner for God: Letters and Papers from Prison*, ET (New York: Macmillan, 1960), especially the letters of April 30 and May 5, 1944, and following, pp. 123-25, 144ff., 156f., 158ff., 162f., 168f.

10. All except one of the parables peculiar to Matthew (21:28) are "parables of the kingdom of Heaven" (13:24, 44, 45; 18:23; 20:1; 25:1; and 22:11; cf. v. 2). On the other hand, none of the parables found only in Luke have this introduction. There is one parable in Mark 4:26 (and one which he shares with Q, Mark 4:31; cf. Matt. 13:23 and Luke 13:18), and two Q parables which are so introduced (Matt. 13:33 and Luke 13:20 and Matt. 22:2; cf. Luke 14:15). One of these may not be from Q but may have existed in two forms. In Luke the Banquet begins "a certain man" (*anthrōpos tis*), with which words five other parables in Luke begin (10:30; 13:6; 15:11; 16:1; 16:9).

11. Wilder, pp. 81, 82, 83.

12. Funk, pp. 155, 156.

13. Via, p. 104.

14. Linnemann, p. 86.

15. Kahlefeld, pp. 34, 36.

16. For an example, see Note 17 in Chapter Three.

17. The expression is probably recalled from a lecture of my teacher, W. Cosby Bell, but I have not been able to find it in his writings.

18. Funk uses the term "temporally open-ended" for both metaphor (p. 142) and parable (p. 214).

19. Funk, p. 213. See his "theses 2, 3," p. 197, where the parable "shifts

attention away from God and from Jesus himself, i.e., from the religious question, to a specific way of comporting oneself with reality. God and Jesus remain hidden." (I obviously have difficulty with the concept of Jesus as "hidden.")

20. See above, Note 14, pages 106-7 in text.

21. See Wilder's comment on Jesus "as an artisan . . . in the marketplace" (p. 85) but cf. his warning about making the parable teaching "banal" (pp. 92f.). See also Cadbury's development of the warning against the mistaken notion that Jesus was "teaching about the secular areas of the illustration and not about the different area to which the illustration was presumably applied." Henry J. Cadbury, "Soluble Difficulties in the Parables" in Harvey K. McArthur, ed., New Testament Highlights, p. 123.

22. Bornkamm, p. 70. See also p. 88, "Wisdom consists not in being indignant but in being prepared."

23. See, e.g., Jeremias, pp. 110-12 for lists.

24. This method is to a considerable extent followed in Perrin. Cf. Funk's statement, p. 180, "What the parables imply, the logia state (e.g., Mt. 21:31) and the Evangelists assume (e.g., Lk. 15:2)."

25. Fuchs, p. 20.

26. Ibid., p. 21.

27. Funk reasons, "Jeremias fails to recognize that the vindication of the gospel is also its proclamation. What from one standpoint is a defense of the gospel, is from another point of view its affirmation" (p. 181). "Secondary" indications of the occasion for Jesus' affirmation of his own way (e.g., Luke 15:1f.) are "secondary" as specific settings for particular parables, but there is evidence that the editors were right in noting this connection of practice and response as typical of Jesus' situation. See Via's judgment, p. 183, "The parables, therefore, need to be seen in relation to the pattern of connections in Jesus' story as well as in relation to the pattern of connections in the finished kerygmatic Gospel."

28. Bultmann, p. 205. These criteria receive a balanced treatment in Perrin, passim, in the course of which the parables are used with discrimination to enlarge the presumption of authenticity.

29. An example is found in J. J. Vincent, "The Parables of Jesus as Self-Revelation," in Studia Evangelica (Texte und Untersuchungen LXXIII, Berlin, 1959). The question of the audience's understanding is an acute aspect of the question. Jeremias lays his method open to question when he too closely identifies the opponents against whom the parables are aimed. Warnings against a premature Christology are found, e.g., in Funk, pp. 70, 215f.; Wilder, p. 94; Via, pp. 133f. This is not to say that the parables do not pose the christological question and have an implicit answer (cf. Via, p. 191, "We would expect an implicit Christology in the parables"). In recent works there has been stress on Jesus' mediation through the parables of his own experience of God and his kingdom, his own decision underlying his demand for a decision. Cf. Via, p. 193, "a clue to Jesus' understanding of his own existence," and, p. 197, "his own decision lay behind the decision he asked of others." See also Wilder, p. 80, "Jesus mediates his own vision and his own faith."

Cf. p. 93. But note p. 94, "But we are saying that they should be understood in relation to the speaker and the occasion; not in connection with his *titles* but in relation *to his way and his goal*" (italics added). Also John D. Crossan ("The Seed Parables of Jesus," *JBL*, 92 [June 1973]), pp. 265f.: "[The thesis here proposed is that] Jesus' parables are the primary and immediate expression of his own experience of God. They are the ontologico-poetic articulation of the Kingdom in-breaking upon himself." (I regret that at this writing I have not received Dr. Crossan's announced book, *In Parables*.) Undoubtedly the parables do express Jesus' own experience, but the danger may arise of seeking to penetrate Jesus' self-consciousness, which, it seems to me, is not open to us.

30. See particularly Bornkamm's fine summary, pp. 60-62. He says (p. 61), "The very nature of his teaching and his actions, so vulnerable, so open to controversy and yet so direct and matter of fact, doom to failure any attempt to raise his Messiahship into a system of dogma through which his preaching, his actions and his history would receive their meaning."

31. A minister at one of my conferences on the book recalled there was a somewhat similar interpretation referred to by Origen. It is found in *Matthew*, 92: "Another interpretation of the passage is that, as the Son of God's love, He according to foreknowledge loved those who were to believe from the Gentiles, and loved the Jews, as the seed of the holy fathers. . . . But, loving these, He saw what they would suffer for seeking Him for death and choosing Barabbas for life; therefore grieving for them He said, 'Father, if it is possible, let this cup pass from me.' "

# INDEX TO NAMES AND SUBJECTS

Crisis, 30, 33-34, 57, 110-14, 117-18, 126-27, 149, 161-62, 193, 201, 205-6, 210, 213-14
Crossan, J. D., 230 nn.2-4, 231 nn.14-15, n.18, 232 n.22, 247 n.29
Cullmann, O., 229 n.14, n.17, 243 n.14

Dahl, N. A., 227 n.11
Dead Sea Scrolls (see *Qumran*)
Delayed parousia (see *Parousia*)
Derrett, J. D. M., 9, 64 (n.27, p. 233), 75-76 (n.9, p. 234), 77, 132 (n.6, p. 240), 133 (n.8, p. 240), 134, 142, 147 (n.26, p. 242), 224, 227 n.8, 235 n.16, n.20, 236 n.30, nn.32-33, 237 nn.6-7, n.10, n.12, 238 n.14, n.17, n.24, 240 n.4, 241 n.19, nn.21-22, 242 n.26
Dibelius, M., 137 (n.14, p. 241), 228 n.1
Dissimilarity, criterion of, 209
Dodd, C. H., 30 (n.8, p. 229), 44, 132, 137 (n.15, p. 241), 139, 146 (n.24, p. 242), 155 (n.34, p. 242), 157-58, 197, 226 n.8, 240 n.6

Enslin, M. S., 106 (n.11, p. 237)
Eschatology, 49, 57-58, 118, 216, 219
Esoteric teaching (see *Parables*)
Example-stories, 15, 104-9, 203-4, 225 n.4, 237 n.6, n.14

Farmer, H. H., 218
Farmer, W. R., 229 n.14
Figs, no time for, 238 n.18
Fishers of men, 231 n.9, 233 n.4
Form-criticism, 27 (n.1, p. 228), 230 n.9, 233 nn.4-5
Fuchs, E., 9, 207 (nn.25-26, p. 246), 208, 224, 227 n.11, 234 n.7, 235 n.23
Fuller, R. H., 229 n.17
Funk, R. W., 9, 197-98 (n.12, p. 245), 200, 224 (n.1), 226 nn.7-8, 237 n.6, nn.9-10, n.14, 238 n.23, 239 nn.24-26, n.28, 244 n.3, 245 n.12, nn.18-19, 246 n.24, n.27, n.29

Gandhi, 154
Genre criticism, 194-95, 215
Gentile mission, 29, 64, 70, 97-98 (n.1, p. 236), 122-23, 131
Gethsemane, 149, 182, 188, 215-16
Glueck, N., 239 n.27
God, 14-15, 70, 78-79, 84, 198
    fatherhood of, 77-79, 85, 214
    grace of, 79-80, 86-87, 89-90, 93, 95, 112, 234 n.13, 239 n.26
    initiative of, 80, 90, 93-94
    judgment of, 93, 110-14, 118, 127, 137, 206, 213, 219
    love of, 85, 95
    mercy of, 15, 83, 97, 219
    sovereignty of, 47, 211
    will of, 66, 72-74, 94, 99, 109
    Word of, 43, 203, 218
Gospel of Thomas, 9, 224, 225 n.2, 228 n.11, 230 n.5, 231 n.10, n.12, 232 n.18, n.22, 233 nn.27-28, n.4, 234 n.7, n.15, 236 n.34, 239 n.26, n.28, 240 n.9, 243 n.11, nn.16-17, 244 n.18
Grant, R. M. and Freedman, D. M., 224, 230 n.5, 232 n.22, 241 n.9, 244 n.18
Growth (see *Parables*)
Guignebert, C., 228 n.4

Guillaumont, A., et al., 224
Guthlac of Crowland, 57

Hahn, F., 230 n.18
Halévy, J., 106
Hatch, W. H. P., 235 n.26
History, 25, 27, 31-32, 49-50, 144, 149, 196
Hunter, A. M., 224

Ignatius, 48 (n.9, p. 230), 155 (n.35, p. 242)
Israel, *passim*

Jeremias, J., 9, 132, 223, 224 n.1, 225 n.2, n.4, 227 nn.10-11, 230 n.2, n.4, n.6, 231 n.10, nn.12-15, 232 n.24, 233 n.4, 234 nn.7-8, n.10, 235 n.19, n.21, n.23, nn.25-26, 236 n.32, 237 n.6, 238 n.19, n.21, n.24, 239 n.25, n.27, 240 n.9, 241 nn.16-17, nn.19-20, 242 n.23, n.31, 243 nn.2-3, n.7, nn.10-12, nn.17-20, 246 n.23, n.27
Jerusalem, 20, 27, 36, 45, 99, 103, 111, 118, 121, 127, 131, 134-35, 141, 161, 193, 238 n.15
Jesus
    as enigma, 36, 38
    as Jew, 18, 31, 194, 205, 209, 215-16, 243 n.3
    as offense, 20, 28, 36, 67
    biography of, 19, 27, 194
    claim (authority) of, 127, 129, 140, 144, 161-62, 172, 190-91, 205-7, 210
    crucifixion of, 11, 19-20, 23, 25-27, 49, 95, 99, 109, 168, 194, 208
    failure of, 27, 39, 228 n.4
    genius of, 12, 34, 108, 124, 168, 204, 208
    historical, 9, 25, 28, 193 (n.1, p. 244), 207, 227 n.11
    mission of, 45, 72, 74, 94, 97-98, 134
    person of, 12, 19-20, 27, 35-36, 112, 118, 162, 173
    rejection of, 11, 19-20, 44-45, 66, 215
    response to, 19-20, 30-31, 35, 38, 118, 126, 204, 210, 217-19
    resurrection of, 11, 23, 25-29, 37, 95, 163, 166-69, 228 n.2
    self-consciousness of, 35-37, 209-11
    strategy of, 26, 66, 77, 143, 194, 216
    temptation of, 39 (n.1, p. 230), 93, 168, 243 n.12
    titles of, 229 n.17, 247 n.29
    trial of, 34 (n.16, p. 229), 36
John the Baptist, 28, 39, 44, 61-62, 99, 111
Johnson, H. L., 231 n.11
Jones, G. V., 9, 200, 223
Jülicher, A., 17 (n.6, p. 226), 198, 237 n.6
Justification, 81, 83, 94-95, 104

Kahlefeld, H., 198 (n.15, p. 245), 208, 223, 227 n.10, 228 n.12, 245 n.15
Kähler, M., 195 (n.5, p. 245)
Kingdom of God, 15, 19, 21, 23, 31-32, 37, 39, 43-44, 47-66, 88, 117, 170-73, 182, 187, 211-18, 241 n.10
Kingsbury, J. D., 223, 226 nn.5-6, 227 n.9, 230 n.7, 231 n.9, n.12, n.15, n.17, 232 n.18, n.23, n.27, 234 n.5
Klausner, J., 31 (n.9, p. 229), 229 n.10, n.14, 230 n.3, 235 n.20
Knox, J., 33 (n.15, p. 229), 229 n.16
Koester, H. (see *Robinson and Koester*)
Kümmel, W. G., 224, 233 nn.4-5, 240 n.2, n.7, 243 n.10

# INDEX TO PARABLES